KT-493-582

Russia

1855–1964

Derrick Murphy ■ **Terry Morris**

◌ **Collins**

237 703

Published by Collins
An imprint of
HarperCollinsPublishers
77–85 Fulham Palace Road
Hammersmith
London
W6 8JB

Browse the complete Collins
catalogue at
www.collinseducation.com

10 9 8 7 6 5 4 3 2

ISBN 978 0 00 726867 2

British Library Cataloguing in
Publication Data
A Catalogue record for this
publication is available from the
British Library

Edited by Graham Bradbury
Commissioned by Michael
Upchurch
Design and typesetting by Derek Lee
Cover design by Joerg
Hartmannsgruber, White-card
Map Artwork by Tony Richardson
Picture research by Celia Dearing
and Michael Upchurch
Indexed by Malcolm Henley, Henley
Indexing
Production by Simon Moore
Printed and bound in Hong Kong

ACKNOWLEDGEMENTS
Every effort had been made to
contact the holders of copyright
material, but if any have been
inadvertently overlooked the
publishers will be pleased to make
the necessary arrangements at the
first opportunity.

Cambridge University Press for the
extract from *The Russian Revolution,
1917* by Rex Wade (2000).
HarperCollins Publishers Ltd for the
extract from *Russia under the
Bolshevik Regime 1919–1924* by
Richard Pipes (1994) and *The
Russian Revolution, 1899–1919* by
Richard Pipes (1990). The Historical
Association for the extract from *The
Russian Constitutional Monarchy
1907–17* by R.B. McKean (1977).
Hodder Headline for the extracts
from *Rethinking the Russian
Revolution* by Edward Acton
(Hodder Arnold, 1990). Indiana
University Press for the extracts
from *Critical Companion to the
Russian Revolution* edited by Acton,
Chernaiev and Rosenberg (1997).
Macmillan for the extracts from
*Imperial and Soviet Russia: Power,
Privilege and the Challenge of
Modernity* by David Christian
(Macmillan, 1997), *The
Industrialisation of Russia,
1700–1914* by M.E. Falkus (1972),
*Lenin, A Political Life, Volume 3: The
Iron Ring* by Robert Service,
(Palgrave Macmillan, 1994) and
European Political Facts, 1848–1918
(Palgrave Historical & Political
Facts) by Chris Cook and John
Paxton (1978). Nelson Thornes Ltd
for the extract from *The Great
Powers, 1814–1914* by Eric Wilmot
(1992). Northern Illinois University
Press for the extract from *The Great
Reforms: Autocracy, Bureaucracy, and
the Politics of Change in Imperial
Russia* by W. Bruce Lincoln (1990).
Oxford University Press for the
extract from *The Russian Empire,
1801–1917* by Hugh Seton-Watson
(1967). Pearson for the extracts
from *Russia in the Age of Reaction
and Reform, 1801–1881* by David
Saunders (Longman, History of

Russia series, 1992), *The Abolition of
Serfdom in Russia* by David Moon
(1978), *The Soviet Union 1917–1991*
by Martin McCauley (Longman,
History of Russia series, 1993) and
*Russia in the Age of Modernisation
and Revolution, 1881–1917* by Hans
Rogger (Longman, History of Russia
series, 1983). Penguin Books Ltd for
the extracts from *An Economic
History of the USSR* by Alec Nove
(1982) and *Stalin: a Political
Biography* by Isaac Deutscher
(1966). Prima Publishing for the
extract from *Stalin: Triumph and
Tragedy* by Dmitri Volkogonov
(1991). Random House Publishers
for the extracts from *A People's
Tragedy: Russian Revolution,
1891–1924* by Orlando Figes (1996).
Routledge for the extracts from *The
Communist Party of the Soviet Union*
by Leonard Schapiro (1960).
Weidenfeld & Nicolson for the
extract from *The Fall of the Russian
Monarchy* by Bernard Pares (2001)

The publishers would like to thank
the following for permission to
reproduce pictures on these pages.
T=Top, B=Bottom, L=Left, R=Right,
C=Centre

akg-images 31(T), 42, 66, 83, 134,
157; akg-images / Erich Lessing
161; akg / Russian Picture Service
168; The Bridgeman Art Library 27;
© DACS / The Bridgeman Art
Library 115; © Bettmann/CORBIS
123, 140; © Hulton-Deutsch
Collection/CORBIS 89; Mary
Evans/Mary Evans ILN Pictures 43;
Mary Evans Picture Library 113;
© Penguin Books Ltd; Unknown 21,
31(B), 64, 101, 111, 133, 141

Contents

Study and examination skills

This section of the book is designed to aid Sixth Form students in their preparation for public examinations in History.

- Differences between GCSE and Sixth Form History
- Extended writing: the structured question and the essay
- How to handle sources in Sixth Form History
- Historical interpretation
- Progression in Sixth Form History
- Examination technique

Differences between GCSE and Sixth Form History

- **The amount of factual knowledge required for answers to Sixth Form History questions** is more detailed than at GCSE. Factual knowledge in the Sixth Form is used as supporting evidence to help answer historical questions. Knowing the facts is important, but not as important as knowing that factual knowledge supports historical analysis.

- **Extended writing is more important in Sixth Form History**. Students will be expected to answer either structured questions or essays.

Structured questions require students to answer more than one question on a given topic. For example:

> (a) What problems faced Tsar Alexander II when he became Tsar in 1855?
>
> (b) How successful was Tsar Alexander II in dealing with Russia's problems?

Each part of the structured question demands a different approach.

Essay questions require students to produce one answer to a given question. For example:

> 'Brutal but effective'. Assess this view of Stalin's rule in the period 1928 to 1939.

Similarities with GCSE

- **Source analysis and evaluation**

The skills in handling historical sources, which were acquired at GCSE, are developed in Sixth Form History. In the Sixth Form, sources have to be analysed in their historical context, so a good factual knowledge of the subject is important.

- **Historical interpretations**

Skills in historical interpretation at GCSE are also developed in Sixth Form History. The ability to put forward different historical interpretations is important. Students will also be expected to explain why different historical interpretations have occurred.

Extended writing: the structured question and the essay

When faced with extended writing in Sixth Form History students can improve their performance by following a simple routine that attempts to ensure they achieve their best performance.

Answering the question

What are the command instructions?
Different questions require different types of response. For instance, 'In what ways' requires students to point out the various ways something took place in History; 'Why' questions expect students to deal with the causes or consequences of an historical event.

'How far' or 'To what extent' questions require students to produce a balanced, analytical answer. Usually, this will take the form of the case for and case against an historical question.

Are there key words or phrases that require definition or explanation?
It is important for students to show that they understand the meaning of the question. To do this, certain historical terms or words require explanation. For instance, if a question asked 'how far' a politician was an 'innovator', an explanation of the word 'innovator' would be required.

Does the question have specific dates or issues that require coverage?
If the question mentions specific dates, these must be adhered to. For instance, if you are asked to answer a question on Stalin's foreign policy it might state 'in the period 1924 to 1939'.

Planning your answer

Once you have decided on what the question requires, write a brief plan. For structured questions this may be brief. This is a useful procedure to make sure that you have ordered the information you require for your answer in the most effective way. For instance, in a balanced, analytical answer this may take the form of jotting down the main points for and against an historical issue raised in the question.

Writing the answer

Communication skills
The quality of written English is important in Sixth Form History. The way you present your ideas on paper can affect the quality of your answer. Therefore, punctuation, spelling and grammar, which were awarded marks at GCSE, require close attention. Use a dictionary if you are unsure of a word's meaning or spelling. Use the glossary of terms you will find in this book to help you.

The introduction
For structured questions you may wish to dispense with an introduction altogether and begin writing reasons to support an answer straight away. However, essay answers should begin with an introduction. These should be both concise and precise. Introductions help 'concentrate the mind' on the question you are about to answer. Remember, do not try to write a conclusion as your opening sentence. Instead, outline briefly the areas you intend to discuss in your answer.

Balancing analysis with factual evidence

It is important to remember that factual knowledge should be used to support analysis. Merely 'telling the story' of an historical event is not enough. A structured question or essay should contain separate paragraphs, each addressing an analytical point that helps to answer the question. If, for example, the question asks for reasons why the Bolshevik Revolution occurred, each paragraph should provide a reason which explains why the October Revolution took place. In order to support and sustain the analysis evidence is required. Therefore, your factual knowledge should be used to substantiate analysis. Good structured question and essay answers integrate analysis and factual knowledge.

Seeing connections between reasons

In dealing with 'why'-type questions it is important to remember that the reasons for an historical event might be interconnected. Therefore, it is important to mention the connections between reasons. Also, it might be important to identify a hierarchy of reasons – that is, are some reasons more important than others in explaining an historical event?

Using quotations and statistical data

One aspect of supporting evidence that sustains analysis is the use of quotations. These can be from either a historian or a contemporary. However, unless these quotations are linked with analysis and supporting evidence, they tend to be of little value.

It can also be useful to support analysis with statistical data. In questions that deal with social and economic change, precise statistics that support your argument can be very persuasive.

The conclusion

All structured questions and essays require conclusions. If, for example, a question requires a discussion of 'how far' you agree with a question, you should offer a judgement in your conclusion. Don't be afraid of this – say what you think. If you write an analytical answer, ably supported by factual evidence, you may under-perform because you have not provided a conclusion that deals directly with the question.

Source analysis

Source analysis forms an integral part of the study of History.

In dealing with sources you should be aware that historical sources must be used 'in historical context' in Sixth Form History. This means you must understand the historical topic to which the source refers. Therefore, in this book sources are used with the factual information in each chapter. Also, specific source analysis questions are included at the end of most chapters.

How to handle sources in Sixth Form History

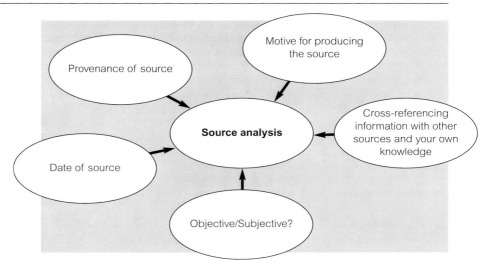

In dealing with sources, a number of basic hints will allow you to deal effectively with source-based questions and to build on your knowledge and skill in using sources at GCSE.

Written sources

Attribution or Provenance and date

It is important to identify who has written the source and when it was written. This information can be very important. If, for instance, a source was written by Lenin in 1917, this information will be of considerable importance if you are asked about the usefulness (utility) or reliability of the source as evidence of Bolshevik policy in that year.

It is important to note that just because a source is a primary source does not mean it is more useful or less reliable than a secondary source. Both primary and secondary sources need to be analysed to decide how useful and reliable they are. This can be determined by studying other issues.

Is the content factual or opinionated?

Once you have identified the author and date of the source, it is important to study its content. The content may be factual, stating what has happened or what may happen. On the other hand, it may contain opinions that should be handled with caution. These may contain bias. Even if a source is mainly factual, there might be important and deliberate gaps in factual evidence that can make a source biased and unreliable. Usually, written sources contain elements of both opinion and factual evidence. It is important to judge the balance between these two parts.

Has the source been written for a particular audience?

To determine the reliability of a source it is important to know to whom it is directed. For instance, a public speech may be made to achieve a particular purpose and may not contain the author's true beliefs or feelings. In contrast, a private diary entry may be much more reliable in this respect.

Corroborative evidence

To test whether or not a source is reliable, the use of other evidence to support or corroborate the information it contains is important. Cross-referencing with other sources is a way of achieving this; so is cross-referencing with historical information contained within a chapter.

Visual sources

Cartoons
Cartoons are a popular form of source used at both GCSE and in Sixth Form History. However, analysing cartoons can be a demanding exercise. Not only will you be expected to understand the content of the cartoon, you may also have to explain a written caption – which appears usually at the bottom of the cartoon. In addition, cartoons will need placing in historical context. Therefore, a good knowledge of the subject matter of the topic of the cartoon will be important.

Photographs
'The camera never lies'! This phrase is not always true. When analysing photographs, study the attribution/provenance and date. Photographs can be changed so they are not always an accurate visual representation of events. Also, to test whether or not a photograph is a good representation of events you will need corroborative evidence.

Maps
Maps which appear in Sixth Form History are predominantly secondary sources. These are used to support factual coverage in the text by providing information in a different medium. Therefore, to assess whether or not information contained in maps is accurate or useful, reference should be made to other information. It is also important with written sources to check the attribution and date. These could be significant.

Statistical data and graphs
It is important when dealing with this type of source to check carefully the nature of the information contained in data or in a graph. It might state that the information is in tons (tonnes) or another measurement. Be careful to check if the information is in index numbers. These are a statistical device where a base year is chosen and given the figure 100. All other figures are based on a percentage difference from that base year. For instance, if 1928 is taken as a base year for steel production, it is given the figure of 100. If the index number for steel production in 1939 is 317 it means that steel production has increased by 217% above the 1928 figure.

An important point to remember when dealing with data and graphs over a period of time is to identify trends and patterns in the information. Merely describing the information in written form is not enough.

Historical interpretation

An important feature of both GCSE and Sixth Form History is the issue of historical interpretation. In Sixth Form History it is important for students to be able to explain why historians differ, or have differed, in their interpretation of the past.

Availability of evidence

An important reason is the availability of evidence on which to base historical judgements. As new evidence comes to light, an historian today may have more information on which to base judgements than historians in the past.

'A philosophy of history?'

Many historians have a specific view of history that will affect the way they make their historical judgements. For instance, Marxist historians – who take the view from the writings of Karl Marx the founder of modern socialism – believe that society has been made up of competing economic and social classes. They also place considerable importance on economic reasons in human decision making. Therefore, a Marxist historian of fascism may take a completely different viewpoint to a non-Marxist historian.

The role of the individual

Some historians have seen past history as being moulded by the acts of specific individuals who have changed history. Alexander II, Lenin and Stalin are seen as individuals whose personality and beliefs changed the course of Russian history. Other historians have tended to 'downplay' the role of individuals; instead, they highlight the importance of more general social, economic and political change.

Placing different emphasis on the same historical evidence

Even if historians do not possess different philosophies of history or place different emphasis on the role of the individual, it is still possible for them to disagree because they place different emphases on aspects of the same factual evidence. As a result, Sixth Form History should be seen as a subject that encourages debate about the past based on historical evidence.

Progression in Sixth Form History

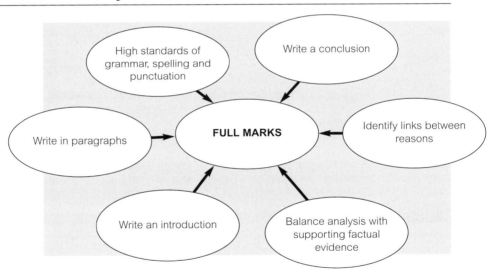

The ability to achieve high standards in Sixth Form History involves the acquisition of a number of skills:

● Good written communication skills

● Acquiring a sound factual knowledge

● Evaluating factual evidence and making historical conclusions based on that evidence

● Source analysis

● Understanding the nature of historical interpretation

● Understanding the causes and consequences of historical events

- Understanding themes in history which will involve a study of a specific topic over a long period of time

- Understanding the ideas of change and continuity associated with themes.

Students should be aware that the acquisition of these skills will take place gradually over the time spent in the Sixth Form. At the beginning of the course, the main emphasis may be on the acquisition of factual knowledge, particularly when the body of knowledge studied at GCSE was different.

When dealing with causation, students will have to build on their skills from GCSE. They will not only be expected to identify reasons for an historical event but also to provide a hierarchy of causes. They should identify the main causes and less important causes. They may also identify that causes may be interconnected and linked. Progression in Sixth Form History will come with answering the questions at the end of each sub-section in this book and practising the skills outlined through the use of the factual knowledge contained in the book.

Examination technique

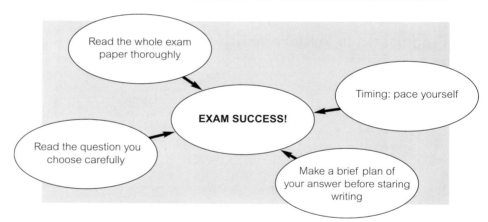

The ultimate challenge for any Sixth Form historian is the ability to produce quality work under examination conditions. Examinations will take the form of either modular examinations taken in January and June or an 'end of course' set of examinations.

Here is some advice on how to improve your performance in an examination.

- Read the whole examination paper thoroughly
  Make sure that the questions you choose are those for which you can produce a good answer. Don't rush – allow time to decide which questions to choose. It is probably too late to change your mind half way through answering a question.

- Read the question very carefully
  Once you have made the decision to answer a specific question, read it very carefully. Make sure you understand the precise demands of the question. Think about what is required in your answer. It is much better to think about this before you start writing, rather than trying to steer your essay in a different direction half way through.

- Make a brief plan
  Sketch out what you intend to include in your answer. Order the points you want to make. Examiners are not impressed with additional information included at the end of the essay, with indicators such as arrows or asterisks.

- Pace yourself as you write
  Success in examinations has a lot to do with successful time management. If, for instance, you have to answer an essay question in approximately 45 minutes, then you should be one-third of the way through after 15 minutes. With 30 minutes gone, you should start writing the last third of your answer.

Where a question is divided into sub-questions, make sure you look at the mark tariff for each question. If in a 20-mark question a sub-question is worth a maximum of 5 marks, then you should spend approximately one-quarter of the time allocated for the whole question on this sub-question.

Revision tips

Even before the examination begins make sure that you have revised thoroughly. Revision tips on the main topics in this book appear on the Collins website:

www.collinseducation.com

1 Russia 1855–1964: A synoptic overview

Key Issues

- How far did Russia's government change from 1855 to 1964?

- How did Russian society and the economy change in the period 1855 to 1964?

- How important were individual Russian rulers in bringing change to Russia from 1855 to 1964?

1.1 Russia in 1855

In 1855 Russia faced national humiliation. It was in the middle of a war on its own soil against Britain, France, Piedmont-Sardinia and the Ottoman Empire. The Crimean War (1854–56) saw the forces of these four powers besiege the southern Russian naval base of Sebastopol, and by 1855 the Russian forces were on the brink of defeat. In 1855 Tsar Nicholas I died, to be replaced by Tsar Alexander II – who become known during his reign as the 'Tsar Liberator'. Alexander II was determined to modernise Russia to prevent such an event happening again. From 1855 until his death, at the hand of assassins in 1881, Alexander II brought about fundamental social and political reform to Russia.

Throughout its history, from 1855 to 1964, Russia saw periods of major social, political and economic change instituted from above. In the twentieth century, there were similar periods of fundamental change, brought about by the Soviet leaders Lenin and Stalin.

In 1855 Russia was one of Europe's five Great Powers. It stretched from Poland in the West to Alaska in North America. It covered approximately 20 per cent of the world's land surface. Although vast in size, it was the most politically and economically backward of Europe's major states. The ruler of the Russian Empire was the Tsar (Emperor) who had complete political power. There was no national parliament or any form of elective government. The Tsar chose the government and determined government policy. He was head of the armed forces and was regarded as the head of the main religion, the Russian Orthodox Church. The vast majority of the Russian population – 80 per cent – were **serfs**, the personal property of their owners. In 1855 Russia had more in common with medieval England than the rest of Europe.

Serf: A person who is the personal property of their owners.

1.2 The reign of Alexander II, the Tsar Liberator, 1855–81

Ukase: A decree (law) introduced by the Tsar.

Alexander II brought about a revolution from above during his reign. In 1861 he issued an Imperial **ukase** which emancipated the serfs. This was even more significant than the freeing of slaves within the United States that took place just a few years later (1863–65). In one imperial act, Russian landowners lost an important part of their property – their serfs. The government compensated landowners, and in return the serfs had to pay for their freedom through redemption payments over 49 years. Alexander II also introduced important political reforms, such as elective local government (**zemstva** and town dumas). By the time of his death in 1881 Alexander II had transformed Russia.

Zemstva: Elected local government in rural areas created in 1864.

In the 1890s the Russian government began a period of rapid economic growth. This 'Great Spurt' towards economic modernisation was orchestrated by the Finance Minister, Sergei Witte, and its centrepiece was the construction of the Trans-Siberian Railway. Witte's economic modernisation of 1893 to 1903 was followed by another period of economic reform under Prime Minister Prince Peter Stolypin (1907–10). Stolypin gave financial support to **peasants** to buy their own land and aided peasant migration to the new lands of Siberia. By 1914 Russia seemed to be well on the road to becoming one of Europe's major economic powers.

Peasant: An agricultural labourer who rents land. The vast majority of serfs became peasants after 1861.

1.3 The coming of the communist state

From the outbreak of the First World War in 1914, however, to the mid-1920s Russia went through a period of crisis. World War was followed by revolution and Civil War. Under Vladimir Lenin (1917–24) and Josef Stalin (1924–53) Russia again went through a 'revolution from above'.

After a brief period of democracy, Lenin established a communist **dictatorship**, which was to last until 1991. Under Stalin, Russia was again transformed socially and economically. Through a programme of forced **collectivisation** of agriculture, Stalin destroyed the independent Russian peasantry between 1928 and 1939.

Dictatorship: Government by a person or group who hold political power without democratic consent.

Collectivisation: The merging of individual peasant farms to create large state-owned farms.

In the same period he embarked on a policy of rapid industrialisation, and by the outbreak of the Second World War Russia had become one of the world's major industrial powers. The strength of its economic power was shown during the Second World War, when Russia defeated Nazi Germany in the 'Great Patriotic War of the Soviet Union' (1941–45). By 1945 Russia had become one of two superpowers which dominated world affairs. In 1949 Russia successfully exploded its first nuclear weapon and from 1957 became the leading world power in space exploration with the launch of Sputnik.

Therefore, from 1855 to 1964 Russia had been transformed from the position of Europe's most socially and economically backward state into a global economic superpower.

The period 1855 to 1964 was also characterised by political repression. From 1855 to 1906 Russia had no national parliament or officially recognised political parties. As a result, opponents of the Tsarist **autocracy** had to operate outside the political system, and some resorted to political terrorism. In 1881, a group of radicals, called 'People's Will', assassinated Tsar Alexander II. In 1887 the same group attempted to assassinate Tsar Alexander III, and by the early twentieth century it seemed that political reform would take place only through revolution. In 1905 revolution engulfed Russia. Among its many causes were Russia's defeat by Japan in a war in the Far East – which undermined support for the government – and peasant unrest due to taxation and the poor harvest which affected large areas of European Russia. An important element in the revolution was the call for political reform and, although the revolution failed to topple the Tsar, it did lead to the creation of Russia's first elected national parliament, the Duma. Control over the government, however, remained firmly in the hands of the Tsar.

Autocracy: Government by one person.

The end of Tsarism was brought about by military defeat in the First World War. By early 1917 Russia was on the brink of defeat at the hands of the German and Austro-Hungarian armed forces. In February 1917 a spontaneous revolution led to the fall of the Tsar and his replacement by a republic which supported the introduction of democracy. From February to October 1917, Russia experienced a period of liberal political reform under the Provisional Government. But this brief period was brought to an abrupt end with the Bolshevik seizure of power. Under Lenin, the Bolsheviks reintroduced political repression from above. Political parties and a free press were banned. Concentration camps for political opponents were established and opponents were arrested and imprisoned by a new secret police, the Cheka. By the time of Lenin's death, in 1924, Russia had a dictatorship more severe and oppressive than anything experienced under the Tsars.

What Lenin had created, his successor – Stalin – took to extremes. In the Great Purges of 1934 to 1939, Stalin launched a terror campaign against the entire Russian population. The secret police, known at the NKVD from 1934, imprisoned millions, and murdered hundreds of thousands. No one seemed to be immune from this government-sponsored terror. Members of the Bolshevik/Communist party and leaders of the armed forces were all subject to Stalin's purges. By 1939 Stalin was the undisputed, all-powerful ruler of Russia in a way that any Tsar would have envied.

1.4 Key themes in Russian history 1855–1964

1. Draw a timeline from 1855 to 1964, highlighting the periods when Russia experienced rapid political, social and/or economic change.

2. In 1964, in what ways had Russia changed since 1855, and in what ways was it still similar?

3. Who do you regard as the ruler who brought most change to Russia in the period 1855 to 1964? Explain your answer.

Therefore, the two major themes of Russian history from 1855 to 1964 were radical reform from above, instigated by Russia's rulers, and political repression. However, for a brief period, from February to October 1917 it seemed that Russian history was going to follow a different path. In February 1917 Tsar Nicholas II abdicated, bringing to an end over 300 years of rule by his family, the Romanovs. From February 1917 Russia seemed to be following a new political course – one towards western-style parliamentary government. However, this experiment towards democracy was short-lived. It was brought down by a variety of factors. Russia's decision to continue fighting in the First World War was deeply unpopular. Also the fall of the Tsar saw a breakdown of government in the countryside, with peasants taking land for themselves. In many ways Russia was in a state of anarchy from February to October 1917. By October it seemed that the Provisional Government that had ruled Russia since the fall of the Tsar would be replaced. In that month, in a military coup, the Bolshevik Party seized power and declared the creation of the world's first communist government. Faced with massive opposition within Russia and intervention by foreign powers such as Britain, France and the USA, the Bolsheviks established a political dictatorship. Once established this dictatorship lasted until the fall of the USSR in 1991. However, attempts were made to 'lighten' communist control. The first came in 1956, when Soviet leader Khrushchev 'denounced' Stalin at the 20th Congress of the Communist Party of the Soviet Union (CPSU). From 1956 the worst excesses of Stalinist rule were removed. These included the excessive use of concentration camps (Gulags) for political opponents. Yet, when Khrushchev fell from power, in 1964, the communists were still firmly in control of Russia. It was still a one-party state without a free press and with central control of both politics and the economy.

2 The Tsarist autocracy, 1855–1894: the reigns of Alexander II and Alexander III

Key Issues

- Why did Alexander II undertake an extensive programme of reforms in the 1860s?

- What was the impact of these reforms upon Russian society and upon the Tsarist regime?

- Why did the Russian regime return to conservative policies in the 1880s?

2.1 What was Russia like in the 19th century?

2.2 What forces were there for continuity and for change within the Russian Empire on the eve of the Crimean War?

2.3 Was serfdom a source of strength or of weakness for the Russian state and the Russian economy?

2.4 What were the domestic political implications of Russia's defeat in the Crimea?

2.5 How effective were the measures taken from 1861 to emancipate the Russian serfs?

2.6 Historical interpretation: To what extent does Alexander II deserve the title of 'Tsar Liberator'?

2.7 How seriously was the Tsarist regime threatened by the opposition that arose during Alexander II's reign?

2.8 Why did Tsarist policy change between reform and reaction in the years 1879–1894?

2.9 Why and with what consequences did the Tsarist government pursue a policy of Russification?

2.10 To what extent was Russia's international prestige restored in the reigns of Alexander II and Alexander III?

2.11 What was the extent of Russia's economic development during the reigns of Alexander II and Alexander III?

Framework of Events

1854	Outbreak of the Crimean War
1855	Death of Tsar Nicholas I; accession of Alexander II
1856	Conclusion of the Crimean War by the Treaty of Paris
1861	Emancipation of the Russian serfs
1863	Polish Revolt
1864	Introduction of *zemstva*. Reform of judiciary system
1872	Russia enters League of the Three Emperors
1873–74	Radical students institute the 'To the People' movement
1874	Introduction of Milyutin's military reforms
1877–78	Russo–Turkish War
1878	Congress of Berlin
1881	Assassination of Alexander II; accession of Alexander III
1889	Introduction of Land Commandants
1894	Death of Alexander III; accession of Nicholas II.

Overview

Tsar: Title of the emperor of Russia. Also spelled Czar and Tzar. Believed to be a shortened form of Caesar (Roman emperor).

IN the first half of the 19th century Russia's status as a great power appeared undeniable. It rested upon the dual foundation of an autocratic political system and a strictly ordered society in which the ownership of serfs by landlords guaranteed the transmission of the **Tsar's** will to the lowest ranks of society. The

Private enterprise: The economic activities of a country or a community which are independent of government control and directed to satisfy private wants.

Autocracy (adj. autocratic): A form of government in which the ruler (the autocrat) exercises absolute political power, unlimited by other factors such as a parliament or a constitution.

disadvantages of such a system lay in the fact that it severely hampered **private enterprise**. The fact that the peasants were not free to pursue greater prosperity, and that many landowners were comfortably cushioned by their privileged position, deprived Russia of the kind of growth that was generating an economic revolution in many parts of western Europe. Awareness of such disadvantages, along with a degree of ideological opposition to **autocracy** and serfdom, was already growing when defeat in the Crimean War emphasised the extent of Russia's decline as a great power. If that war sometimes appears to be little more than a footnote in French or British history, it was a key event for Tsarist Russia. The Crimean War stimulated attitudes and triggered policies in Russia that had simmered below the surface for decades.

Under these circumstances, Tsar Alexander II introduced a programme of reforms that was undoubtedly the most radical and far-reaching of any attempted by a European government in the 19th century. Over 40 million people were released from slavery, and a series of further reforms was implemented that appeared to be based upon liberal institutions in western Europe. Nevertheless, a profound paradox ran through this programme. While it introduced a degree of personal and legal freedom previously unknown in Russia, it did so by an act of the monarch's autocratic will. Indeed, the preservation of the Tsar's authority, and the consolidation of conservative interests, were among the fundamental aims of the programme. Does this mean, as Soviet historians usually claimed, that the 'great reforms' were confused and sterile? Was it all a hopeless attempt to preserve a doomed political system? Or is it better to follow the interpretation often reached by liberal, western historians, who see these reforms as steps that could have taken Russia forward into a modern age of political reform and economic progress?

The tragedy of Alexander II's great reform programme was that he and his ministers only partly understood the implications of their actions. They hoped for peace and stability in the countryside, for a more prosperous and contented peasantry, and for a degree of industrial growth that would strengthen and modernise both the economy and the army. Yet the reforms transformed most of the existing social, political and economic relationships within the state. They were bound to hasten Russia into a new world of market forces and political debate that was incompatible with the habits of command and blind obedience upon which Russian government had been based for centuries. Perceived as a short, sharp burst of radical change which would earn widespread gratitude for the 'Tsar liberator' (Alexander II), the reforms opened a troubled era of Russian history. As governments sought, alternately, to advance modernisation or to apply the brake, so various sections of the population tried to exploit the momentum towards change, or recoiled from its implications. The assassination of Alexander II in 1881 was a result of these political tensions. It guaranteed that for a generation, Russia's rulers would recognise the dangers of reform more clearly than they recognised its benefits, and that they would abandon that path. For three decades before the outbreak of the First World War, the Tsarist regime attempted to restore the effectiveness of traditional forms of government, without the bedrock institution of serfdom, upon which those traditional forms had been based.

At the same time as it struggled with the domestic problems that the Crimean War had highlighted, the Russian government also had to confront the diplomatic implications of the war. Recently regarded as the European continent's strongest military power – the 'gendarme of Europe' – Russia now found itself isolated and vulnerable. In addressing this problem, the government employed two different strategies. On the one hand, it attempted to find a working relationship with the other powers of continental Europe, especially with the new German state that emerged in 1871. On the other, in a fashion that resembled the westward expansion of the USA, it sought to exploit the vast 'virgin' regions that lay to the east. It sought power in Asia as a compensation for weakness in Europe. In the short term, there is a good case for arguing that Russia had regained its status as a great power by the end of Alexander III's reign. In the longer term, the steps taken in foreign policy led directly to Russia's disastrous involvement in the wars of 1904 and 1914. In foreign affairs, as in domestic policy, these decades prepared the ground for the traumas that Russia experienced in the first decades of the 20th century.

Tsars of Russia

Nicholas I
    1825–1855
Alexander II
    1855–1881
Alexander III
    1881–1894
Nicholas II
    1894–1917

2.1 What was Russia like in the 19th century?

1. Which of the factors in the mind map do you regard as examples of reform and which do you regard as examples of repression? Give reasons for your answer.

2. What do you regard as the most important event in Russian history in the period from 1855 to 1894? Explain your answer.

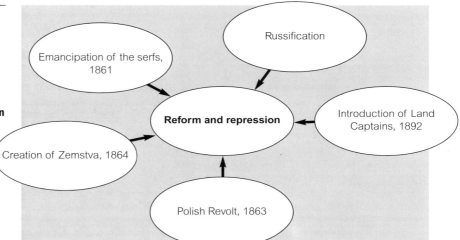

What was Russia like geographically?

The map of Russia's expansion into Europe gives some idea of how the Russian Empire had grown from the its beginnings around Moscow in the 13th century, while the map of Russian Asia shows the vast stretch of land Russia commanded to the east. This Empire was still growing. The first map shows the territories Russia annexed as it expanded to the west and south in the first 15 years of the 19th century: Georgia (1801–06), Azerbaijan (1805–13), Finland (1809), Bessarabia (1812) and Poland (1815). These borders were to be pushed still further in the course of the 19th century. To the east (see the second map), the Russian Empire absorbed Alaska (1789–1867), territory around the Amur river, the east coast of Manchuria and a large area to the east of the Caspian Sea. It has been calculated that during the period 1683–1694, Russia expanded at a rate of 55 square miles a day, on average.

According to the historian Norman Davies, in *Europe – a History* (1997), 'a country that already possessed more land than it could usefully exploit kept on indulging its gargantuan [huge] appetite'. In 1800, European Russia contained around 35–40 million people; by 1815, around 52 million. These numbers increased, as a result of conquest and population growth, to 56.1

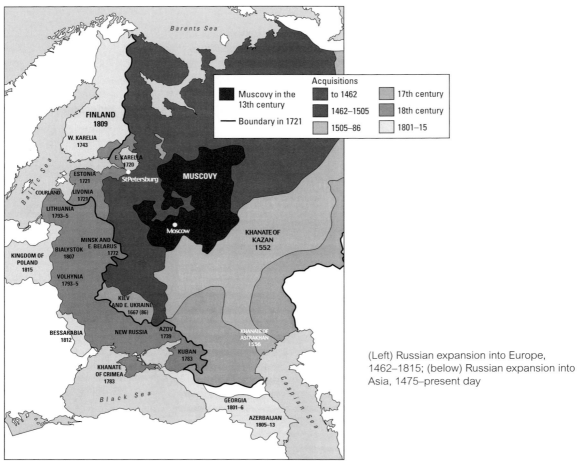

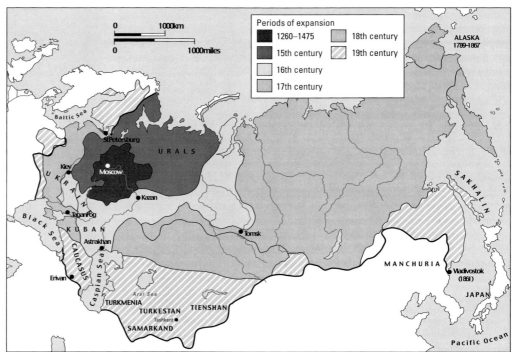

(Left) Russian expansion into Europe, 1462–1815; (below) Russian expansion into Asia, 1475–present day

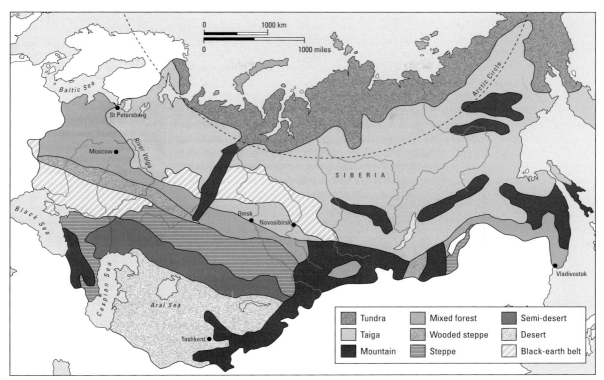

Physical map of Russia showing belts of vegetation

million by 1831 and 97.7 million by 1880. By 1815, Russia covered almost a sixth of the total land surface of the world.

Although vast in extent, much of the Empire was of limited productive use because of its geography and climate. As can be seen on the map, Russia's Empire can be divided into a series of zones of vegetation running east–west, broken in part by mountains. The main zones are:

- the Tundra in the very north around the Arctic Ocean;

- the *taiga* – vast areas of coniferous forest covering the northerly parts of Russia and Siberia;

- mixed coniferous/deciduous forest in a thin strip which broadens to the west to include the Baltic region;

- another thin strip of wooded steppe (treeless open grassland), mainly found along a line from the Ural mountains westwards to Kiev;

- the steppe extending from the Black Sea to the central Asian area (the Caucasus). This turns into semi-desert and desert proper further east. (As Russia expanded into the area to the east of the Caspian Sea, it acquired yet more desert land.)

The tundra, desert and mountainous regions could sustain little human activity. However, the *taiga* offered potential for hunting and timber while, beneath the thick grass roots of the steppe, the 'black earth' was rich and fertile. Within both these areas, the main settlements were along the river valleys.

The northerly situation and continental climate of Russia also caused difficulties. Although warm in the *taiga* in summer, the season was too short to ripen crops reliably. Also, the soil was poor and often swampy. The steppe, on the other hand, with a low rainfall, risked drought. The 'black earth' was extensively ploughed, and could dry out disastrously.

The two thin belts between these major Russian zones were much easier to exploit. The mixed forest was easier to clear than the *taiga*, the soils were better and the climate more temperate. The wooded steppe was better watered and easier to cultivate than the main steppe area further south. Consequently, the most developed part of the Russian state – between Kiev, Moscow and St Petersburg – lay within these areas.

What was Russia like economically?

Russia was an overwhelmingly rural country, and agriculture was the mainstay of the economy. As well as feeding its vast population, the grain, grown primarily in the south and west, was Russia's most valuable export. Although Russia had immense natural resources, such as iron ore in the Ural mountains and coal in the Donetz basin (around Taganrog, north of the Black Sea), industry was limited. Russia did produce a fair amount of iron. In fact, it provided a third of the world's iron production in 1800. But as the century wore on, Russia increasingly fell behind in comparison with the western European powers, as the following table shows:

Output of pig iron in metric tonnes

	Austria	France	Germany	Great Britain	Sweden	Russian Empire
1850	155,000	406,000	210,000	2,285,000	142,000	228,000
1875	303,000	1,448,000	1,759,000	6,467,000	351,000	428,000

The same was true of Russia's woollen, coal and chemical industries, although the cotton industry fared rather better, using new technology from England. By 1850, it was the fifth largest in the world. The success of cotton, in comparison with the other industries, gives one indicator as to why the Russian economy failed to grow as fast as that in much of western Europe. The cotton industry was a relatively new industry and was free from stifling restrictions. Most of the traditional industries were hampered by controls and were too established in their practices to institute significant change.

A variety of factors was holding Russian industry back:

● Russian industry was 'protected' by duties on foreign imports and, therefore, felt little pressure from its overseas' competitors.

● Government 'monopolies' controlled trade and industry. They hedged them round with complex restrictions thus preventing those outside the monopoly from challenging it.

Joint stock companies: 17th-century forerunner of the present 'limited company'. These grew out of ventures entered into by several people, usually on the agreement that the profits would be shared out in relation to each person's original investment.

● **Joint stock companies** were restricted by state legislation, so that it was impossible to finance large enterprise by raising money in 'shares' and by giving these shareholders a stake in the success of the business.

● State and private banks were unstable, making it difficult for anyone who wished to raise capital to do so in the form of bank loans.

● Reliance on plentiful serf labour meant that there was little incentive to invest in machinery to reduce labour costs.

● The absence of a strong middle class, and the aristocratic distaste for trade and industry, meant that there was no group interested in enriching itself through business enterprises. This meant that capital was tied up in land and not available for industrial development.

● The costs of transporting goods in the huge empire were very high.

● Resources, such as the coal and iron ore, were often a long way from the centres of population. Communications were poor and transport slow.

Although the Russian economy did grow in the 19th century, in relation to other European economies its record was poor, as the following statistics confirm:

Output of coal in metric tonnes

	Austria	France	Germany	Great Britain	Sweden	Russian Empire
1850	77,000	4,434,000	5,100,000	50,200,000	26,000	300,000
1875	4,471,000	16,957,000	47,800,000	135,400,000	64,000	1,700,000

Length of railway in kilometres

	Austria	France	Germany	Great Britain	Sweden	Russian Empire
1855	1,588	5,037	7,826	11,744		1,049
1875	9,344	10,331	19,357	27,970	23,365	19,029

What was Russia like socially?

The structure of society in Russia in 1900 (see poster) was no different from that of a century earlier. The percentages of the total population given for each group are based on a table of statistics produced by K. Arseniev, who used the **census** returns of 1812 and 1816.

Census: Official survey of the population of a country. It is carried out by the government in order to get details of the number of people living in the country, their ages and occupations, where they live etc.

Poster of a cartoon put out by Russian socialists in Geneva, showing a representation of the structure of Russian society in the 19th and early 20th centuries. From the bottom: the workers; capitalists, saying 'We do the eating'; the army, 'We shoot you'; the clergy, 'We mislead you'; and the royal family, 'We rule you'.

- At the top, beneath the imperial eagle, sits the Tsar and his wife. The Tsar holds autocratic power and his word is law.

- Beneath the Tsar stands the court, ministers and civil servants appointed by the Tsar to carry out his policies. (All officials: 3.7%)

- The Greek Orthodox Church supports the Tsarist autocracy. (Clergy: 1.1%)

- The Army was large and powerful and could be used to crush internal unrest, as well as for expansion elsewhere. (Military: 5%)

- The nobility was an established hereditary class of wealthy landowners who frequently enjoyed a life of idleness. (Nobility: 1.1%)

- The 'workers' at the bottom supported the rest. The only difference between this illustration and conditions in the early 19th century is that a few industrial workers are portrayed here. In the first half of the 19th century, this group was virtually non-existent. (According to Arseniev, this group consisted of 4.2% merchants, shopkeepers and artisans, 32.7% state peasants, 50.7% serfs and 1.5% 'others' – mainly more peasants.)

While the top four tiers of society formed the 'unproductive' classes and comprised 10.9% of the population, the lowest tier of 'productive' classes made up 89.1% (83% of these were state peasants or serfs).

Serfdom

Serfdom had developed in Russia in the 15th and 16th centuries and had been legitimised by Alexis I in 1649. Serfs were essential to the Russian idea of the 'service state', which had been established in this period. The nobility held land in return for 'service' to the Tsar, government and the army, while peasants worked their land. To ensure the nobles' income, these peasants were legally 'fixed' to it, and so became serfs, subject to some state protection. Peter the Great (1682–1725) strengthened the service state and in the 18th century serfdom was more efficiently enforced. However, the serfs' position worsened as they were increasingly regarded as their master's possessions.

Serfs fulfilled their obligations by working a number of days, often three a week (*barschina*) for their landlord, or by paying a rent (*obrok*). The *obrok* was more usual where the land was poor. It meant the serfs could take up other jobs, perhaps in the towns, with their master's permission. A landlord was responsible for his serfs' **poll tax**, while the village commune (*mir*), run by the most senior members of each serf family, distributed land and tasks. Serfdom was not slavery, but there were many restrictions on the lives of serfs, and state peasants were slightly better off.

State peasants were mainly either those working on the crown estates, or non-Russians. They were tied to their villages. They were also liable to conscription, like the serfs, but they were able to engage in any activity so long as they paid their taxes. Their greatest fear, however, was that they could be, and often were, sold into private ownership, at any time.

Serfs were the property of the landowners, who might do whatever they wished with them. They could sell serfs in the market place, sell the serfs' land, sell the serfs without land, split up families, take them into domestic service, arrange marriages and administer justice as they saw fit. Only **capital punishment** was forbidden. A nobleman's status depended on the number of 'souls' he owned and the stability of Russia was felt to depend upon the allegiance of serf to landowner.

The nobles were freed from their service to the state in 1762, but it was not until 1861 that the serfs were legally freed. Even then, although their legal status altered, their conditions of work had not changed greatly by 1870 (see section 2.5).

Poll tax: A sum of money which had to be paid to the state for every serf (a poll is literally a head).

Capital punishment: Execution. This should not be confused with corporal punishment or beatings, which were permitted

The structure of society, as shown in the poster on page 21, is also interesting in that it reveals the absence of any 'middle class'. Arseniev's figures show a small number of tradesmen, but there was no powerful 'factory owning' or business class, such as had already emerged in Great Britain and was developing in most of western Europe in the early 19th century.

Finally, the poster emphasises the static nature of Russian society. Men were born into a class, and there they remained. There was comparatively little movement between ranks.

What was the effect of the Russian social structure on the country's development?

The hierarchical and hereditary structure of society was one of the causes of Russia's political and economic backwardness in the 19th century.

The structure stifled ambition. The nobility grew used to depending on their serfs for everything. They were increasingly discouraged from exerting themselves and showing any initiative. Many of them continued to serve the Tsar, if only to give themselves some purpose in life. However, the general picture of the nobility, as often portrayed in Russian novels of the 19th century, is of a bored class, which did little more than provide corrupt administrators and incompetent army officers.

The structure restricted the development of industry. The 'unproductive classes' were not prepared to involve themselves in business and trade,

---

Autocracy, Orthodoxy and Nationality

Autocracy

This was the Russian system of government by which the Tsar had no limits on his power and was accountable to no one but God. It was believed that he was divinely appointed and that God supported his actions. The Tsar had advisers but he was not bound to listen to their advice, nor was he obliged to take it. Laws were made by a decree from the Tsar and his will was supreme. This made the authority of the Romanov Tsars the 'most absolute' in Europe. One of the Tsar's strongest supports came from the Orthodox Church.

Orthodoxy

In the 11th century, the Christian Church had split into the western 'Roman Catholic' and eastern 'Orthodox' branches. In 1453, the centre of the Orthodox Church moved from Constantinople (which fell to the Turks) to Moscow. Here, the Orthodox Church developed its own rituals and beliefs, and became quite separate from western influences. By the 19th century, it still enforced superstitious practices that had scarcely changed since the Middle Ages.

The Orthodox Church supported the Russian monarchy as the representative of God on earth and, in return, received state protection. Authority within the Church rested with the Patriarch of Moscow who worked closely with the Tsar. Beneath him were the metropolitans, archbishops and bishops. These were followed by the arch-priests and archdeacons, who were known as the 'black' or monastic clergy, and mainly lived in monasteries, under an 'archimandrite'. At the lowest level, the 'white' clergy of priests and deacons served the parishes. They married, and their sons generally continued their way of life.

Orthodoxy taught its followers to accept that conditions on earth were God's will. Good Orthodox Christians should never question their earthly lot, but trust to God's goodness in the world to come. Such teaching, coupled with ancient traditions and a reluctance to embrace change, helped make the Orthodox Church a symbol of the isolation and backwardness of Russia.

Nationality

Many of the people who lived in Russia were of non-Russian nationality. There were the Finns, Poles and Germans in the western part of the Empire. Between the Black and Caspian Seas lived Georgians and Armenians with their distinctive non-Slavic languages, and the Azerbaijanis, who were among the many Turks absorbed into the Empire as it had expanded in the 19th century. In central Asia there were Kazakhs, Bashkirs, Turkomens, Uzbeks, Kalmuks and Kirghiz. There were other races living in eastern Siberia, including Eskimos (now referred to as Inuits).

Altogether there were around 170 different ethnic groups, with the Russians or East Slavs comprising just under half the total population. However, together with the Ukrainians and Belorussians, who were closely related, they were a clear majority and the regime tended to favour them over the non-Russians in the same way that it favoured the Orthodox Church over other religions. Although 'Russification' (a policy of the later 19th century by which non-Russian peoples were forced to accept the Russian language and culture) was not official policy in the time of Nicholas I, the Tsar's clear preference for the Russian nationality was.

which was considered beneath them, whilst most of the 'productive classes' were tied to the land. While the ratio of town to country dwellers in the 1840s was one to two in Great Britain and one to five in France, in Russia it was one to over 11. Such enterprise as there was remained in the hands of the small group of town dwellers. Many of the poorer labourers, artisans and shopkeepers engaged in business within strictly defined rules about how much they might buy and sell. A few managed to gain acceptance into a merchants' guild, which enhanced their status, but left them hampered by restrictions. Furthermore, since vast numbers of serfs and peasants were tied to the land (and even after 1861 it was near impossible for rural peasants to leave their farms), it was hard to attract a labour force to support any industrial development in towns.

The system acted as a brake on the development of efficient agriculture. Reliance on the plentiful labour of the serfs and peasants discouraged labour-saving practices and innovation. Farming continued from generation to generation with the same primitive methods. The controlling elders of the *mir* were usually the very men most committed to the traditional practices of their younger days, and were hostile to change. The strip system, once common in medieval England, was used to allocate land, so fallow land was wasted and holdings were usually scattered and difficult to farm efficiently.

On the whole, the class structure was regarded as 'normal', and ordained by the will of God and the Tsar. Since everyone had a place in life, there was no incentive to improve one's lot and few possessed the power to do so. The nobles remained isolated from the people that served them. Many lived at Court and spoke French rather than Russian, which they regarded as fit only for the use of the lower classes. The serfs (and from 1861 'peasants'), busy providing for their families and masters, had little time to consider their position. If they complained, it was usually about some local injustice rather than about the system as a whole. In any case, they could hardly be expected to have any understanding of 'rights', given their illiterate state.

What was Russia like politically?

All decision making in Russia was in the hands of the autocratic Tsar. He was regarded by his people as the 'little father' and was responsible only to God, a belief reinforced by the powerful Orthodox Church. In theory, at least, he protected and cared for his subjects, as a parent looks after their children – guiding, helping and punishing when necessary. This was a role which the Tsar's subjects, with few exceptions, accepted without question.

However, in a country of the size and complexity of Russia, the Tsar obviously needed help not only in reaching his decisions, but also in ensuring that they were carried out. Consequently, a small band of chosen ministers and a huge army of civil servants, known as the 'bureaucracy' assisted him. The country was divided into provinces, the provinces into districts and the districts into villages. Since communication was slow, local governors were relied on to make decisions, and some wielded a good deal of power. Their corruption was often a focus of 19th-century protests, although these men were sometimes made scapegoats for the Tsar, who was remote from everyday life. There was little encouragement for initiative in a system where length of service counted for more than efficiency.

1. Why might the geography of 19th-century Russia be important to a historical understanding of this period?

2. With reference to Russia's economic development in the 19th century, explain the statistics given in the tables on pages 20 and 21.

3. Which were the more important barriers to progress, Russia's climate and landscape or her social and political institutions?

2.2 What forces were there for continuity and for change within the Russian Empire on the eve of the Crimean War?

Autocracy

As Russia went to war in 1854, the reign of Tsar Nicholas I was nearing the end of its third decade. Throughout that period the Tsar had rigidly maintained the traditional, autocratic forms of government. Under this system, all executive political authority was concentrated in the hands of one man, and his edict (*ukaz*) was the only source of law. In principle, the Tsar's relationship with the Russian people was that of a loving, but authoritarian, father. 'His subjects,' as a senior police official explained, 'are his children, and children ought never to reason about their parents.' Just as it would be a dereliction of responsibility by a father to allow children to make decisions about the future of the family, so all political decisions lay in the hands of the Tsar. Although a variety of opinions existed in Russia on political and social issues, it remained difficult to express them, and virtually impossible to implement them unless one could enlist the support of the Tsar himself. This was the principle that was expressed by Tsar Paul I (1796–1801) when he informed an official that 'no one is important in Russia except the man who is speaking to me, and then only when he is speaking to me'.

The roles of the nobility and of the Orthodox Church

It remained a more difficult matter to implement the Tsar's authority throughout the vast Russian Empire (see map on page 30). At the centre, the main tool of government was His Imperial Majesty's Private Chancery. The Third Section of this Chancery was in charge of state security, standing at the centre of a complex web of censorship and surveillance. The work of the censors extended from the strict limitation of any reporting of events in western Europe, to the banning of any criticism of social conditions within Russia. It also involved the control of any careless or dangerous expression in any form of literature. In the reign of Nicholas I, the Third Section shadowed some 2,000 persons and dealt with around 15,000 security cases annually. In the distant provinces, the regime relied heavily upon the Russian nobility. Some of these served the Tsar as provincial governors, but all landowners had a vested interest in local law and order, ruling their estates and their serfs (peasants) almost as miniature Tsars. In the early years of the 19th century, this consensus of political and social interests provided Russian government with a considerable degree of unity. 'The landowner,' commented NicholasI's Chief of Police, 'is the most faithful, the unsleeping watchdog guarding the state; he is the natural police magistrate.' It remained unclear how the Russian Empire could be governed if that cohesion were ever dissolved.

Throughout the 19th century the Orthodox Church, with its message of faith in God and unquestioning submission to God's will, was the major support of the Tsarist regime. It endorsed the regime's claim that its power was an expression of the Divine Will. There were numerous other religious groups within the Empire. A commission set up in 1839 reported 9.3 million non-Orthodox Christians alone. However, for most of the century it was claimed, with varying degrees of coercion, that only members of the Orthodox faith could really be true and reliable subjects of the Tsar.

The political beliefs of Nicholas I

As has already been explained, any project for political or social change in 19th-century Russia would be totally dependent upon the reaction of the

Tsar himself. Several factors dictated, during the long reign of Nicholas I, that the Tsar's attitude would be rigidly conservative. Nicholas, for instance, was profoundly influenced by the dramatic Decembrist revolt that accompanied his accession in 1825. This was an unsuccessful attempt by liberal intellectuals and army officers in St Petersburg to place Nicholas' brother Constantine at the head of a constitutional monarchy. It filled Nicholas with horror. It convinced him that, despite the defeat of France in 1815, Europe was not safe from the radical ideas of the French Revolution, from blasphemous attempts to undermine the authority of monarchs who were God's representatives on earth. The fear and revulsion inspired by such **radicalism** were renewed at regular intervals: by the deposition of Charles X by the French in 1830; by the Polish revolt of 1831; and by the European revolutions of 1848. Nicholas' pretension to act as the 'gendarme of Europe' in Wallachia (1848) and in Hungary (1849) typified the role that he felt compelled to play throughout his reign – that of defender of the old discipline against the influences of 'rotten, pagan France'.

Radicalism: The belief that there should be great or extreme changes in society.

Slavophiles

The conservative principles of Nicholas I were part of a broader system of beliefs that dominated Russian thought in the 19th century. This was the conviction that Russian social organisation, religion, government, culture and philosophy were superior, by virtue of their isolation from the mainstreams of western European development. It was thus the duty of all Russians to protect these blessings against all external (i.e. western) threats. Those who wished to preserve and consolidate the essentials of Slav culture, and to spread that culture throughout the Empire, became known as 'slavophiles'. There can be no doubt that, for 30 years before the Crimean War, the Russian government shared the views of such slavophile thinkers. To the west, the reaction of Nicholas I to the Polish Revolt of 1831 showed very clearly his deep concern at the spread of western liberalism and **nationalism**. The rising was ruthlessly suppressed and many important elements of Polish national identity were subsequently attacked. The constitution was withdrawn, the universities closed and the Russian language was vigorously imposed in Polish public life. To the south, consistent attempts were made to support the Slav inhabitants of the declining Turkish Empire and to turn them into clients of Russia. Indeed, Nicholas' attempts to exert influence over the Sultan's Orthodox Christian subjects were a major cause of the Crimean War (see later section). The most spectacular expansion of Russian culture and political influence occurred to the south and south-east. The acquisition of Persian Armenia (1828), was followed by the establishment of influence over Dagestan and the Caucasus in the 1830s and 1840s, and of control over the Uzbeks and the Kazakhs in the same decades.

Nationalism: The growth and spread of loyalty towards a nation, rather than towards an individual ruler.

Westernisers

The alternative view was that Russia would be strengthened and modernised by the adoption of some western technical and philosophical ideas. Such 'westernising' beliefs comprised the major forces for change that operated within 19th-century Russia, but they made little headway during the reign of Nicholas I. Such ideas clearly lay behind the Decembrist revolt of 1825, and their association with that event condemned them in the eyes of the Tsar. The failure of the revolt drove liberal ideas underground and for the next 30 years they found expression mainly in literature and in the discussions of intellectuals. If those intellectuals were too outspoken in their statements, they might expect severe consequences. Alexander Pushkin, arguably the greatest of Russia's poets, had his work personally censored by the Tsar. It is

Dmitri Milyutin (1816–1912)
His early life was divided between military and academic circles, and he had some experience of travel in western Europe. Dmitri was Deputy Minister for War (1860) and Minister for War (1861–81), introducing expansive reforms of the Russian army. Milyutin resigned upon the death of Alexander II, but continued to sit on the Council of State until 1905.

Nikolai Milyutin (1818–1872)
Younger brother of Dmitri, and prominent among the 'enlightened bureaucrats' at the end of the reign of Nicholas I. As a high official in the Ministry of the Interior, he played a major role in the drafting of the legislation for the emancipation of the serfs (see page 00), but was dismissed for the radicalism of his views in 1861.

possible that Pushkin's political views contributed to his death in a duel (1837). Pyotr Chaadaev was officially pronounced insane after the publication of an anti-government essay in 1836.

Nevertheless, indirect criticism of the existing social system could be expressed in more subtle forms. Nikolai Gogol exposed provincial corruption in his play *The Government Inspector* (first performed in 1836) and satirised the institution of serfdom in his novel *Dead Souls* (1842). The publication of 224 new magazines from 1826 to 1854 indicates that ideas continued to circulate in Russia during the reign of Nicholas I, even if the Tsar remained unmoved by most of them. Similarly, the number of university students in Russia doubled between 1836 and 1848. This was mainly due to the government's desire to educate an administrative élite, but inevitably a proportion of this group would learn to think for themselves. Indeed, one of the most important developments of Nicholas' later years was the emergence of a group identified as the 'enlightened bureaucrats'. These younger officials emerged from the education system into official positions, fully aware of some of the weaknesses of the Russian system. They were eager to remedy them if their political masters would permit it. The Milyutin brothers, Dmitri and Nikolai, fit into this category. They

1. Where do you think the painter of this picture stood in the contemporary debate between westernisers and slavophiles?

2. What evidence is there in this work of the artist's attitude towards Russia's past and present?

A work by the Russian artist Vasili Perov, painted between 1865 and 1875 and entitled 'A monastic refectory'.

Patrons: Those who could offer jobs, promotion or favours to other individuals.

Paternalism: 'Fatherly' attitude shown by a ruler or government. All decisions are made for the people, thus taking away personal responsibility.

1. Outline the means by which the Tsar maintained his control in Russia in the first half of the 19th century.

2. Summarise the forces that resisted liberal and modernising reforms in Russia at the opening of Alexander II's reign.

3. On what issues did 'slavophiles' and 'westernisers' disagree in 19th-century Russia?

found influential **patrons** in such major political figures as Count Lev Perovski, the Minister of Internal Affairs, and Nicholas' younger son, the Grand Duke Constantine Nikolaevich.

The greatest weakness of such thinkers was that they had no alternative to Tsarist autocracy, but merely sought to give it a more humane, or a more efficient form. They were powerless as long as the Tsar refused to entertain their arguments. Nicholas steadfastly refused to do so, not because he rejected change, but because he remained extremely wary about the means of change. As the historian David Saunders (1992) concludes, 'the Tsar knew that changes had to be undertaken, but was determined not to allow them to be promoted by any movement or group beyond the control of the government. He believed that reform could be achieved by the government acting alone.' Nevertheless, the last years of Nicholas I's reign remained unpromising for the westernisers. The European revolutions of 1848–49 destroyed any positive elements that remained in the Tsar's **paternalism** and he reacted sternly against any hint of liberalism within Russia. The campaign against any freedom of thought or expression was typified by the formation of the Buturlin Committee to supervise and regulate the work of the existing censors, and by the attack (April 1849) upon the intellectual circle of M.V. Petrashevsky. This circle was influenced by the works of the French socialists, and included in its ranks the young writer Feodor Dostoevsky. With the appointment of a new Minister of Education, Platon Shirinsky-Shikhmatov, school fees were duly raised, the number of university students was reduced (from 4,600 in 1848 to 3,600 in 1854), and the study of such 'dangerous' subjects as philosophy and European constitutional law was suppressed.

2.3 Was serfdom a source of strength or of weakness for the Russian state and the Russian economy?

What was serfdom?

While intellectuals debated in St Petersburg and Moscow, and while ministers issued decrees, the social and economic life of the Empire centred overwhelmingly upon the vast Russian countryside. The population of the Russian Empire in 1858 was 74 million, of whom nearly 85% worked on the land. Of these peasants, some 22.5 million were serfs; that is, they were the personal property of the landowners for whom they worked and on whose estates they lived. In addition, over 19 million were 'state peasants', tied to lands owned by the Crown. The authority of these owners, sometimes delegated to the elders of the peasant commune (the *mir*), was almost absolute. It extended over the allocation of land, labour dues, taxes and corporal punishment, to the actual sale of the serf to a new master.

The institution of serfdom constituted the most difficult domestic problem facing the government, just as it had for more than a century. The moral objections to such a system had been recognised, but swept under the carpet for more than half a century before the Crimean War. 'There is no doubt,' Nicholas told his Council of State in 1842, 'that serfdom in its present situation in our country is an evil, palpable and obvious to all, but to attack it now would be something still more harmful.' Under Nicholas I, legislation did away with some of the most inhuman aspects of the institution:

● forbidding the splitting up of families by the sale of individuals (1833)

● banning the auctioning of serfs (1841).

Such tentative reforms did little to still the peasant discontent that had been a constant feature of Russian politics for a century. There were 712 outbreaks of revolt between 1826 and 1854, half of them between 1844 and 1854. In addition to these issues of social stability, there were also increasing economic arguments in some well-informed quarters for the abolition of serfdom. As the rural population increased, and as agricultural practices in Russia slipped further behind those in western Europe, serfdom made less and less economic sense. Serf labour found it increasingly difficult to produce enough grain both to feed the local population and to provide a surplus for the landowner to put on the market. Many landowners found their debts mounting, to such an extent that, by 1860, 60% of private serfs had in fact been mortgaged to the state. Yet two compelling reasons stood out against the abolition of serfdom. One was that the monarchy scarcely dared to challenge the vast vested interest of the nobility and landowners, whose financial and social status depended upon the number of 'souls' that they owned. The other was that the monarchy itself derived great benefit, not only as the owner of the 'state peasants', but also from the role played by the landowners in the maintenance of local order and stability.

Serfdom and industrial backwardness

While slavophiles stressed the importance of serfdom in the preservation of political and social stability, westernisers emphasised its role as a brake upon Russia's economic development. Essentially, although not exclusively a rural institution, serfdom placed severe restrictions upon the development in Russia of an urban middle class, and of an urban workforce. In 1833 the total urban population was about two million. Even then, most towns were market and administrative, rather than industrial, centres. Russia lacked the basis for any serious industrial development on the scale of western Europe. The Soviet historian P.A. Khromov estimated that only 67,000 people were employed in textile manufacture in 1830, and only 20,000 in the iron and steel industries. Russia's cotton industry in 1843 had only 350,000 mechanised spindles, compared with 3.5 million in France and 11 million in Britain. Its share of world iron production dropped, as the industry developed faster abroad, from 12% in 1830 to 4% in 1859. The classic indication of Russia's industrial backwardness was the slow growth of its railways. The first, a short line for the use of the Imperial family from St Petersburg to the summer residence at Tsarskoe Selo, was built in 1837. The first train did not run between St Petersburg and Moscow until 1851.

1. What powers did Russian landowners have over their serfs?

2. Why has serfdom usually been regarded as a force that held back economic growth in Russia?

2.4 What were the domestic political implications of Russia's defeat in the Crimea?

Allied troops landed on Russian soil at Eupatoria (14 September 1854) and within two weeks had laid siege to Sevastopol, Russia's major naval base on the Black Sea. The year-long siege showed both facets of the Russian military machine. The gallantry of the common soldiers defied all attempts to take the town, but weaknesses of strategy and supply contributed to the defeat of a number of relief operations, at Balaclava (October 1854), at Inkerman (November 1854) and at the Chornaya (August 1855). The fall of Sevastopol in September 1855 fulfilled the main objectives of the British and the French and paved the way for a peace settlement.

A superficial consideration of the peace terms concluded in Paris in 1856 suggests that Russia escaped lightly. Despite the neutralisation of the Black Sea and the loss of its influence over the Romanian principalities,

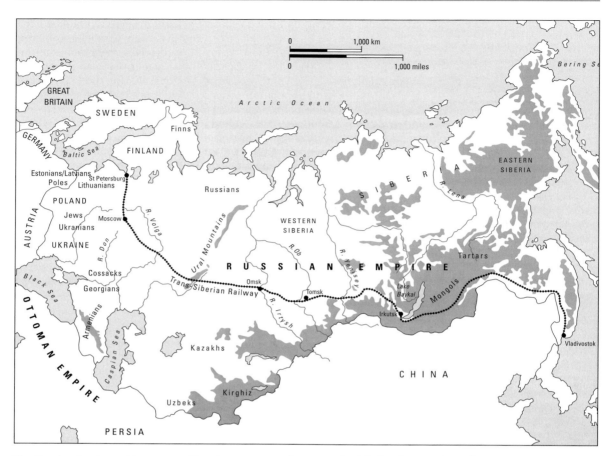

The Russian Empire and its nationalities, 1914 – showing the Trans-Siberian railway

Russia was never threatened with the destruction of its 'great power' status – as France had been in 1815. The nature and causes of its defeat, however, had more serious implications for the Tsarist regime. Russia's vast military strength had proved to be an illusion. Partly because of the need to maintain forces on other frontiers, but largely because of the lack of a modern system of communications, Russia was never able to muster in the Crimea more than 60,000 of its one million soldiers. Worse still, Russian industry proved largely incapable of equipping these troops properly. It could provide no more than one musket for every two men at the start of the war. It could equip only 4% of Russian troops with the newer, long-range percussion rifle, when 33% of French troops and 50% of British troops used this weapon. The implications of such failures can hardly be exaggerated. The strongest justification for autocracy, and the most persuasive argument of the slavophiles, was that the existing system guaranteed Russian stability and greatness. So its failure seemed to call into question the very bases of Russian politics and society. The defeat in the Crimea appeared to justify the crushing verdict delivered by the government censor A.V. Nikitenko: 'the main shortcoming of the reign of Nikolai Pavlovich [Tsar Nicholas I] consisted in the fact that it was all a mistake'.

In the aftermath of the defeat, one of the major preoccupations of the Tsar's government was with the state of the Russian army. Various examples of incompetence on the part of the British and French commanders could not hide the fact that they commanded superior armies, which were better equipped and more effectively organised. Bravely as Russia's serf soldiers had fought, it was clear that they could not be relied upon as the basis of an effective, modern army. Above all, the Crimean War demonstrated to the

Russians the advantages of a western-style army in which soldiers served for a relatively short period, before returning to civilian life as members of a trained military reserve. Serfdom made it impossible to implement such a system in Russia, for the traditional practice had been to free serf soldiers at the end of their marathon, 25-year stint of military service. To continue such a practice after a shorter term of service would mean the liberation of large numbers of serfs by instalments. To return men to serfdom at the end of their period of military service would mean a steady accumulation in the provinces of discontented serfs with military training. In this respect, as in many others, the Crimean War reinforced the arguments of those who saw the abolition of serfdom as an inevitable preliminary to other forms of reform and modernisation within Russia.

1. What weaknesses were revealed by Russia's defeat in the Crimean War?

2. Why did Alexander II decide to adopt a programme of reforming measures at the end of the Crimean War?

2.5 How effective were the measures taken from 1861 to emancipate the Russian serfs?

Alexander II (1818–1881)
Tsar of Russia from 1855. Deeply influenced by Russia's defeat in the Crimean War (1854–56), he embarked upon an extensive reform of Russian government and society. Remembered as the 'Tsar Liberator' for his emancipation of the serfs (1861), he was also responsible for reforms relating to the systems of law, local government and military service. He was unwilling, on the other hand, to compromise over the principle of autocracy, an inconsistency that left him isolated from reformers and conservatives alike. His reign saw an increasing degree of radical political opposition, and he was eventually the victim of an assassination by the terrorist group, the People's Will.

The process of emancipation

In the midst of the crisis of the Crimean War Tsar Nicholas I died (2 March 1855), apologising to his son for the state in which he left the empire. Alexander II came to the throne at the age of 36, the undisputed heir, and far better prepared and trained for the succession than his father had been. It was never the intention of the new Tsar to depart from the principles of autocracy. Yet he was less of a disciplinarian than his father, more open to the arguments of others, and was convinced, by the experience of the war and by the more liberal group of ministers that he chose to consult, that fundamental changes had to be made.

The new Tsar became responsible for the introduction of the most spectacular social reform of the 19th century. Speaking to the nobility of Moscow in April 1856, and referring both to the Crimean War and to renewed peasant disturbances, Alexander said that 'the existing order of serfdom cannot remain unchanged. It is better to abolish serfdom from above than to wait for the time when it will begin to abolish itself from below.' The early months of Alexander's reign saw an unparalleled degree of discussion in intellectual, noble and administrative circles, and an unusual consensus in favour of change. The peasantry, too, was in a state of unusual agitation. Under these pressures, Alexander may appear less as a far-sighted reformer than as a dutiful ruler forced to confront challenges of great complexity.

Women barge haulers in Russia

The terms of the Edict of Emancipation

The Edict of Emancipation was issued on 19 February 1861 and constituted a fundamental break with Russia's past.

- The serfs were granted their personal freedom over a period of two years.

- They now possessed the same legal freedoms enjoyed by other Russians, such as the freedom to own land, to marry without interference, and to use the law courts.

- The freed peasants were granted ownership of the houses in which they lived, and the plots around those houses, which they had previously worked.

- The Edict confirmed the landlords' legal ownership of the land on their estates, but provided (from 1863 onwards) for the purchase of some of that land by the peasants. Maximum and minimum prices were laid down based upon the productivity of the land in different regions, but the precise details were to be negotiated between peasant and landlord.

- The government was to compensate landlords for land transferred to the peasantry, paying them the purchase price in the form of government bonds.

- To recoup its losses, the government charged the peasants 'redemption dues' in the form of regular repayments over a period of 49 years.

- The same terms applied to state peasants, although in their case the period of transition to freedom was five years.

- Domestic serfs who had not previously worked the land did not receive land under the terms of the Edict.

The lapse of five years between Alexander's Moscow speech and the Edict of Emancipation of February 1861 (see panel above) reflected the difficulty of the task that the Tsar had undertaken. It also provides some important clues to the forces that shaped the final Edict. Undoubtedly there were those within the government who worked for far-reaching reform that would help to reshape Russian society. Even if, as historian David Saunders concludes in *Russia in the Age of Reaction and Reform, 1801–1881* (published in 1992), 'none of the enlightened bureaucrats of the reign of Alexander II was a social revolutionary, all of them sought greater social fluidity. Like the Tsar, they were determined to maintain order, but they were also anxious to discover new sources of energy.' Few of the 232,000 serf owners were sufficiently scared to co-operate unreservedly with the Tsar. Only the Lithuanian nobility accepted his invitation to submit plans for emancipation in their region. The greatest problem was land. Land could only be granted to the peasants at the expense of the landlords, and such a step would come dangerously close to accepting the radical doctrine that the land truly belonged to those who worked it. To liberate the serfs without land, on the other hand, would merely have served to create a vast and dangerous mass of destitute third-class citizens. So difficult was it for the Russian landowners to grasp this that it required a direct order from the Tsar, the Nazimov Rescript (November 1857), to make it clear to them that the serfs were to receive land along with their personal liberty.

How great a reform was the emancipation?

No European government in the 19th century broke with its social and economic past so emphatically as Russia did in 1861. Yet, the political system that initiated these reforms, supposedly to strengthen its own position, had collapsed within 60 years of their introduction. It is hardly surprising that historians have found it difficult to agree about the success of the emancipation. Many have felt constrained to dismiss it as a fraud, and to show the Tsar embarking on a course of false liberalism, only to recoil from the true implications of his actions. The historian Hugh Seton-Watson, in *The Russian Empire, 1801–1917* (1988), makes a valuable comparison when he set the Tsar's reforms alongside the emancipation of the black American slaves at the same time. He stresses that the American reform was carried out less peacefully and was far less successful in guaranteeing the personal freedom of those that it supposedly liberated. A more recent authority on the Russian peasantry, David Moon (*The Russian Peasantry 1600–1930*, published in 1999) echoes this judgement, adding that the guarantee of land was a major benefit that was not shared by the American slaves. David Christian, in his book *Imperial and Soviet Russia* (1997), supports such views by emphasising that the emancipation of the serfs was in fact wholly successful in achieving its immediate objectives. 'The peasant disturbances which had continued for so long, like approaching thunder, died away to a distant rumble for 40 years after 1862. The government had succeeded in the complex task of abolishing serfdom without provoking an immediate rebellion. That was a considerable achievement.'

Much depends upon the criteria that one uses to evaluate the emancipation. If one judges it in terms of rights and liberties, it is difficult to remain unimpressed, for the legal status of some 40 million Russians was transformed at a stroke. If one considers, as most of the peasants probably did, the impact of the reform upon the wealth and the living standards of the former serfs, the short-term effects do not appear so positive. Although the reform ended an era of Russian social history, its immediate impact was lessened by a host of practical problems in its implementation. Above all, it could not be implemented in the localities without the co-operation of the landlords, and was thus often applied in ways that served their interests. The process was always slow and the land settlement made upon the ex-serfs was usually unsatisfactory. The areas granted were often too small, resulting in an average holding of about nine acres (four hectares), and the landlords rarely hesitated to compensate themselves for the loss of free serf labour by inflating the estimated value of the land. Many peasants found themselves saddled with **redemption payments** far greater than the actual productive value of the land that they farmed. David Moon estimates that peasants may have been overcharged by as much as 20% in the more fertile 'black earth' regions, and by as much as 90% in less productive regions. Besides, many peasants were convinced that the land was really theirs in the first place, and thus greatly resented the purchase by redemption payments of their own 'property'. Lastly, although freed from the landowner, the peasant often remained bound to the *mir*, which continued to exercise many restrictions upon travel and freedom of enterprise.

In the shorter run, too, emancipation did not seem to solve the problem of industrial backwardness. The inadequacy of peasant land holdings ruled out the rapid rise of a prosperous class of peasant consumers. As late as 1878 it was estimated that only 50% of the peasantry farmed allotments large enough for the production of surplus goods. This proportion failed to increase largely because of a dramatic 50% rise in the rural population of Russia between 1860 and 1897. Nor did the government's reforms help to create a landowning class with the funds for substantial agricultural or

Redemption payments: The sums of money which peasants paid every year to the government to purchase the land they had been granted in 1861.

1. What did the Russian serfs gain by the Edict of Emancipation?

2. Why did it take so long after the Crimean War to complete the legislation for the emancipation of the Russian serfs?

3. Did the emancipation of the Russian serfs accomplish what it set out to achieve?

industrial investment. The majority of the landowners before emancipation were so deeply in debt that it has been estimated that 248 million of the 543 million roubles paid to them by the government by 1871 was used to pay off existing debts and mortgages.

Why did the emancipation of the serfs entail a further programme of reforms?

In some respects, the landowning nobility found it harder than the serfs did to adjust to the new economic world created by the emancipation. Many simply abandoned that world by selling their land-holdings. Thus, whereas in 1862 the nobility owned 94.8 million hectares of land in Russia, their landed property in 1911 amounted to only 46.9 million hectares. It could be argued that, by undermining the landed interests, and the role of the nobility in local government, the emancipation struck a serious blow at the effectiveness of Tsarist government. It was inevitable, therefore, that emancipation should be followed by a wider programme of reforms aimed at repairing the damage that had been done in this respect.

The zemstva

This wider programme also owed much to the liberal thinking of those who now surrounded the Tsar. Particularly notable was a series of proposals put forward by the nobility of Tver province. The essentially liberal nature of these proposals is illustrated by the fact that they included the suggestion of a national, elected assembly to advise the Tsar. Although this notion was rejected out of hand, what Alexander accepted certainly constituted a substantial step in the direction of liberal local government. An Imperial decree of 1864 established a series of local governmental assemblies known as *zemstva*. Potentially such elected assemblies, supplemented from 1870 by similar urban assemblies, were as radical a measure in an autocracy as the emancipation of serfs itself. It is clear, however, that Alexander saw them as props for the autocracy, rather than as a step away from the traditional system of government. Thus the hopes of Russian liberals were dashed almost before they were raised. Both the system of voting and their established local reputations made it easy for the conservative nobility to dominate these assemblies, and at provincial level they occupied 74% of all *zemstvo* seats in 1865–67. Furthermore, when *zemstvo* representatives had the audacity to suggest that delegates from each assembly should gather to form a central, national body, they were sharply reminded by the Tsar of the limitations upon their powers. At this point, Alexander stood at the crossroads between autocracy and liberal reform. Having whetted the appetite for the latter, he remained committed to the former.

Legal, military and educational reforms

The emancipation of the serfs also required substantial reform of the Russian legal system, now that the summary justice of the landlord could no longer be so easily applied in the localities. From 1865 onwards measures were introduced to ensure that:

● legal proceedings were conducted in public;

● they were uniform for all classes of society;

● a jury system prevailed for the trial of all charges;

● judges were independent of the government.

Martial law: Military law when applied to civilians. Normal civil rights are suspended, allowing the government to arrest individuals and detain them without trial. Suspects could be tried by military court (without a jury) and given the death penalty if found guilty.

Although the government retained the power to impose **martial law** in emergencies, and did so to a wide degree during the terrorist crisis of the 1870s, these were remarkable reforms. They ensured that, in Seton-Watson's words, 'the court-room was the one place in Russia where real freedom of speech prevailed'.

If all these reforms were directly or indirectly a response to the military disasters of the Crimea, then it was only logical that the Russian military establishment should also be re-examined. Army life had traditionally reflected the state of Russian society, with privileges for the noble officers and savage penalties for the peasant soldiers. The task of bringing greater equity and efficiency into this system fell to the Minister of War, Dmitri Milyutin. He was perhaps the leading liberal figure in Russia in the 1860s, and was hailed by Florinsky and other Russian historians as one of the few outstanding statesmen of imperial Russia. During his tenure of office Milyutin reduced the term of service in the army from the 'life sentence' of 25 years to a period of six years. He also introduced universal military service (1874) to which all males were now liable at 20 years of age, without the loopholes that had frequently allowed the nobility and richer classes to escape the obligation to serve their country. The abolition of more brutal forms of punishment, and of military service as a form of punishment for criminal offences, went far to humanise conditions in the Russian army. A further victim of Milyutin's reforms were the 'military colonies' to which the sons of long-term recruits had been sent to be trained as the next generation of soldiers.

Lastly, education, always an accurate barometer of the philosophy of Russian governments, was liberalised. The Minister of Education, A.S. Norov, reversed most of the repressive measures of the previous reign. The numbers of university students were allowed to rise (1855) and lectures were permitted once again on European government (1857) and on philosophy (1860). A new University Statute (1863) gave the universities more autonomy in the conduct of their affairs than at any previous point in their history.

1. What further reforms did Alexander II carry out with the emancipation of serfs?

2. To what extent were Alexander II's reforms in the 1860s motivated by a desire for a more modern state and society in Russia, and to what extent did they bring about such results?

3. How profound, and how effective, were the great reforms of the 1860s in Russia?

Source-based questions: The impact of emancipation

SOURCE A

The Tsar outlines his expectations of the emancipated peasants

The serfs will receive in time the full rights of free rural inhabitants. At the same time, and with the consent of the nobility, they may acquire in full ownership the arable lands and other properties which are allotted them for permanent use.
And now We confidently expect that the freed serfs will appreciate and recognise the considerable sacrifices which the nobility has made on their behalf. They should understand that by acquiring property and greater freedom, they have an obligation to society and to themselves to live up to the letter of the new law. Abundance is acquired only through hard work, wise use of strength and resources, strict economy, and above all, through an honest God-fearing life. And now, Orthodox people, make the sign of the cross, and join with Us to invoke God's blessing upon your free labour.

Part of the Emancipation Edict, 1861

SOURCE B

A British traveller and journalist comments upon the economic impact of emancipation upon the Russian peasants

If the serfs had a great many ill-defined obligations to fulfil [before emancipation], they had, on the other hand, a good many ill-defined privileges. They grazed their cattle during part of the year on the manor lands; they received firewood, and occasionally logs for repairing their huts; and in times of famine they could look to their master for support. All this has now come to an end. Their burdens and their privileges have been swept away together, and been replaced by clearly-defined, unbending legal relations. They now have to pay the market price for every stick of firewood that they burn, and for every acre of land on which they graze their cattle. If a cow dies, or a horse is stolen, the owner can no longer go to the proprietor in the hope of receiving a present.

From a contemporary account written by Sir Donald McKenzie

Source-based questions: The impact of emancipation

SOURCE C

A radical landowner describes the peasants' response to emancipation on one of his estates

I was in Nikolskoye in August 1861, and again in the summer of 1862, and I was struck by the quiet, intelligent way in which the peasants had accepted the new conditions. They knew perfectly well how difficult it would be to pay the redemption tax for the land, which was in reality an indemnity to the nobles in place of the obligations of serfdom. But they so much valued the abolition of their personal enslavement that they accepted the ruinous charges – not without murmuring, but as a hard necessity – the moment that personal freedom was obtained.

Peter Kropotkin, *Memoirs of Prince Kropotkin* (published in 1930)

(a) Study Source C.

From this Source and your own knowledge, explain the reference to 'the redemption tax for the land'.
[20 marks]

(b) Study Sources C and D.

To what extent do the figures in Source D confirm the impression stated in Source C that the emancipated peasants would find it difficult to pay the redemption dues imposed upon them? [40 marks]

(c) Study all of the Sources.

Using all of these Sources and your own knowledge, examine the view that the Russian peasantry lost more than they gained through the Edict of Emancipation. [60 marks]

SOURCE D

Statistics for the repayment of redemption dues in different regions of Russia

(The table covers the years 1876–80.)

	Sums due*	Arrears*	Arrears as % of sums due
Northern provinces	8,527	3,968	46
Baltic provinces	1,686	161	10
North-western provinces	11,999	2,646	22
South-western provinces	12,928	1,125	9
Industrial regions	24,344	5,402	22
Central black-soil provinces	40,574	6,443	15
Eastern provinces	22,220	7,975	36
Southern provinces	9,329	3,128	33
Ukraine	11,408	1,021	9

*(thousands of roubles)

Taken from: E. Wilmot, *The Great Powers 1814–1914*

2.6 To what extent does Alexander II deserve the title of 'Tsar Liberator'?
A CASE STUDY IN HISTORICAL INTERPRETATION

There can be no doubt that Alexander II bore direct responsibility for the great reforms that occurred in Russia during his reign. One of the peculiarities of Russian government, as we have seen, was the fact that all executive power lay in the hands of the Tsar, and that there were simply no means by which political initiatives could be implemented without his authority. Whatever pressures might be generated by economic or social forces, only the Tsar could trigger change. Reform, therefore, took place in the 1860s for two reasons. While the impact of defeat in the Crimean War was an extremely important factor, nothing could have been achieved in Russia without a new ruler whose response to that defeat was to listen to reformers. The accession of Alexander II raised great hopes for an end to blank and sterile reaction, and the first actions of the new Tsar seemed to justify those hopes. Political prisoners were released, censorship was relaxed, tax arrears were cancelled, and some of the liberties of Poland and of the Catholic Church were restored.

Yet it is impossible to view Alexander II as a liberal in any real sense. Coming to the throne at the age of 36, he was less of a soldier and less of a disciplinarian than his father. Also he was made more aware by the Crimean War of the faults in the social and governmental systems of Russia. Yet his reforms were motivated by a desire to strengthen autocracy rather than to replace it. Those historians who have denied Alexander credit as a great reformer have often done so on the grounds that at the end of his reign, 'the concept of the state embodied in the person of the auto-crat was in no way altered' (the words of W. Bruce Lincoln in *The Great Reforms, Autocracy, Bureaucracy and the Politics of Change in Imperial Russia*, 1990).

What then were Alexander's motives? Did he act predominantly in the interests of the traditional political establishment? Russian Marxist histo-rians insisted that the Tsar was motivated by the desire to benefit his noble supporters rather than the serfs, and that emancipation was mainly a means of putting money in the pockets of a regenerated land-owning class. Others have emphasised other motives, equally beneficial to the establish-ment. Dmitri Milyutin, one of the most prominent of Alexander's reforming ministers, consistently stressed the beneficial impact that eman-cipation would have upon the army, perhaps because he felt that this was the kind of argument to which his master would be most susceptible.

Machiavellian: A term describing a form of political activity which is guided by cynical self-interest and advantage, rather than by any form of abstract principle. The term derives from the 15th-century Italian, Niccolo Machiavelli, who was an advocate of such political activity.

This is probably unfair to Alexander, for there is little in his life to suggest that he was cynical or **Machiavellian**. Most historians agree that he did not have the mental agility to operate in that way, and none suggests that the reforms of the 1860s sprang from Alexander's superior political vision. He was not a clever man, and was not at ease in the company of clever people. As a contemporary cruelly noted, 'when the Emperor talks to an intellectual he has the appearance of someone with rheumatism who is standing in a draught'. The most satisfactory explanation may be to view Alexander's reforms as arising from the specific strengths and weaknesses in his personality. The **anarchist** Pyotr Kropotkin, who served at court before embracing radical politics, observed that the Tsar was a complex and confusing man:

Anarchist: One who believes in 'anarchy', or the absence of government. This philosophy believes that society should be self-ordering, and should not be directed by orders and sanctions decreed by a central government.

> 'Two different men lived in him, both strongly developed, struggling with each other. He was possessed of a calm, reasoned courage in the face of a real danger, but he lived in constant fear of dangers that existed only in his brain.'

Such a personality is well reflected in the inconsistent nature of the Tsar's reforms. As an autocrat, he recognised it as his duty to rectify a system that had manifestly failed Russia in the Crimea, yet he was uncertain how best to go about the task, and apprehensive whenever he glimpsed the more radical implications of his policy. A number of recent historians have based their evaluation of Alexander's policies upon this sort of contradiction. Perhaps David Saunders, in *Russia in the Age of Reaction and Reform, 1801–1881* (1992), captures the Tsar's state of mind most accurately when he concludes that 'the laws which freed the serfs emerged from a process that the Tsar barely understood and over which he had only partial control.' A little earlier, both W.E. Mosse in *Alexander II and the Modernisation of Russia* (1958) and Hugh Seton-Watson in *The Russian*

Empire, 1801–1917 (1967) had seen Alexander II confronting the choice between autocracy and modern constitutional development. They saw him refusing to abandon the former, and failing mainly because he sought to reach an unrealistic compromise between the two.

In the final analysis, however, it seems harsh and unhistorical to criticise Alexander II because he could not or would not turn his back on the philosophy of his ancestors. Even if they did not solve the problems that they addressed as thoroughly as the government anticipated, and even if they did not quite address the right problems, the reforms of the 1860s were staggering in the breadth of their conception and extremely far-reaching in their impact. Historian David Saunders grudgingly accepts this in his judgement that although they were 'conceptually limited, poorly executed, incomplete, unsustained and insecure, the measures enacted by Alexander II nevertheless transformed the Russian Empire'. Some might prefer this more charitable judgement made at the time by the Russian liberal, B.N. Chicherin:

1. Why have historians found it difficult to decide how much credit should be given to Alexander II for his domestic reforms?

2. Comment upon the view that Alexander II's reputation as a reformer has been greatly exaggerated.

'Alexander was called upon to execute one of the hardest tasks that can confront an autocratic ruler: to completely remodel the enormous state which had been entrusted to his care, to abolish an age-old order founded on slavery, to replace it with civil decency and freedom, to put a repressed and humiliated society on its feet and to give it the chance to flex its muscles.'

The kind of political and social liberation that emerged from all this may not have been the kind that either Alexander or Chicherin envisaged, but it was liberation nevertheless.

2.7 How seriously was the Tsarist regime threatened by the opposition that arose during Alexander II's reign?

Instead of strengthening and stabilising the regime, and earning universal acclaim for the 'Tsar Liberator', the reforms of Alexander II drew fierce criticism from many sections of the political spectrum. The Tsar suffered the classic fate of those who try to enjoy the best of both worlds, and became trapped in a cross-fire of criticism. Conservatives resented the loss of influence and privilege, while liberals became frustrated at the Tsar's refusal to take his reforms to their logical conclusion. Many governmental departments became the scenes of bitter personal and political rivalries, such as that between Dmitri Milyutin and P.A. Shuvalov at the Ministry of War. The disappointment of conservatives and liberals alike, however, was muted by the need to rally against the more radical and revolutionary forms of opposition that developed as Alexander's reign progressed. This opposition was, in some cases, fuelled by a fierce ideological hatred of the regime, and encouraged by the freer political atmosphere created by the Tsar's reforms.

The Polish Revolt

The bitter disillusion that Alexander II felt at the reaction to his role as the 'Tsar Liberator' was quickly fuelled by the revolt of his Polish subjects in 1863. Poland had fallen under the power of the Tsars as a result of a compromise made at the Congress of Vienna in 1815. Rather than allow the former independent kingdom of Poland to become part of the Russian Empire, the allies had preserved its nominal independence. However, they had allowed the Tsar to rule as King of Poland, thus effectively combining the two states. This special status, and the vague paternalism of

Alexander II, had combined to give Poland rather freer institutions than existed anywhere else in eastern Europe. Poland enjoyed a constitution, a parliament, and the use of Polish as an official language. The first Polish rebellion (1831) had resulted, however, in the suppression of many of these liberties by Nicholas I. Poland nevertheless, like other parts of the Empire, had reason to greet the accession of Alexander II with optimism. The Tsar's gestures included the filling of the vacant Catholic archbishopric of Warsaw (1856) and the formation of a new Agricultural Society (1857) to promote new techniques of cultivation.

On the surface it appeared that the question of land reform was the most pressing of Poland's problems. Unlike the rest of the Empire, however, the demand for such reform was directly connected with the desire to re-establish Polish nationhood, a desire to which no Tsar could agree. It was nationalist demonstrations in Warsaw that set off a train of events in February 1861. In April the Agricultural Society was dissolved on account of its links with nationalist unrest, and in the demonstrations which resulted up to 200 were killed. In May 1862 the Tsar's brother, Constantine, a liberal by reputation, was appointed **viceroy** in an attempt to defuse the situation. He came close to assassination in his first month in office. Further concessions were proposed, including the emancipation of Polish Jews and the opening of a university in Warsaw. A proposal for the conscription of Poles into the Russian army nullified any calming effect, and armed insurrection broke out in January 1863.

This was largely a rural rebellion, with the majority of the landowners more or less favourable to the rebels, but with the attitude of the peasants remaining highly **ambiguous**. It took nearly a year to control and was not properly over until August 1864. In that year **agrarian** reform was at last carried through, giving **freehold tenure** to 700,000 peasant families, without any redemption payments to the Russian government. Although some historians have seen the reform mainly as an attempt to separate the peasants from the nationalist landowners, it was consistent with Russia's relatively liberal treatment of Poland between 1855 and 1863. The Tsar saw its general failure as further evidence of ingratitude and of the futility of conciliatory gestures. In reality, the failure demonstrated the impossibility of reconciling such beliefs as Polish nationalism with Tsarist autocracy. Henceforth Russian policy towards all the nationalities of the Empire would be one of Russification (see later section).

The growth of radical opposition; from Herzen to Nihilism

The most important names on the Russian left in the 1850s and 1860s were those of Alexander Herzen, Nikolai Chernyshevsky and Dmitri Pisarev. Herzen, already an exile from Russia by 1848, had moderated his stance as a result of the revolutions of that year and became more willing to accept and applaud reforms, even if they came from the Tsarist government. His journal *The Bell* (*Kolokol*) was published from London and regularly reached influential persons in Russia by unofficial channels.

Chernyshevsky took the opposite path. Originally part of the literary radicalism of the 1850s and enthusiastic about the emancipation of the serfs, he came to realise that further worthwhile reform was impossible without a fundamental alteration of Russia's political and economic bases. Thus he stands on the threshold of a new generation of Russian radicals who paved the way for the philosophy of the 1917 revolution. Chernyshevsky himself was largely dismayed by the increasing use of violence by those who claimed to be his disciples. Nevertheless his novel *What is to be Done?* (1862) inspired the next generation and provided the title for one of Vladimir Lenin's most important works.

Viceroy: Governor of a country or province acting in the name and the authority of the ruler (i.e. a vice-king; from 'roi', French for king.)

Ambiguous: Unclear or confusing because it can be understood in more than one way.

Agrarian: Relating to the ownership and use of land, especially farmland.

Freehold tenure: Originally a form of ownership which required a tenant to give only services and obligations as were worthy of a freeman (i.e. not a serf).

'**Nihilism**': Belief that rejects all political or religious authority and current ideas, in favour of the individual. From the Latin *nihil* – nothing.

Populism: Belief that all political activities or ideas are based on the interests and opinions of the ordinary people.

To a limited extent, Pisarev supplied an answer to Chernyshevsky's famous question. Rejecting revolution as impossible for the present, Pisarev advocated a thorough examination and revision of the moral and material bases of society, in order to provide a better future basis for justice and equality. His followers were advised not to 'accept any single principle on trust, however much respect surrounds that principle'. From this desire to accept nothing of the existing society without question, the novelist Ivan Turgenev (1818–1883) named this philosophy '**nihilism**'. Pisarev liked the term and accepted it.

Populism

Many young radicals were reluctant, however, to wait for revolution – as Pisarev thought necessary. Broadly, they envisaged two possible answers to the question 'What is to be done?' One of these was **populism**, a movement that dominated Russian radicalism in the mid-1870s. The founders of populism, Nikolai Mikhailovsky and Pyotr Lavrov, viewed the Russian peasantry not as a force of great revolutionary potential, but as one which needed thorough re-education. Thus in 1874–75 some 3,000 young radicals invaded the countryside to open the eyes of the population to their plight and to the sources of their salvation. This movement – 'To the People' (*v narod*) – was a depressing failure. Hugh Seton-Watson notes that 'some peasants listened with sympathy, many were hostile, and most understood hardly anything of what they heard'. Over 1,600 of these populists (*narodniki*) were arrested between 1873 and 1877, often handed over to the police by the very peasants, blindly loyal to the Tsar, that they sought to help. Learning from these failures, a breakaway group calling itself 'Land and Liberty' (*zemlya i volya*) made some progress in the following years with a revised plan that involved living with the peasants for longer periods to understand their mentality better. Perhaps the most lasting legacy of populism was the foundation by members of 'Land and Liberty' of the first unions for Russian industrial workers in Odessa (1875) and in St Petersburg (1878).

The rise of terrorism

For those with equal conviction but less patience, the more attractive alternative was conspiracy and terrorism. The first attempt on the life of the Tsar occurred in 1866 when a student named Karakozov shot at him in the streets of St Petersburg. The best claim to be the founder of the conspiratorial activism that triumphed in 1917 belongs, however, to Sergei Nechayev. Apparently motivated by a mixture of idealism and ambition, he created a complex system of revolutionary cells up to 1869 by ruthless methods. This system collapsed when internal arguments caused him to murder a fellow conspirator, and the trial that followed gave full publicity to Nechayev's unsavoury aims and methods. The real 'heyday' of terrorism as a means towards political change followed a split in 1879 in the ranks of 'Land and Liberty'. One wing, led by Georgi Plekhanov and Pavel Axelrod and calling itself the 'Black Partition' (*chorny peredyel*), favoured further peaceful work among the peasants. The other, 'The People's Will' (*narodnaya volya*), advocated violence as the trigger to general revolution. Although other government officials were among their early victims, their chief target was always the Tsar himself. Within a period of a year, Alexander survived: another attempt to shoot him (April 1879); an attempt to dynamite the royal train, which blew up the wrong train (December 1879); and an explosion in the banqueting hall of the Winter Palace (February 1880).

Although by the end of 1880 the radical opposition within Russia had achieved nothing of worth, many of the methods and preconceptions of the 1917 revolutionaries can be seen in the process of formation during the reign of Alexander II.

Conclusion

No member of the Tsar's government could have remained complacent about the wave of violence that Russia experienced between 1878 and 1881. When the Tsar himself was added to the list of the terrorists' high-ranking victims in March 1881, it became clear that the revolutionaries could indeed strike successfully at any member of the political establishment. The Tsar's assassination made it equally clear, however, that they could neither destroy nor replace that establishment. It remained as true as ever that social and political power lay in the hands of a narrow élite, and that no political change could be brought about by anyone outside that group.

Alexander II's son succeeded peacefully to the throne and pursued policies that crippled the revolutionary organisations for a generation. Terrorism failed to destroy Tsarist government for at least three reasons.

1. By its very nature – intellectual, exclusive and secretive – it could not mobilise the considerable resources of peasant discontent that constituted the major threat to political stability.

2. It offered no practical alternative to the existing government, no regime that could replace Tsarism if indeed it did collapse under the weight of the terrorist assault.

3. It failed because conservative interests in Russia were far too strong. If those interests were less automatically sympathetic to the Tsar than they had been before the emancipation, they could never support the violent and ill-defined alternatives that the terrorists seemed to propose. If the Tsar's government could, in future, form a stronger alliance with those conservative interests, it was highly likely to survive the onslaught of the radicals.

---

1. What alternatives to Tsarist rule were offered by Russian radicals during the reign of Alexander II?

2. How effective were opposition groups (both Russian and non-Russian) within the Tsarist Empire in the period 1855–1890?

2.8 Why did Tsarist policy change between reform and reaction in the years 1879–1894?

Alexander II's return to reformism

By the beginning of the 1880s Alexander II was, according to the historian W.E. Mosse, 'isolated from the Russian people, unpopular with the educated public, and cut off from the bulk of society and the Court. His fate had become a matter of indifference to the majority of his subjects.' This was largely the result of his indecision between the two policies of reform and conservatism. Even at Court he was increasingly unpopular because of his embarrassing passion for a much younger woman, the Princess Dolgoruky. She bore Alexander a number of illegitimate children, and he married her with indecent haste upon the death of his first wife in 1880. The passion contributed directly to the further confusion of imperial policy in the last years of Alexander's life. While the Tsar grew more and more disillusioned and conservative, the princess remained the friend and patron of a number of liberal politicians. Thus the government's reaction to the violence of 1879–80 was a mixture once again of repression and concession. Executions took place, but the major political event was the appointment as Minister of the Interior of Mikhail Loris-Melikov, a member of Princess Dolgoruky's liberal circle.

Mikhail Loris-Melikov (1825–1888)
Originally a professional soldier with distinguished service in the Russo–Turkish War. Military governor of the Ukraine (1879), where he gained a reputation for firm administration based upon the rule of law. Appointed Minister of the Interior (1880–81) through the patronage of Princess Dolgoruky. Retired from public life after the assassination of Alexander II.

The Loris-Melikov ministry

Despite the misgivings of the Tsar, within a year (January 1880 – February 1881) Mikhail Loris-Melikov had abolished the Third Section, replaced the reactionary Dmitri Tolstoy at the Ministry of Education, and steered Alexander II to the verge of the most fundamental reform of his reign. By February 1881 plans were prepared for the calling of a national assembly, partly of nominated members, but partly of elected representatives of the *zemstva* and the town councils. It was thus a limited body, but a logical and significant step away from total autocracy. The Soviet historian P.A. Zaionchkovsky, in *The Abolition of Serfdom in Russia* (1978), conceded that 'in the conditions of an increasingly complex situation it might have been the beginning of the establishment of a parliamentary system in Russia'. The Tsar had just given his personal approval to the measure when the luck of the 'People's Will' changed, and on 13 March Alexander was killed by the second of two bombs thrown at his sledge in a St Petersburg street.

Alexander III and the return to reaction
The heir to the throne was Alexander's son by his first marriage, who succeeded as Alexander III. The death of his father did not initiate the conservatism of the son, but the horrible circumstances of that death, and the cruel irony of its timing confirmed it most strongly. The greatest influence on the views of the new Tsar was that of his former tutor and trusted adviser, Konstantin Pobedonostsev. Pobedonostsev's sympathies lay with autocracy against **democracy**, with Orthodoxy against all other sects, and with Russians against all other nationalities of the Empire. For him **universal manhood suffrage** was 'a fatal error'; the principle of the sovereignty of the people was 'among the falsest of political principles'; parliamentarianism was the 'triumph of egoism'; the freedom of the press was 'one of the falsest institutions of our time'. As Pobedonostsev also served the new Tsar as tutor to his eldest son, Nicholas, his influence stretched unbroken from 1881 to the turmoil of 1905.

Although of less direct influence, another major 'prophet' of the new temper in Russian thought, and especially in Russian foreign policy, was Nikolai Danilyevski. In his most influential work, *Russia and Europe* (1871), he rejected the enthusiasm of westernisers for Western philosophy and technology. Instead he argued that as Russia had a quite different history and development, it should ignore the Roman and Germanic worlds and concentrate upon its Slav nature and inheritance. This view differed from the old slavophile notions in that it was more aggressive, preaching a union of all Slav nations under Russian leadership stretching from the Baltic to the Adriatic. This regeneration of aggressive, autocratic nationalism was called '**pan-slavism**'.

Democracy: A system of government in which people choose their rulers by voting for them in elections.

Universal manhood suffrage: The right that all males over the age of consent have to vote, in order to choose a government or a national leader. °

Pan-slavism: A political doctrine which advocated the political union of all Slav peoples. This was widely viewed in other European states as a cover for the political ambitions of Russia.

Konstantin Pobedonostsev (1827–1907)
Leading theorist of Russian conservatism and autocracy. Professor of Civil Law at Moscow University (1858). Procurator of the Holy Synod (leading government official responsible for the Orthodox Church) from 1880. Tutor to the sons of Alexander II and Alexander III.

Alexander III (1845–1894)

Married Dagmar (1847–1928), daughter of Cristina IX of Denmark and sister to Queen Alexandra of Britain, in 1866. Succeeded his father, Alexander II, as Tsar of Russia in 1881. Pursued a reactionary policy, persecuting Jews and promoting Russification (see page 44). In foreign affairs, Alexander III followed a policy of peace and non-intervention.

Members of the 'People's Will' movement on their way to be executed for the assassination of Alexander II.

Conservative legislation, 1882–1892

It was scarcely surprising that the bomb that killed Alexander II also destroyed the careers of his more liberal ministers and the policies that they advocated. Mikhail Loris-Melikov was replaced as Minister of the Interior by Nikolai Ignatiev, who later gave way to Dmitri Tolstoy. At the heart of the new policy lay the hope of restoring the Russian nobility to the position of strength and influence that it had held before the emancipation. In July 1889 the office of justice of the peace was abolished in local government and a new office, that of Land Commandant (*zemsky nachalnik*), was created. The essential qualification for this office was membership of the nobility, and the holder enjoyed senior administrative and judicial power in the locality, over-riding the authority of the *zemstva*. The partly elective *zemstvo* became a prime target for the reactionaries. Laws of 1890 and 1892 revised the franchise in rural and urban assembly elections to restrict the popular vote. In St Petersburg the combined effect of the laws was to reduce the electorate from 21,000 to 7,000. Furthermore, the assemblies frequently found their most apolitical proposals obstructed and undermined by the objections of a government fundamentally opposed to the principle of elected assemblies.

Russian intellectual life in a period of reaction

Naturally, educational policy also felt the impact of this revision of government thinking. The Minister of Education from 1882 to 1898 was I.V. Delyanov, a man essentially opposed to any 'dangerous' advance in education such as had been proposed in the reforms of Alexander II. Policies

Illiteracy: State of not knowing how to read or write.

1. By what means did Alexander III attempt to stabilise government and society in Russia?

2. In what respects did Alexander III's response to Russia's internal problems differ from that of Alexander II?

towards the universities included the limitation of their administrative autonomy (1884) and the raising of their tuition fees (1887). The raising of fees was also a useful method in primary and secondary education to ensure that the 'children of coachmen, servants, cooks, washerwomen, small shop-keepers, and persons of similar type should not be brought out of the social environment to which they belong'. Only parish elementary schools, safely under the influence of the local clergy, were allowed any real expansion during Delyanov's term of office. Consequently, by the end of the 19th century Russia presented an educational paradox. Its élite contained some of the most famous figures of the century: scientists (Pavlov, Mendeleiev), writers (Chekhov, Tolstoy, Gorky), historians (Klyuchevsky), musicians (Tchaikovsky) of world repute. Yet this brilliant surface of Russian society hid a substructure of rottenness and ignorance represented as late as 1897 by a staggering **illiteracy** rate of 79%.

2.9 Why and with what consequences did the Tsarist government pursue a policy of Russification?

What was Russification?

Referring specifically to Poland, the conservative writer Y.F. Samarin described nationalism in the 1860s as 'a dissolving agent as dangerous, in a different way, as the propaganda of Herzen'. The policy of Russification – that is, of attempting to suppress the local characteristics of various regions within the Empire, and to spread Russian characteristics to all the Tsar's subjects – was not an invention of Alexander III but was applied by his government with fresh vigour and determination.

The Russians were, in fact, in a minority within their vast empire, 55% of the total population belonging to other racial groups. The largest groups within the population were as shown in the table below.

Nationalities of the Russian Empire

(according to the 1897 census)

Great Russians	55.6 million
Ukrainians	22.4 million
Poles	7.9 million
White Russians	5.8 million
Jews	5.2 million
Tartars	3.4 million
Germans	1.8 million
Armenians	1.2 million
Georgians	0.8 million

'Disloyal' subjects

The total population of the Empire at that time was a little over 125 million. The historian J.N. Westwood has divided these racial groups into three main political categories, which he labels 'mainly loyal, mainly disloyal and the Jews'. In the 'disloyal' category it was the Poles who, after the nationalist outbreak of 1863, could most expect to be the subject of rigid Russification. The measures taken by the subsequent governors of defeated Poland, F.F. Berg (1864–1874) and P. Kotzebue (1874–1880), set the pattern for future policies elsewhere. The property of the Polish Roman Catholic Church was seized (1864) and Warsaw's university was closed

(1869). Russian replaced Polish as the administrative language, and more and more Russians replaced Poles in the ranks of the administrators. Similar measures were adopted in the Ukraine, but as there had been no comparable nationalist demonstrations there, they were mainly directed against a small group of radical intellectuals. The other main components of the 'disloyal' group were the Tartars and the Georgians. In both cases the Orthodox Church played a leading role on behalf of the state. By 1900, it had converted an estimated 100,000 Tartars. It also fought a fierce conflict, that went as far as political assassination in some cases, against the Georgian Church. Islam and the Georgian Church both put up fierce resistance, however, and the problem of separatism among the Tartars and the Georgians was still very much alive in 1917.

Finland, Armenia and the Baltic provinces

Much more damaging to the autocracy of the Tsar were the counter-productive efforts to 'russify' areas whose loyalty had not previously been in doubt. Into this category fell Finland, Armenia, and the Baltic territories of Estonia, Latvia and Lithuania. The Finns had been especially well treated under Alexander II and the use of their own language had not merely been permitted, but was actually made compulsory in local administration. Now disadvantageous trade tariffs were imposed. Russians and their language intruded more and more into Finnish government. The process culminated in 1903 with the suspension of the Finnish constitution, a direct breach of the terms upon which Alexander I had absorbed Finland into the Empire in 1815. The Armenians, too, were essentially well disposed to Russian rule, for it had done much to protect them from their major enemy, the Turks. Their reward, under Alexander III, included the confiscation of the property of the Armenian Church and the suppression of the Armenian language. Similarly, the Baltic Germans had enjoyed privileged treatment at the hands of the two previous Tsars, who employed several high-ranking ministers from that region. Now, in contrast, the reconstruction of the great Orthodox cathedral in Riga (1885) and the increasing proportion of Russian students at the famous University of Dorpat (now officially known by its Russian name of Yuriev) constituted symbols of uncompromising Russian domination.

The Jews

Characteristically, the worst blows fell upon the Empire's long-suffering Jewish population. Even the Jews had experienced some improvement in their conditions under the previous reign. Recruitment of Jews into the army had been put on the same basis as that of Russians and the laws forbidding settlement beyond the '**pale**' had been relaxed. Now, however, Alexander III's regime combined the 'official' religious **anti-semitism** of the Orthodox Church with the crude, popular hostility that arose from the Jews' economic role. Associating the Jews in **propaganda** with the Polish rebellion and with the assassination of Alexander II, but also happy to use them as scapegoats on which popular discontent could be vented, the Russian government permitted and even encouraged **pogroms**. An estimated 215 such disturbances occurred between the first outbreaks in May 1881, in the Ukraine, and the 'great' pogrom of 1905 in Odessa in which nearly 500 Jews were killed. As Minister of the Interior, Dmitri Tolstoy was less keen to countenance such actions, not out of any concern for the victims, but out of a general uneasiness at the idea of civil disorder. In their place he instituted a series of less violent, but equally discriminatory, measures. No new Jewish settlers were allowed in rural areas, even within the Pale of Settlement. Jews were forbidden to trade on Christian holy

The 'pale': The area in western Russia to which Jewish settlement was legally restricted. It had been established in the 18th century by Catherine the Great. Also known as the Pale of Settlement.

Anti-semitism: Hostility to Jews or the Jewish religion (Judaism).

Propaganda: Information, often exaggerated or false, which is spread by political parties in order to influence the attitudes of the general public.

Pogroms: Violent attacks upon Jewish communities and upon their property.

Zionist movement: A form of Jewish nationalism, which advocated the establishment of a Jewish state.

1. Which groups within the Russian Empire felt the impact of the policy of 'Russification'?

2. Did the policy of 'Russification' do more to strengthen or to undermine the authority of the Tsarist regime?

days. As they already closed on Jewish holy days, this made it hard for them to compete with non-Jewish rivals. Strict quotas for Jews were set in schools and universities, which never rose above 10% even within the Pale. In 1886 in Kiev, and in 1891 in Moscow, all 'illegal' Jews were expelled, which provided a useful opportunity to harass 'legal' settlers as well.

Apart from emigration, two other courses presented themselves for Jews who had had enough of such treatment. One was militant nationalism, which took the form of the **Zionist movement**. The other was revolutionary agitation as seen in the formation of the Bund (1897), a Jewish socialist organisation which was to play an important part in the development of revolutionary socialism in Russia in the next two decades. Thus, in the long run, the policy of Russification proved to be an even more dangerous 'dissolving agent' than the nationalism that it originally set out to combat.

Source-based questions: Alexander II as 'Tsar Liberator'

SOURCE A

How successful were the 'Great Reforms'? The government had undertaken a radical overhaul of the social, economic, political and military structure of the Russian Empire. This was a complex and potentially dangerous task. So the best measure of the government's success is the fact that it survived the reforms unscathed, unlike the reforming government of Mikhail Gorbachev 130 years later. However, the reforms left serious problems for future governments. In trying to balance the interests of nobles and peasants, while retaining its own powers intact, it alienated both the major classes of traditional Russian society. For Russian society as a whole, the reforms marked an important, though painful, step towards modernity.

From *Imperial And Soviet Russia* by David Christian (1997)

SOURCE B

Norman Pereira [in *Tsar Liberator: Alexander II of Russia,* 1983] has drawn attention to four points between 1856 and 1861 at which, but for the Tsar, forward movement might have come to an end. First, the publication of the Nazimov Rescript at the end of 1857. Second, on a tour of the provinces in 1858 Alexander made plain to backwoodsmen that their committees should take a positive view of the reform. Third, when the provincial gentry still did not take up the cause of reform with alacrity, the Tsar bypassed them by appointing a majority of reformers to the Editing Commissions. Fourth, when draft legislation came before the Main Committee in 1860 Alexander stood firm for change in the face of obdurate resistance from aristocrats.

The determination that Alexander showed as a war leader undoubtedly resurfaced on a number of occasions, but explaining the emancipation of the serfs by depicting him as a latter-day Peter the Great oversimplifies Russian politics between 1855 and 1861. It was 1859 before Alexander gave reformers their head by granting them control of the Editing Commissions, and by then the prestige of the throne would have suffered far more from the abandonment of emancipation than from allowing a version of it to go through. The laws which freed the serfs emerged from a process which the Tsar barely understood and over which he had only partial control. The complicated narrative of the emancipation cannot be reduced to the proposition that Alexander sensed he was facing a crisis and believed that attack was the best form of defence.

Adapted from *Russia In The Age Of Reaction And Reform, 1801–1881* by David Saunders (1992)

SOURCE C

Alexander was subject to liberal influence in his closest circle. His brother Constantine had become an ardent supporter of emancipation. Possibly even more effective was his aunt, the Grand Duchess Elena Pavlovna. Her magnificent work for the wounded during the [Crimean] war had increased her standing in Russian public life. Her palace was a centre of liberal ideas, and she herself gave her protection to liberal officials such as N.A. Milyutin. The influence of these two members of the Imperial family is not so well documented as that of the officials who carried out the reform, but it cannot be doubted that it was very great. The experts prepared the legislation, but it was largely due to the advice of Constantine and Elena that the Tsar was induced to force it through.

From *The Russian Empire 1801–1917* by H. Seton-Watson (1967)

SOURCE D

Certainly Dmitri Milyutin's path would have been much easier if Alexander II had been a more consistent and a wiser man. The War Minister's own conviction that the autocracy was the absolutely necessary agent for Russia's progress was based upon the principle that the autocrat was the partner of the Russian people and, standing above the interests of all groups, he was able to ensure the organic unity and the equality of the entire nation. Quite on the contrary, Alexander allowed himself to be insulated from reality by [conservative politicians such as] Shuvalov, and in these years often served the interests of the gentry. Certainly one gets the impression that Alexander was never really a reformer except for his conviction that the serfs had to be freed and that

all subsequent reforms were dictated by circumstances.

From *Dmitri Milyutin*, by Forrestt A. Miller (1968)

(a) Use Source A and your own knowledge.

Explain what is meant by the statement that, in the Edict of Emancipation, Alexander II tried to 'balance the interests of nobles and peasants'. [5 marks]

(b) Compare Sources B and C and use your own knowledge.

How fully do Sources B and C explain the political problems that faced Alexander II as he sought to emancipate the serfs? [10 marks]

(c) Use Sources A, B, C and D and your own knowledge.

With reference to these sources and your own knowledge assess the view that 'the reputation of Tsar Alexander II as a reformer has been considerably exaggerated'. [15 marks]

2.10 To what extent was Russia's international prestige restored in the reigns of Alexander II and Alexander III?

Just as the end of the Crimean War signalled a turnabout in domestic policy, with substantial reform taking the place of rigid reaction, so a change of equal proportions came about in the foreign policy of the Russian Empire. The defeat, the evidence that it provided of Russian weakness, and the preoccupation of the government with domestic changes all limited the one-time 'gendarme of Europe' to a largely passive role from 1856 until the early 1870s.

Russia's relations with the western European powers

Black Sea clauses: Those clauses of the Treaty of Paris (1856) which forbade Russia to maintain a fleet in the Black Sea. Their aim was to limit Russian influence in the affairs of the Ottoman Empire.

Nevertheless, Russian diplomacy did have one major aim during this period, and it was an uncharacteristic one. The defeat in the Crimea had transformed the greatest conservative power into a revisionist power, eager especially to revise the **Black Sea clauses** of the Treaty of Paris that placed such humiliating restrictions upon its naval power in that area. Between 1856 and 1863, the best means of achieving this end seemed to be to cultivate the friendship of France with a view to gaining a diplomatic agreement at some future date. Thus at the Paris conference (May–August 1858), which effectively formed Wallachia and Moldavia into an independent Romanian state, Russia eagerly co-operated with the French 'line'. In March 1859 Russia even agreed to remain neutral in the event of French action in northern Italy, in stark contrast to its attitude to disturbances in the Austrian Empire ten years earlier. By the early 1860s, however, the understanding with France was on its last legs. French interference with the 'legitimate' regimes of Italy was more than Alexander II could tolerate, and the breaking point came with evidence of French sympathy for the liberalism and the Catholicism of the Polish revolt in 1863.

For ten years from 1863 Russia was almost wholly isolated in European diplomacy. The sole exception was its relations with Prussia, which were improved by General von Alvensleben's mission in that year to offer aid against the Polish rebels. If it was beneath the Tsar's dignity to use the forces of a lesser power to control his own subjects, the friendly gesture was appreciated in contrast to French, Austrian and British hostility. Russia extended benevolent neutrality towards Prussia in its anti-Austrian adventures of the 1860s. Indirectly, Prussia's adventures led to the achievement of Russia's main ambition. With Europe preoccupied with the Franco–Prussian War from July 1870, Russia sensed that this was the moment to renounce the Black Sea clauses. The foreign minister, Alexander Gorchakov, informed the powers in November 1870 that Russia no longer accepted this section of the Treaty of Paris. Although the action was condemned at a conference in London two months later, the powers were forced to recognise that no retaliatory action could be taken.

In the longer term, the main result of the Franco–Prussian War was that Russian diplomacy had to come to terms with the new German Empire, a more powerful neighbour than it had ever known before. The conclusion of the League of the Three Emperors between the rulers of Russia, Austria and Germany gave a false air of stability to the politics of eastern Europe. Behind its facade, a series of factors kept alive Russian resentment at rising German power and at Austrian pretensions in the Balkans. The settlement engineered by Bismarck at the Congress of Berlin, which limited Russia's gains from its conflict with Turkey, struck a serious blow to Russo–German relations. Shortly afterwards, in 1883, Romania formally associated itself by treaty with Germany and Austria. It was a measure of the tension between Russia and Austria that Alexander III refused (April 1887) to renew the Three Emperors' Alliance, as the League had become in 1881. The Reinsurance Treaty concluded with Germany alone two months later maintained the facade of stability. It was a dubious piece of opportunism, partially at odds with Germany's undertakings towards Austria, but it provided an encouraging indication of Germany's desire to maintain good relations with Russia. Thus the refusal of a new German Kaiser to renew the Reinsurance Treaty in 1890 seemed to be a specific rejection of Russian friendship, and starkly renewed Russia's international isolation.

The result was a revolution in Russian diplomacy whereby it turned towards republican France, different in every important aspect of recent history and culture, but well placed strategically to the west of Germany. Russian approaches to Germany in 1893 have suggested to some historians that the exercise may have been planned as a lever to force Germany into warmer relations. There being no favourable reaction from Berlin, an *entente* with France became the mainstay of Russian foreign policy, for want of anything better.

Russian foreign policy in the Balkans

The renunciation of the Black Sea clauses gave Russian policy in the Balkans a new lease of life. This policy continued to be motivated by the familiar blend of concern for national security and the search for prestige in the face of domestic difficulties. This time, extra spice was added by the

Alexander Gorchakov (1798–1883)
Ambassador to Vienna (1854); Foreign Minister (1856–82); Tsar Alexander II's chief minister from 1866. Gorchakov was the chief Russian representative at the Congress of Berlin (1878).

Entente: Friendly agreement between two or more countries.

doctrine of pan-slavism, although Gorchakov's policies in south-east Europe in the early 1870s were conducted more in a spirit of cautious realism. In 1875, however, a series of revolts began among the Serbian and Bosnian subjects of the Turkish Sultan, which set off much pan-Slav agitation for the dispatch of Russian aid. The brutal suppression of the associated Bulgarian revolt in 1876 further excited both Russian feelings and foreign suspicion. Gorchakov quietened Austrian misgivings by an agreement concluded at Reichstadt (July 1876) whereby Russia would regain southern Bessarabia, lost in 1856, and Austria would receive part of Bosnia and Herzegovina in the event of a successful Russian clash with Turkey. Such a war was brought closer, as it had been in 1854, by the inflexible attitude of Turkey. In the first three months of 1877 the Sultan rejected proposals for reform from several of the major European powers, and Russia formally opened hostilities in April of that year.

The Russo–Turkish War was fought on two fronts. In the Caucasus the Turks used the tactic of stirring up local rebellion to keep the Russian forces occupied, and not until late in the year did the latter gain decisive successes. They won a major victory at Aladja Dag in October and captured their main objective, the fortified town of Kars, in November. In the European theatre the initial Russian advance was checked at Plevna, which held out from mid-July until early December 1877. The fall of that town paved the way to a victory that Russia sealed at the decisive battles of Plovdiv and Shipka (January 1878). It had been, as Lionel Kochan notes in *The Making of Modern Russia* (1997), 'a war between the one-eyed and the blind – so many errors of strategy and judgement were committed'.

Nevertheless, Russia briefly enjoyed considerable gains. The Treaty of San Stefano (3 March 1878) ignored its Reichstadt undertakings to Austria and created a large Bulgarian state, wide open to Russian influence. The diplomatic hostility caused by such success, however, forced Russia to agree to a revision of the treaty formulated at an international congress in Berlin. The size of Bulgaria, and thereby the extent of Russia's influence in the Balkans, was reduced. Russia was, nevertheless, left with southern Bessarabia and the Caucasian gains of Kars and Batum. It was a clever settlement, but left pan-Slavs and Russian nationalists bitterly offended, especially with Bismarck whose 'honest broker' stance seemed to them to hide anti-Russian and pro-Austrian intent. In the development of Russian relations with its central European neighbours, the events of 1877–78 foreshadowed greater conflicts to come.

Russian penetration into Asia

If the aftermath of the Crimean War left Russia badly placed to take initiatives in European affairs for several decades, no such restrictions existed along its eastern frontiers. These regions are described by Lionel Kochan as 'the happy hunting-grounds of Russian imperialist adventurers, dubious carpetbaggers, and pseudo-viceroys'. Some voices were indeed raised in St Petersburg against the risks and costs of such uncontrolled expansion, but it proved impossible to check the ambitions of provincial generals and their followers. Motivated by **chauvinism**, by a sense of a civilising mission, and often by pure greed, Russian control spread steadily into the Caucasus region, across the Caspian Sea, and into Siberia. Turkestan was penetrated by stages that included the taking of Tashkent (1865) and of Samarkand (1868), and the Khanate of Bokhara acknowledged indirect Russian rule in 1875. The integration of these areas into the Empire was slowly effected by settlement by Russian peasants, especially during Pyotr Stolypin's period as premier, and by a number of ambitious communications projects, such as the construction of the Transcaspian railway in 1886–98.

Chauvinism: Aggressive and unreasoning patriotism.

---

1. What were the main aims of Russian foreign policy during the reigns of Alexander II and Alexander III?

2. Compare the degrees of success achieved by Russian foreign policy in this period in:

(a) eastern Europe

(b) Asia.

The spreading of Russian influence in Siberia was a longer process. Substantial areas of territory were gained from China by the treaties of Aigun (1858) and Peking (1860), and the foundation of Vladivostok in 1861, on the shores of the Pacific itself, completed the most successful example of European territorial expansion in the 19th century. Here, too, great feats of communication were undertaken. Work on the Trans-Siberian railway – one of the great engineering feats of the 19th century – was begun in 1892.

2.11 What was the extent of Russia's economic development during the reigns of Alexander II and Alexander III?

Stimuli to industrial expansion

Although the great social reforms of the 1860s did not immediately stimulate general economic growth, the reigns of Alexander II and Alexander III did form a period of overall industrial development. This development was, however, uneven and fluctuating. In the 1860s the difficulties of the emancipation of the serfs, and the 'cotton famine' that resulted from the civil war in America, were retarding factors. In the 1870s, however, the Russian economy benefited from the increase in railway building and from the policy of low **tariffs**, which facilitated the import of raw materials. The economic historian, A. Gerschenkron, has written of the former that Russia's 'greatest industrial upswing came when the railway building of the state assumed unprecedented proportions and became the main lever of the rapid industrialisation policy'. The development of Russia's railways was not only substantial in quantity, but also showed much greater economic logic than the earlier lines had displayed. Lines such as those between Moscow and Kursk, Moscow and Voronezh and Moscow and Nizhni Novgorod linked major areas of industrial production to important markets. Similarly, the Kursk–Odessa and Kharkov–Rostov lines linked these towns, and areas of agricultural production, to the ports of the Black Sea. The Batum–Baku railway (1883) linked the Caspian with the Black Sea, and served greatly to increase oil production. The steady growth of the Russian railway system is illustrated in the table below.

Following the initial policy of freer trade, tariffs began to rise steadily as it became clear that low tariffs were causing a heavy influx of foreign goods and creating a substantial trade imbalance. The first major increase came in 1877, followed by further acts in 1881 and 1882. The policy culminated

Tariffs: Customs duties; applied to goods coming into the country as a percentage of the value of the goods.

The development of Russia's railway system	
Date	**Kilometres constructed**
1861–1865	443 km
1866–1870	1,378 km
1871–1875	1,660 km
1876–1880	767 km
1881–1885	632 km
1886–1890	914 km

Russian coal and pig-iron production		
Date	**Coal (poods)**	**Pig-iron (poods)**
1860–1864	21.8 million	18.1 million
1865–1869	28.4 million	18.9 million
1870–1874	61.9 million	22.9 million
1875–1879	131.3 million	25.9 million
1880–1884	225.4 million	29.2 million
1885–1889	302.6 million	37.6 million
1890–1894	434.3 million	66.9 million
1895–1899	673.3 million	120.9 million

1 pood = 36 lb = 16.3 kg

From M. E. Falkus, *Industrialisation of Russia* (1972)

in the great protective tariffs of 1891, which especially affected iron, industrial machinery and raw cotton. The beneficial effect on domestic coal and pig-iron production is shown in the table on the previous page.

In judging the level of Russia's industrial development one certainly sees the truth of the judgement that Lenin passed in 1899: 'If we compare the present rapidity of development with that which could be achieved with the modern level of technique and culture, the present rate of development of capitalism in Russia really must be considered slow.' In the longer term, one can also appreciate the judgement passed by a later economic historian, W.O. Henderson. 'If the Russian economy was still backward in some respects, it was also true that vigorous state action, foreign capital and foreign machinery had given Russia a powerful impetus on the road to industrialisation.'

1. In what respects was the Russian economy modernised during this period?

2. How convincing is the argument that the reigns of Alexander II and Alexander III saw the emergence of Russia as an industrial power?

Source-based questions: Terrorism and the State

SOURCE A

The purpose of terroristic activities is to break the spell of government power, to give constant proof of the possibility of fighting against the government, to strengthen in this way the revolutionary spirit of the people and its faith in the success of its cause, and, finally, to create organisations suited and accustomed to combat.

From the manifesto of the 'People's Will' organisation, January 1880

SOURCE B

Recent events have clearly demonstrated the existence in Russia of a gang of evildoers which, if not very numerous, nonetheless persists in its criminal delusions and strives to undermine all the foundations of the structure of state and society. Not confining themselves to propagating, by means of secretly printed and circulated proclamations, the most revolting doctrines aimed at subverting religious teaching, family ties, and property rights, these scoundrels have made repeated attempts on the lives of the highest dignitaries of the Empire.

From the Tsar's emergency decree, April 1879

(a) Study Sources A and B.

How far do these two sources agree in their view of the threat that terrorism posed to the Russian state?
[5 marks]

(b) What means did radicals use in the 1870s, other than terrorism, to bring about social and political change in Russia?
[7 marks]

(c) What, if anything, had Russian radicals achieved up to the death of Alexander III in 1894? Explain your answer.
[18 marks]

Further Reading

Texts designed for AS and A2 Level students

Russia 1815–81 by Russell Sherman (Hodder & Stoughton, Access to History series, 2002)

Alexander II, Emancipation and Reform in Russia, 1855–1881 by Maureen Perrie (Historical Association pamphlet, 1989)

Russia 1848–1917 by Jonathan Bromley (Heinemann Advanced History series, 2002)

More advanced reading

The Russian Empire, 1801–1917 by Hugh Seton-Watson (Oxford University Press, 1967)

Russia under the Old Regime by Richard Pipes (Weidenfeld & Nicolson, 1974)

Russia in the Age of Reaction and Reform, 1801–1881 by David Saunders (Longman, History of Russia series, 1992)

Imperial and Soviet Russia: Power, Privilege and the Challenge of Modernity by David Christian (Macmillan, 1997) provides a concise overview of recent work on modern Russian history.

The Industrialisation of Russia, 1700–1914 by M.E. Falkus (Macmillan, 1972) provides a good, concise guide to economic developments during this period.

The Russian Peasantry 1600–1930 by David Moon (Longman, 1999)

3 Russia under Nicholas II: the crisis of Tsarism, 1894–1914

Key Issues

- What political and economic problems faced Russia at the beginning of the 20th century?

- What problems contributed to the outbreak of revolution in Russia in 1905, and how did Tsarism survive?

- How strong was the Tsarist regime on the eve of the First World War?

3.1 How well suited was the new Tsar to tackle the problems that confronted Russia in the 1890s?

3.2 In what respects and with what success was Russia's industrial economy modernised between 1892 and 1905?

3.3 To what extent did political opposition to the regime become more dangerous during this period?

3.4 What were the causes of the Russo-Japanese War?

3.5 Why did Russia lose the Russo-Japanese War and what were the consequences of its defeat?

3.6 Why did revolution break out in Russia in 1905?

3.7 How did the government survive the 1905 Revolution?

3.8 Did the Dumas represent a real constitutional advance in Russia?

3.9 What impression of Russian society is conveyed by scientific and cultural developments in the two decades before the outbreak of war?

3.10 Historical interpretation: How stable and how strong was the Russian regime on the eve of world war?

Framework of Events

1892–1903	Witte in office as Finance Minister
1894	Accession of Nicholas II
1897	Russian currency placed upon gold standard
1900	Formation of Socialist Revolutionary Party
1903	Formation of Russian Social Democratic (communist) Party, which splits into Bolshevik and Menshevik factions
1904–05	Russo-Japanese War
1905	January: 'Bloody Sunday' massacre
	May: Formation of first Soviet
	October: Major strikes in St Petersburg. Issue of October Manifesto
1906–11	Stolypin in office as chief minister
1906	April–July: First Duma
	November: Stolypin's agrarian reforms
1907	February–June: Second Duma
1907–12	Third Duma
1911	Assassination of Stolypin
1912–17	Fourth Duma
1914	Outbreak of First World War.

Overview

**Nicholas II
(1868–1918)**
Tsar of Russia
(1894–1917). He was
dominated by his wife,
Tsarina Alexandra,
who was allegedly
under the influence of
Rasputin (see page
83). Nicholas'
mismanagement of
Russian internal affairs
and of the Russo-
Japanese war led to
the revolution of 1905.
Although the revolution
was suppressed, the
Tsar was forced to
grant limited
constitutional reforms.
Nicholas took Russia
into the First World
War, but was forced to
abdicate in 1917 after
the Russian Revolution
(see Chapter 4). The
Tsar and his family
were executed in
1918.

Romanov dynasty: The
imperial crown of Russia
had been passed from
generation to generation of
the Romanov family since
Michael Romanov had been
proclaimed Tsar in 1613.

Duma: The semi-
constitutional assembly in
Russia between 1906 and
1917.

I N 1894 a new Tsar came to the Russian throne to be confronted by some familiar problems. Like his immediate predecessors, Nicholas II had to decide upon the balance that his government would strike between the traditional political structure of Tsarist Russia, and the massive socio-economic forces that were operating within the Russian Empire. In some respects, the problems that he faced were more acute than those faced by his predecessors, for the forces unleashed by the great reforms of the 1860s were now making an increasing impact upon the economic and political life of his Empire. Although Russia could scarcely rival the great industrial economies of western Europe, it was no longer the exclusively agrarian society that it had been 50 years earlier. It was also now clear that Russia's international status depended heavily upon continued industrial growth. At the same time, the majority of Russian workers were still engaged in agricultural production, and there remained many agrarian problems to be solved before the aim of the Edict of Emancipation – a freer and more prosperous peasantry – was achieved. On a domestic, political level, several decades of freer expression had given rise to a variety of political groupings for whom unquestioning obedience of the Tsar's autocratic will was no longer acceptable.

Alexander III's response to these pressures had been to dig in his heels and to resist social and political change wherever possible. The response of Nicholas II suggests that he had more in common with his grandfather, Alexander II. Nicholas listened to ministers who recognised the need for economic modernisation, but he too failed to appreciate that this was likely to entail a significant degree of political change. There is little doubt that Nicholas' ideal vision of Russia's future included a more modern and efficient economy, combined with a political system that retained the traditional features of autocracy. The great revolutionary outburst of 1905 was largely the result, therefore, of the government's failure to adapt politically to the substantial social and economic changes that had taken place.

The 1905 revolution was the most concentrated outburst of domestic opposition that the **Romanov dynasty** had so far faced. It indicated that the regime faced opposition, not only from the peasantry and the rapidly expanding urban workforce, but also from significant sectors of the educated middle class who were no longer willing to tolerate government by an autocratic Tsar and his closed bureaucracy. Yet the government survived because it had some important cards to play. Faced with mounting crisis, Nicholas again accepted the need for reform, or at least for the appearance of reform. The measures implemented by his chief minister, Pyotr Stolypin, aimed to win back the support of his more moderate opponents, and to create a viable, conservative base of support for the monarchy. Constitutional reforms, of which the most important was the establishment of a **Duma** (parliament), offered the educated classes some real hope that they might now be involved in the processes of government. At the same time, Stolypin's agrarian reforms offered concessions and encouragement to the more prosperous and enterprising of the peasants, who might fulfil similar, conservative functions in the countryside.

In short, the reforms proposed a new power base for the Russian monarchy in place of that which had been undermined by the great agrarian reforms of the 1860s. In 1905, as in 1861, the monarchy stood at the crossroads between limited but significant reform, and stubborn reaction.

It is easy to write off Stolypin's experiment as a failure. There is much evidence that the Tsar saw it only as a temporary expedient, as a way of warding off the immediate danger. Within 10 years, the First World War set off the train of events that would destroy the Romanovs forever. The fact remains, however, that by 1906 the Russian monarchy had introduced a constitution, and had embraced some of the most important economic implications of the emancipation of the serfs. These were remarkable advances from the situation that had existed at the end of the Crimean War, just 50 years earlier. For many years the dominance of communism in Russia made this brief period of 'constitutional monarchy' appear a pathetic and doomed response to the great determinist forces that were bearing down upon the Russian conservatives. With the recent collapse of the Union of Soviet Socialist Republics (USSR), many historians find it meaningful once more to consider whether this period really formed a viable basis for the long-term survival of a reformed Romanov monarchy.

3.1 How well suited was the new Tsar to tackle the problems that confronted Russia in the 1890s?

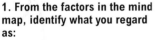

1. From the factors in the mind map, identify what you regard as:

(a) The long-term causes of the 1905 Revolution

(b) The short-term causes of the 1905 Revolution

(c) The immediate cause of the 1905 Revolution.

Write a sentence against each factor, giving a brief reason for your choice.

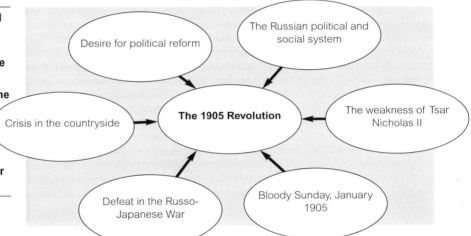

The death of Alexander III in October 1894 brought his 29-year-old son, Nicholas, to the throne. A determined and dominant father had produced a shy and less assertive successor. There is a rare agreement among historians that the new Tsar was not equal to the tasks that confronted him. Hans Rogger speaks for many when he writes, in *Russia in the Age of Modernisation and Revolution 1881–1917* (1983), that:

> 'Nicholas had no knowledge of the world or of men, of politics or government, to help him make the difficult and weighty decisions that the Tsar alone must make. The only guiding stars that he recognised were an inherited belief in the moral rightness of autocracy, and a religious faith that he was in God's hands, and his actions were divinely inspired.'

In an attempt to achieve a balanced assessment, many commentators have drawn attention to Nicholas' private qualities, especially those as father and husband. However, as historian J.N. Westwood comments, in *Endurance and Endeavour: Russian History 1812–1980* (1981), 'family happiness has never yet saved a dynasty'.

The main influences on the Tsar had been conservative in the extreme. Such factors as the assassination of his grandfather in 1881, and his education at the hands of Konstantin Pobedonostsev, had left the new Tsar determined to maintain the autocracy of his predecessors. In the year of his succession, Nicholas was married to Princess Alice of Hesse-Darmstadt, and this only compounded the difficulties of the reign. Alexandra, as she became upon conversion to the Russian Orthodox faith, shared her husband's political incompetence. Being a stronger character and equally devoted to the principle of autocracy, she was better able to resist the good advice of those who might have saved the monarchy.

The probable course of the reign was indicated at an early stage. Meeting representatives of the *zemstva* and the town councils in January 1895, Nicholas dismissed their hopes 'for public institutions to express their opinion on questions which concern them' as evidence that they were 'carried away by senseless dreams'. To the horror of those who hoped for some relaxation of the oppression of his father's reign Nicholas pledged himself to 'uphold the principle of autocracy as firmly and unflinchingly as my late, unforgettable father'. In terms, however, of the social and economic development of Russia, and of the development of foreign affairs, Nicholas was on the verge of a very different world from his father's.

How had Russia's agrarian problems developed by the 1890s and by what means did the government of Nicholas II address them?

The peasant problem
The early years of Nicholas II's reign brought little respite for the peasantry, or for many of the smaller gentleman landowners, from the problems that had beset them since the emancipation of the serfs. The official government policy of low bread prices meant a low income for the farmers even when harvests were good, and harvest failures were frequent (notably in 1891, 1892, 1898 and 1901). Steady population growth in European Russia also increased the pressure upon peasant holdings that were already inadequate. It has been estimated that the average peasant holding shrank from 35 acres (14.5 hectares) in 1877 to 28 acres in 1905 due to subdivision within the growing family. The result, quite apart from frequent outbreaks of agrarian violence, was that arrears in taxation and in redemption payments accumulated rapidly.

Government initiatives
Motivated by concern for its own income, and for the future of the landed gentry and nobility, the government attempted two solutions to these problems. One was the formation of an improved Land Bank in 1886. The bank was equipped with funds and with reserves of land, much of it former state land, to encourage the purchase of holdings that might satisfy the pressing '**land hunger**' of the peasants. Within two years of its formation the interest rates charged by the bank upon its loans were as low as 4%. The second was to exploit a larger proportion of Russia's vast land resources by encouraging settlement on '**virgin land**' in the east. In 1896, the government founded its Resettlement Bureau to stimulate migration to Siberia. As a further encouragement, and to improve the public image of Siberia, the shipment of criminals there was suspended in 1900.

Neither project was wholly unsuccessful, but neither could hope to do more than scratch the surface of an enormous problem. It is true that the total amount of land in peasant hands increased substantially, by over 26 million hectares between 1877 and 1905, but that in the hands of the nobility declined by nearly 21 million. Equally, the fact that 750,000 peasants migrated to Siberia in the last four years of the 19th century needs to

---

1. What factors formed the political views of Nicholas II?

2. How similar were the personality and political philosophy of Nicholas II to those of Alexander III?

'**Land hunger**': A term used to describe the problem encountered by the Russian peasantry, who had no other means of livelihood than agriculture, but who did not always farm enough land to make an adequate living. As the population increased, the demand for more land to farm grew dramatically.

'**Virgin land**': Land that has not previously been farmed or exploited.

be set against the huge total peasant population of nearly 97 million reflected in the census of 1895.

The survival of agrarian problems

By the revolutionary year of 1905 there were still several obstacles between the peasant and a lasting solution to the land problem. One was the continuing existence of the peasant commune, the *mir*, to which many were still bound by the legislation of 1861. In many cases the *mir* continued to impose restrictions upon travel and freedom of enterprise that counteracted government initiatives. Secondly, the consistent lack of direct financial investment in agriculture meant that the Russian peasant was still using primitive farming methods totally outdated by comparison with western Europe. The magnitude of Russian agricultural production was a reflection of its land resources, and not of the efficiency with which they were exploited. In 1898–1902, for example, an average acre of Russian farmland produced 8.8 bushels, compared with 13.9 in the USA and 35.4 in Great Britain.

The fact, therefore, that Russia became the world's largest supplier of wheat to foreign markets in 1913 by exporting 3.33 million tons, conceals the truth that much of this was what came to be referred to as 'starvation exports'. The phrase reflects the fact that wheat was often exported despite domestic demand for the product, in order to pay for the industrial raw materials and machinery upon which the government, by the late 1890s, was staking the future of Russia.

---

1. What were the main difficulties facing Russian agriculture at the end of the 19th century?

2. How justified is the statement that, at the start of the 20th century, the Russian government was taking realistic and effective steps to solve the state's agrarian problems?

3.2 In what respects and with what success was Russia's industrial economy modernised between 1892 and 1905?

Count Sergei Witte (1849–1915)

Russian statesman of Dutch origin. His family had achieved noble status by service to the state, and Sergei rose to high office by the unusual route of outstanding service in railway administration (he oversaw the construction of the Trans-Siberian railway). He was thus highly unusual among Russian ministers in that he was attuned to the needs and priorities of business and industry. Minister of Finance (1892–1903). Witte urged the rapid industrialisation of Russia, and took measures to stabilise the rouble and to attract foreign loans. Removed from office as a result of criticism of the results of his policies, but was recalled in the summer of 1905 to help negotiate peace with Japan and to quell revolution at home. After a six-month spell as Prime Minister, he was again dismissed from office.

Sergei Witte's view of the future of Russia

For all the political shallowness of Nicholas II, he was served by two ministers who might have saved the monarchy, given the right circumstances and consistent support. The first of these was Sergei Witte, who became Minister of Finance in August 1892 and held office until 1903. Witte did not regard himself as a narrow financial specialist. Self-confident and dynamic, he regarded the ultimate aim of his policies as being the salvation of Russia and the creation of a strong, modern state, but his political views were confused and uncertain. Although he professed himself dedicated to the maintenance of the autocracy, he cannot wholly have failed to foresee the political effects that the economic transformation of Russia would have. This curious mixture of energy and miscalculation naturally made Witte a controversial character among contemporaries and historians alike. Political opponents accused him of extravagance and of unpatriotic concessions to foreign capitalists. A number of more recent historians have criticised him for being insufficiently aware of the need for agricultural reform. Others have been impressed by the extent of his practical ability, and by the vision that he showed in advocating, for the first time in Russia's history, a coherent programme of industrial growth. Historian Hugh Seton-Watson, in *The Russian Empire, 1801–1917* (1988), is not alone in regarding Witte as 'one of the outstanding statesmen of the 19th century'.

Witte's measures

Witte understood that the key to Russia's future greatness lay in industrialisation. Russia's only alternative was to become a 'European China', a vast market unable to supply its own needs and thus 'the eternal handmaiden of states that are economically more developed'. His views were not original, being largely those of the previous Minister of Finance, I.A. Vyshnegradsky (1887–92). Witte was also influenced by Bismarck's policies in Germany. His real contribution was the coherent programme that he proposed in the 1890s to carry out this desired industrialisation. The basis of the policy was the strengthening of protective tariffs to guard infant Russian industries against the destructive competition of stronger European economies.

But how was Russian industry to develop when the vital investment capital was lacking, when the total amount of capital lying in Russian banks amounted to only 200 million roubles? How would foreign powers react if their access to so valuable a market were to be restricted? Witte's solution was to invite these foreign powers to continue to participate in the Russian economy, but by investing capital in it rather than by off-loading their consumer goods on to it. Thus the capital would be provided for the development of Russian industry. Industrial growth would also safeguard the government against social unrest by providing fuller employment and, in the long run, higher wages and cheaper goods. Protective tariffs, the attraction of foreign capital and the placing of the Russian currency on the **Gold Standard** (January 1897) – in order to inspire greater foreign confidence – were the three prongs of Witte's policy to create a great industrial Russia.

Gold Standard: A system whereby a state regulates the value of its currency, and the amount of currency in circulation, according to the quantity of gold that it has in its reserves. The object is to create greater international confidence in the national currency.

The development of heavy industries

At the time of the outbreak of the First World War, Russia was still a modest industrial power by comparison with much of Europe and with the USA. For example, in 1912 it produced only 5.6% of the world's pig iron, and only 3.66% of its steel. In 1910 only 30% of Russia's total national production was industrial, compared with 75% in Britain, 70% in Germany, and even 47% in Austria-Hungary. In purely Russian terms, nevertheless, progress had been rapid. An annual industrial output valued at 1,502 million roubles in 1890 had increased to 5,738 million by 1912. It should be remembered that this period included a major economic slump (1899–1902) and serious foreign and domestic disruptions (1904–06). Development differed from area to area and from industry to industry. Industrial production was largely concentrated in four regions: in St Petersburg and the shores of the Baltic, in Moscow and the provinces of Nizhni Novgorod and Vladimir, in Poland, and in the Donbas and Krivoi Rog regions of the south. Textile production continued to dominate, accounting in 1910 for 40% of Russia's industrial output. The table shows that, although they may not have compared so favourably with their more developed world rivals, other industries made impressive advances.

Russian industrial production (thousand tons)				
	Coal	Petroleum	Iron ore	Steel
1880	3,290	382	–	307
1885	4,270	1,966	–	193
1890	6,010	3,864	1,736	378
1895	9,100	6,935	2,851	879
1900	16,160	10,684	6,001	2,216
1905	18,670	8,310	4,976	2,266
1910	25,430	11,283	5,742	3,314

From Cook and Paxton, *European Political Facts, 1848–1918*

Attracting foreign investment in Russian industry

Certainly, those industries detailed in the table above were among those that benefited most from the influx of foreign capital stimulated by Witte's policies. There is no recent study of the exact extent to which foreign powers and individuals involved themselves in Russian industry, but older studies show that it was vast. A Soviet commentator, P. Ol, showed 214.7 million roubles of foreign capital invested in Russia in 1890, 280.1 million in 1895, and then a very substantial upsurge to reach 911 million in 1900, and 2,000 million before the outbreak of war in 1914. About half of this went into the mining and metallurgical industries of the south, and it is possible that by 1900 as much as 90% of the finance behind these sectors of the economy came from foreign investment. Oil production and banking were the next largest recipients of foreign funds. The greatest financial friend to Russia was its closest political ally, France, whose investment was about 33% of the total in 1914. The other most important suppliers of capital were Great Britain (23%), Germany (20%), Belgium (14%) and the USA (5%).

Railway development and foreign trade

The development of Russian railways also produced some impressive growth statistics, although these pale by comparison with those of more advanced countries. While Russia had built only 5,800 kilometres of track between 1861 and 1890, the rate of railway construction accelerated to produce a national system of 59,616 kilometres by 1905. The imagination of the world was captured by the vast engineering feat of the construction of the Trans-Siberian Railway, linking European Russia to its most easterly outpost of Vladivostok (1891–1904). The greatest years of industrial expansion, however, coincided with a tailing-off of railway construction. The five years between 1908 and 1913 saw the slowest rate of growth since the 1880s, and although Russia boasted the world's second largest railway network in 1913, there was a substantial gap between Russia and the only state of comparable size. Its network totalled 62,200 kilometres, compared with 411,000 kilometres in the USA. Other forms of communication in Russia remained wholly inadequate. Only the major inter-city roads of European Russia matched up to general European standards, and the merchant marine was remarkably small, nearly all of Russia's substantial foreign trade travelling in foreign ships.

This foreign trade formed the last major feature of Russia's pre-1914 industrialisation. The table below indicates the steady increase in trade in both directions. It should be remembered, however, that while the balance remained favourable to Russia, its exports were mainly of agricultural produce. The balance in industrial goods, therefore, remained very much to Russia's disadvantage. Russia was most heavily involved with Germany, to whom it exported 453 million roubles' worth of goods in 1913, and from whom it received 652 million roubles' worth. Great Britain held second place in both respects.

Russia's balance of trade (million roubles)

	Imports	Exports
1904	651.4	1,106.4
1906	800.6	1,094.8
1908	912.6	998.2
1910	1,084.4	1,449.1
1912	1,171.7	1,518.8

The growth of an urban proletariat

The steady industrialisation of the Russian economy accentuated the breakdown of the traditional social structures that had begun in 1861. It combined with Russia's continuing agrarian problems to accelerate the drift of workers from the impoverished countryside to the developing centres of industrial production. In 1900, 2.5 million workers were employed in factory or workshop production. Taking into account their families and dependants, this probably meant that 10–13 million Russians were now reliant upon an industrial wage. This was a relatively small proportion of Russia's total population of 116.5 million (1895), but was probably three times the figure that had applied in 1880.

Of equal importance was the increase in the size of units of production. The next table, indicating an increase of about 30% in the number of factories while the workforce doubled, makes it clear that the workforce of the average factory grew substantially. Nearly half of Russia's industrial workforce in 1902 worked in factories employing 1,000 men or more.

Russia's industrial workforce

	Factories	Workers
1887	30,888	1,318,000
1890	32,254	1,434,700
1897	39,029	2,098,200
1908	39,856	2,609,000

The results of these changes were typical of the early stages of industrialisation elsewhere in Europe. The dramatic growth rates of the major towns between 1867 and 1997, such as Moscow (197%), Warsaw (253%), Baku (702%) and Lodz (872%), suggest the problems of urban overcrowding that now developed. Living and working conditions are suggested by the trickle of social legislation wrung from a reluctant government by a wave of strikes at the turn of the century.

● The employment of children under 12 was forbidden (1892).

● Female labour was banned in mines (1892).

● An eleven-and-a-half-hour working day was legally instituted (1896), although the law was widely ignored by employers.

● Factory inspectors were finally introduced in 1903.

Nevertheless, major problems persisted, such as overcrowding in factory barracks, and the illegal payment of part of the worker's wages in kind. Strikes, although illegal until 1905, were frequent: 68 were recorded in 1895, 125 in 1900, culminating in 14,000 outbreaks in the revolutionary year of 1905.

1. What steps did Sergei Witte propose to modernise Russian industry?

2. How convincing is the claim that, at the start of the 20th century, industrial development was making Russia a more stable and prosperous country?

3. In what ways did the state of the Russian economy in 1900 pose problems for the Tsarist government?

3.3 To what extent did political opposition to the regime become more dangerous during this period?

Given the ultimate success of the Marxists in 1917, it is easy to understand how a number of western historians, as well as their Soviet counterparts, should have emphasised their importance in the years before 1914, and diminished the importance of other radical groups. The later collapse of Soviet communism makes it easier to appreciate, however, that this was not the inevitable outcome of contemporary Russian politics, and that there were other forces at work which might have moderated, or even replaced, the power of the Tsar. In the context of the time, at least two other opposition movements had far greater support and played a far more positive role in the events of the years 1905–14.

Russian liberalism

The events of 1905–14 provided encouragement above all for Russian liberalism. This was a diverse movement, made up of many different groups, of varying degrees of radicalism. Prominent among them were the liberal politicians who had been active in the localities as members of the *zemstva*. Some of these, led by D.N. Shipov, persisted in their hopes for a representative assembly that would provide some form of consultation between the Tsar and his people on the lines of the old *Zemsky Sobor*. Many *zemstvo* politicians, supported by a more radical group known as the 'Third Element', expressed less interest in political institutions than in practical reforms within the existing social system. Among their demands were the abolition of corporal punishment and of the power of the Land Commandants over the peasantry, and the introduction of primary education for all children. In the light of the events of the decade 1905–14, these liberals might claim to have been the most successful of the opposition groups within Russia.

Until 1905, the two courses of action proposed by liberals had borne little fruit. For a while it had seemed that direct representations to the government might work. The then Minister of the Interior, Ivan Goremykin, seemed willing to introduce *zemstvo* institutions into Lithuania, Byelorussia and other areas where none existed. By 1902, however, he had lost both the debate on the subject within the council of ministers and his official post. The other course, common to many opposition groups, was to found a party and a journal in the safety of foreign exile. Both the influential liberal newspaper *Liberation* (*Osvobozhdeniya*) and the Union of Liberation (*Soyuz Osvobozhdeniya*) were established in 1903. The dramatic realisation of several liberal demands was, however, to be brought about by events of a quite different nature.

The Socialist Revolutionaries

To the left of such liberal politics, the largest and most dangerous socialist grouping was the Socialist Revolutionary Party, founded in 1901. The SRs, as they came to be called, were essentially second-generation populists (see page 40), their cause revived by agrarian distress in 1891 and by the release of some earlier leaders from Siberia. They followed a path recognisable to the earlier generation, but modified to meet changed circumstances, such as the undeniable development of Russian capitalism. It is common for historians to refer to the Socialist Revolutionaries as 'the party of the peasants', but their views and policies extended beyond purely agrarian concerns. This enabled the SRs to build up a much broader membership. The various groups established in Moscow, in Saratov and in the Ukraine in the 1890s placed a common emphasis upon the need to spread their views among the urban workers. They differed, however, in the confidence that they placed in the peasantry, and in the importance that they attached to terrorism as a revolutionary weapon. As agrarian discontent spread, especially in the Ukraine in 1902, the revolutionary role of the peasantry became a more prominent element in party theory. When party policy was officially formulated, the peasantry was placed in the role of the army that would follow the 'vanguard' of the **urban proletariat**. The main plank of the party's platform was the redistribution of agricultural land to the peasantry on the basis of how much each could profitably use.

The terrorist branch of the SRs also achieved spectacular, if sterile, successes. The deaths of the Minister of Education, Bogolepov (1901), the Minister of the Interior, Sipyagin (1902), his successor Plehve (1904), and the governor of Moscow (1905), were all the work of its members. The apparent success of peasant agitation and terrorist conspiracy thus made

---

Zemsky Sobor (Russian – Assembly of the Land): A representative assembly that sometimes assembled in 16th- and 17th-century Russia. It had some of the characteristics of an early form of parliament.

Ivan Goremykin (1839–1917)
Minister of the Interior (1895–99). Prime Minister (1906 and 1914–16). Arrested and executed by the Bolsheviks in the course of the revolution.

Urban proletariat: Term used by Marx to describe those who lived in towns and cities who owned no property and had to sell their labour to survive. Sometimes used more closely to mean 'working class'.

Vyacheslav Plehve (1846–1904)
Director of Police in Russia (1880–84). State Secretary for Finland (1889–1902), where he pursued a policy of strict Russification. Minister of the Interior (1902). Assassinated by Socialist Revolutionaries.

the SRs a party of action, while the Marxists seemed to remain a party of faction and theory. 'More than any other party,' wrote Richard Charques, 'it was the party of youth.' This immediate, superficial appeal made the SRs the most popular of the radical opposition groups until 1917.

The limited scale of Russian Marxism in the 1890s

> **Vera Zasulich (1849–1919)**
> Populist activist. Attempted assassination of governor of St Petersburg (1877), was arrested but acquitted by jury. Abandoned terrorism in favour of Plekhanov's early Marxist movement.
>
> **Pavel Axelrod (1850–1928)**
> Prominent in the movement 'To the People' (1875). Co-founder of *Iskra* (1902). Consistently supported Menshevik faction of communists, and fiercely opposed the October Revolution.

Meanwhile, the ideas of Karl Marx had made only slow progress in Russia. That the arguments of a German socialist thinker advanced at all was partly due to the enthusiasm of Georgi Plekhanov, but also in part to the curious leniency of the Russian censors. Plekhanov was originally a populist prominent in the 'Land and Liberty' movement. Observing the growth of Russian industry, he became convinced that Marx, and not those who concentrated upon the Russian peasant and his commune, held the key to Russia's future. Vera Zasulich and Pavel Axelrod were other figures who formed a bridge between populism and Marxism. By 1894 the writings of Plekhanov had given Russian readers their most coherent summary of Marx's thought. That they were able to read it at all was largely due to censors who allowed Marxist works in the belief that they would weaken the terrorist threat of populism. *Das Kapital* was thus available in a Russian translation as early as 1872.

It is only with hindsight that any political importance can be given to the earliest Marxist groups in Russia. A number of very small cells existed from 1889 in St Petersburg, Moscow, Vilna and Kiev. Their only real claim to fame at this point was that one of the St Petersburg groups was joined in August 1893 by a young lawyer from Simbirsk named Vladimir Ilyich Ulyanov. He was later to adopt the 'cover' name of V.I. Lenin (see page 000). Not until March 1898 did representatives of the various groups meet secretly in Minsk to found the Russian Social Democratic Labour Party (RSDRP). Even then the immediate arrest of eight of the nine delegates rendered Marxism a modest force in Russian politics at the turn of the century.

1. What were the main political objectives of (a) the Russian liberals and (b) the Socialist Revolutionaries at the start of the 20th century?

2. How convincing is the claim that Marxism posed the most serious threat to the Tsarist government by 1905?

At this stage the Russian Marxists rejected the use of terror as counter-productive and chose to concentrate instead upon industrial agitation and propaganda. Marxists were active alongside other opposition groups in the industrial disturbances in St Petersburg in 1895, 1896 and 1897.

3.4 What were the causes of the Russo-Japanese War?

The colonial collision in the Far East

Power vacuum: A term used to describe a region in which no state exercises effective control. Such areas are always liable to be occupied by expansionist powers.

The Russo-Japanese War was the direct result of the clash of two sets of imperialist ambitions attempting to expand into the same **power vacuum**. Russian economic activity in the Far East had a long history. The development of Vladivostok dated from the 1860s but, although important, the port was of limited value as it was closed by ice for three to four months of the year. The decision to begin the Trans-Siberian Railway in 1891 represented a more substantial commitment to eastward expansion. Between 1891 and the turn of the century, Russia gained substantial advantages from the collapse of the Chinese Empire. The construction of the Chinese Eastern Railway across Manchuria (1897) brought valuable political and economic penetration of that region. In 1898, to offset German gains in China, Russia demanded and received a 25-year lease on the ice-free port of Port Arthur, together with its **hinterland**, the Liaotung **Peninsula**.

Hinterland: The area behind a coast, which is linked to it economically.

Peninsula: A body of land surrounded on three sides by water.

When Chinese resentment of foreign encroachment made itself felt in the Boxer Rebellion (1900), Russian troops were most prominent in the protection of European lives and interests, creating a dangerous confidence in their ability to defeat any oriental foe.

Japan watched Russian progress with apprehension and resentment. Japan's recent modernisation and westernisation contrasted starkly with China's decay, and it had taken advantage of that decay to prosecute long-standing territorial claims. The Chinese–Japanese War of 1894–95 had established Japanese control over Korea, Port Arthur and the surrounding Manchurian territory, much of which it had been forced to relinquish by pressure from the European powers established in China. Russia's subsequent acquisition of much of this territory was naturally a source of great indignation among nationalists in Japan.

The collapse of Russo-Japanese relations

1. What factors caused Russia and Japan to clash in the Far East in 1904?

2. Were the causes of the Russo-Japanese War mainly political or economic?

Two years of effort (1901–03) by Japan to reach an understanding about spheres of influence in Manchuria and Korea failed, largely due to Russian apathy. When, in February 1903, Russia failed to remove its 'temporary' garrison from Manchuria, it looked suspiciously as if it had ambitions to dominate both regions. There is little evidence to suggest a deliberate desire for aggression on Russia's part, but many factors left it inclined to accept a

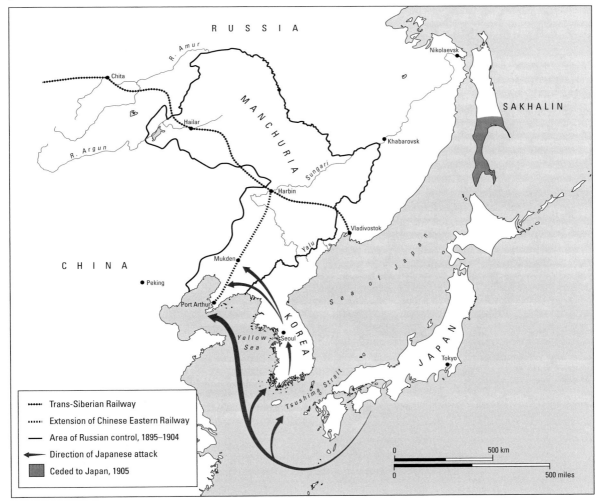

Far East at the time of Russo-Japanese War, 1904–05

military solution if the necessity arose. The so-called 'Bezobrasov Theory', whereby Russian arrogance in the Far East was largely due to the work of an adventurer of that name, is no longer widely held. The historian G. Katkov, for example, has helped to show that the government was more closely connected with eastern financial adventures than was originally thought. The blame placed upon Bezobrasov and his like was partly a campaign by prominent politicians, including Witte, to distract attention from their own role. Nevertheless, influential figures did have large financial interests in economic ventures such as the Russian Timber Company of the Far East. Furthermore, the Tsar received considerable personal encouragement for adventures in the east from the German Kaiser, happy to see Russian attention diverted from eastern Europe by a cultural 'crusade' against the 'Yellow Peril'. Last, but not least, the domestic political tensions in European Russia made a foreign distraction welcome to the Tsar and his ministers. There were doubtless many in high places who shared Plehve's judgement that 'to stem the tide of revolution, we need a successful little war'.

In February 1904, their patience exhausted, and aware of the lack of Russian preparation, the Japanese launched a naval attack on Port Arthur without a formal declaration of war. They laid mines to blockade the Russian fleet in the port.

3.5 Why did Russia lose the Russo-Japanese War and what were the consequences of its defeat?

The balance of military power

What images of Russia and Japan are projected in this cartoon?

The general assumption of international observers was that Russia could expect a quick and easy victory over a minor power such as Japan, yet such expectations should not have survived intelligent and detailed examination. Although Russia's population was three times that of Japan and its

A cartoon by the French commentator, Caran d'Ache, which appeared in *Le Figaro* in 1904. It shows the Russian bear impertinently challenged by Japan.

territory was vastly greater, Japan enjoyed much easier access to the theatre of war (see map on page 63). Russian communications were dependent upon the Trans-Siberian Railway, which operated on a single track for much of its length and which still had a gap of 150 kilometres in it in the region of Lake Baikal. Russian forces in the Far East totalled only 100,000 men at the beginning of hostilities, which the railway could only reinforce at the rate of 35,000 per month. Political developments in the west made it desirable to keep large numbers of experienced and reliable troops available for action there. Naval reinforcements posed even greater problems with the Black Sea fleet effectively 'locked up' there by the terms of the Straits Convention of 1841. Lastly, the Russian command structure was crippled by the rivalries between the regular army commanders and the court favourites who directed political affairs in the Far East.

Japan, on the other hand, had the capacity to put 180,000 men into the field immediately and to reinforce them by a short sea route. For all the endurance and bravery that they showed, the Russian troops never fought with the nationalistic and semi-religious fanaticism that the Japanese soldiers frequently displayed.

The loss of Port Arthur

On land, the Russian forces quickly found themselves unable to contain the numerically superior Japanese, and by May 1904 Port Arthur was cut off. The land campaign then centred upon the respective needs to take or to relieve the port. The eventual surrender of Port Arthur in January 1905 followed a siege of 156 days and cost the Russians 17,200 casualties. Japanese casualties, however, totalled 110,000. As stores and ammunition remained in fair supply, the surrender led to subsequent charges of treason against the Russian commander, General Stoessel. Russian hopes of regaining the vital port faded when they failed to break Japanese forces at the Battle of Mukden (February–March 1905), a larger battle than any in the 19th century, involving some 600,000 men.

The establishment of Japanese naval supremacy

Admiral Stepan Makarov (1849–1904)
Saw distinguished service in the Russo-Turkish War (1877–78). Commander of the Baltic Fleet (1897), then Commander of Russian naval forces in the Far East during the Russo-Japanese War.

Even so, as Russia still had the potential for reinforcement while Japan's resources were quickly stretched to their limits, the truly decisive factor in the war was the naval campaign. Without command of the sea Japan would have been unable to supply or to reinforce its troops on the Korean mainland, but Russian attempts to wrest the initiative were spectacularly unsuccessful. In April 1904 the most popular and successful of the Russian commanders, Admiral Makarov, died when his flagship, the 'Petropavlovsk', struck a Japanese mine. Only twice afterwards did the fleet stationed at Port Arthur venture out to sea before the surrender of their base.

In May 1905 the powerful Baltic fleet arrived in eastern waters, having completed an epic voyage around the globe, without rest at anchor, and refueling its huge coal-burning battleships at sea. To reach the theatre of war was a great achievement in itself, but it was the fleet's only achievement. On 27 May 1905, attempting to pass the Straits of Tsushima to reach Vladivostok, it encountered the Japanese battle fleet under Admiral Togo. It lost 25 of its 35 ships in battle. Most of the survivors were held in neutral ports for the duration of the war.

The peace settlement and its impact

The Russians had lost largely as a result of numerical and strategic disadvantages. Equally, the incompetence of their officers and administrators contrasted, as it had done in the Crimea, with the bravery and sacrifice of

---

1. What advantages did Japan have in the campaigns of 1904–05?

2. How true is it that Russia lost the Russo-Japanese War largely because the government underestimated the difficulties of fighting a campaign in the Far East?

3. Would you agree that Russia's defeat in the Russo-Japanese War was neither very surprising nor very serious?

---

the common soldier. The greater effectiveness of Japan's modern equipment has caused historian J.N. Westwood to ask 'which of the two belligerents was western and which oriental?' Despite these factors, Europeans' convictions of their own racial superiority rendered the outcome of the war acutely embarrassing for the Russian state.

On the face of it the peace settlement arrived at through American mediation at Portsmouth, New Hampshire (August 1905) let the Russians off lightly. Although Port Arthur and the Liaotung Peninsula were surrendered to Japan, Witte's tough negotiations ensured that Russia paid no war indemnity, kept half of the island of Sakhalin, and retained its dominance in Manchuria. The Treaty of Portsmouth, nevertheless, marked a turning point in the foreign policy of Tsarist Russia. Russian interests in the Far East were not ended, but strict limitations were placed upon them. The result was that for the first time in nearly 25 years the foreign prestige of the Russian Empire depended mainly upon developments in Europe.

3.6 Why did revolution break out in Russia in 1905?

The union movement and 'Bloody Sunday'

Military failure and humiliation added to the revolutionary pressure already upon the Tsarist government at the end of 1904. Most of the ingredients for a flare-up were now present. Peasant unrest had recurred sporadically since 1902, industrial strikes had occurred between 1902–04 in most cities, and several explosions of student unrest had taken place in Moscow and St Petersburg in the same years. The spark that set them all off was provided by the 'Bloody Sunday' massacre of 22 January 1905.

'Bloody Sunday' marked the spectacular failure of a daring experiment in the control of revolutionary elements. Sergei Zubatov, the chief of police in St Petersburg, had proposed the concept known as 'police socialism' in 1902. Under this scheme the police provided semi-official encouragement of moderate workers' organisations, aiming at genuine improvements in wages and working conditions, in the expectation that members would then refrain from more dangerous political demands. One of the largest of these organisations was the Assembly of Russian Factory Workers, founded in 1903 and boasting 8,000 members within a year. Its leader was

---

Sergei Zubatov (1863–1917)
Abandoned radical activity to join the *Okhrana* (1886). Chief of Moscow *Okhrana* (1895). Leading police official in St Petersburg (1902).

Tsarist troops fire on the crowd, St Petersburg, on 'Bloody Sunday', 22 January 1905. This image is from a 1925 film.

Georgi Gapon (1870–1906)
Orthodox priest and social and political activist. Founded Assembly of Russian Factory Workers (1903). Organised strikes and petitions that culminated in 'Bloody Sunday' massacre (1905). Discredited, he was murdered by Socialist Revolutionaries (1906).

the Orthodox priest, Georgi Gapon, a controversial figure. After 1905, left-wing suspicion of Gapon's motives was so bitter that he was 'executed' by SR agents (1906). Definite evidence of treachery, however, has never been uncovered. Strict control over the activities of his society was difficult, and the plan to present a loyal petition for redress of grievances to the Tsar in St Petersburg on 22 January 1905 carried Gapon along with it.

The demonstration of more than 150,000 people in front of the Winter Palace was perhaps the last occasion on which the Russian people genuinely approached the Tsar in his traditional role as the 'Little Father' of his people. The panic that led the Imperial troops to fire upon the crowd, killing an estimated 1,000, finished off 'police socialism', mortally wounded the reputation of the autocracy and triggered the 1905 revolution. 'It did more than perhaps anything else during the whole of the reign,' wrote the historian Richard Charques, 'to undermine the allegiance of the common people to the throne.'

The popular response to 'Bloody Sunday'

Gapon's subsequent denunciation of the Tsar summed up the hatred felt by much of the Russian population. 'The innocent blood of workers, their wives and children lies forever between you, the murderer of souls, and the Russian people. May all the blood that must be spilled fall on you, you hangman.' In Russian industry this anger was reflected in an unprecedented strike movement. In February 1905, 400,000 workers went on strike, and the total exceeded 2.7 million by the end of the year. No strike had greater effect than that of the railway workers in October, as a result of which the Russian cities were in imminent danger of starvation and the Russian economy was brought to the verge of collapse. No major city in European Russia escaped the dislocation of its fuel supplies and of its administration.

The relatively small size of Russia's urban proletariat made its revolt, although serious, a problem that might be contained. A general revolt of the peasantry, however, was a much more serious prospect. The first peasant revolt broke out in the Kursk Province in February and by April discontent had spread to most of the prime agricultural regions of European Russia. The peasant unrest was originally spontaneous, but was subsequently exploited by the radical political parties. Thus the All-Russian Peasant Union, formed by regional delegates in May 1905, put forward views similar to those of the SRs.

At a local level, demands and action were far less coherent, inspired by the hatred of past wrongs and by hope of present gain, especially in the form of land. Of these localised disturbances, 3,228 were serious enough to require the intervention of troops, and damage to an estimated value of 29 million roubles was inflicted upon Russian landowners in the course of the year.

Further afield, the separatist demands of various national minorities within the Russian Empire provided another threat to its survival. Socialist and nationalist tendencies combined to produce a rash of nationalist parties and groups, including the Ukrainian 'Enlightenment' group (1905), the Ukrainian Social Democratic Party (1905), the White Russian Community (1903), the Moldavian Democratic Party (1906) and the All-Estonian Congress (1905). Their activities and demands varied from the publication of books and journals, through the desire for a representative assembly within the Empire, to the demand for complete independence.

The armed forces

The key to the success or failure of the revolution lay in the attitude of the armed forces. An ominous element in the 1905 disturbances was the sporadic outbreak of mutinies in army units, but more especially in the navy. Rebellions occurred at Kronstadt in the Baltic and at Sevastopol on the Black Sea. Perhaps the most famous was the mutiny on board the battleship 'Potemkin', in the Black Sea in June. Rebelling against the squalor of their conditions of service and the harshness of their officers, the crew seized control of the ship, killed a number of the officers and bombarded Odessa. The prospect of general mutiny posed a grave threat to the survival of the regime, but it did not materialise. The 'Potemkin' was forced to seek asylum in a Romanian port, and mutinies on other ships were suppressed. The larger part of the army remained loyal. The Imperial manifesto published in December, promising better pay and fairer treatment, had the desired effect upon troops mainly of peasant origin. By clever use of non-Russian troops against Russian mutineers, and vice-versa, the government had largely restored military discipline by the end of the year.

The political response to 'Bloody Sunday'

The summer of 1905 witnessed a rapid crystallisation of opposition groups as each came to believe that its hour was at hand. Two main liberal groups emerged. In October the Union of Liberation, supported by some of the *zemstvo* politicians, established the Constitutional Democratic Party, soon known by the abbreviated title of the 'Kadets'. Its demands included an assembly elected by direct and universal suffrage and the restoration of ancient national rights to Poland and Finland. They were rather more radical than the Union of Unions formed in February by representatives of a number of professional bodies.

The Russian left was caught unawares and in a state of disarray by the events of 1905. The emergence in October of a Council (**Soviet**) of Workers' Deputies in St Petersburg was not the work of established socialist leaders, but a direct action by politically conscious workers to co-ordinate their strike action. Its 400–500 members represented five trade unions and 96 factories. Once the established leftist groups stirred themselves to tap the potential of the organisation, the Soviet came to represent mainly the **Menshevik** tendency of the RSDRP, with **Bolsheviks** and SRs in a distinct minority. Of those who returned from exile, none made a greater impact than Leon Trotsky, an associate of Lenin, but more sympathetic at this point to the more democratic Menshevik views. Trotsky's intellectual and oratorical skills made him one of the leading figures in the political chaos that reigned in the Russian capital.

How much importance should one attach to this first Soviet? To the historians of the USSR its significance was as a 'dress rehearsal' for 1917. On the other hand, the Soviet in St Petersburg lasted only 50 days. It was not responsible for the huge strike in October, and the second general strike that it called in November fizzled out into anti-climax. It is true that its importance outside St Petersburg was negligible, but its significance is in the lead that it gave to later revolutionaries and in the brief influence that it enjoyed in the capital.

Soviet (Russian – Council): The term has come to be understood particularly as referring to the councils of workers' representatives favoured by Russian socialists from 1905 onwards.

Menshevik: A term used to describe the people who belonged to that branch of the Russian communist movement which favoured a more popular, loose-knit form of party organisation and discipline, with more democratic leadership.

Bolsheviks: Used to describe the supporters of the ideas and the political system that Lenin argued for and introduced in Russia after the Russian Revolution in 1917.

---

1. What groups opposed the authority of the Tsar's government in the course of 1905?

2. Did any of the elements that rebelled against the Tsar in 1905 seriously threaten his control of the country?

3. 'The 1905 revolution represented every element of discontent within the Russian Empire.' Did this make the revolutionary movement stronger or weaker?

Leon Trotsky (1879–1940)
Born Lev Davidovitch Bronstein. Became involved in revolutionary activities as a teenager. Exiled to Siberia, from where he escaped (1902) and joined the Social Democratic Party. He opposed Lenin's call for a united group of revolutionary leaders; instead he worked abroad, earning his living as a left-wing journalist (1905–17). Joined the Bolshevik Party on his return to Russia and played a major role in the October Revolution. Became Commissar for War and was involved in a power struggle with Stalin after Lenin's death in 1924. He was ousted from the Communist Party and expelled from Russia (1929).

3.7 How did the government survive the 1905 Revolution?

Concessions to the liberals and to the peasantry

Frightened by his government's loss of control, the possibility of further military disobedience, and the actuality of peasant rebellion – which was the oldest fear of the Russian nobility – the Tsar had the choice of two courses of action. In early October he seemed ready to resort to outright military dictatorship but, faced with the objections of most senior ministers and some prominent members of the royal family, he finally recognised the need for concessions. The October Manifesto (30 October 1905) was, superficially, an acceptance of most of the classic liberal demands. It granted freedom of person, of speech, of religion, of assembly and of organisation. Above all, it confirmed the proposal made in August for the summoning of an elected parliament, or 'duma'.

In direct response to the agrarian unrest, a further set of concessions in November cancelled redemption payments and called for the peasants in return 'to preserve peace and order, and not violate the laws and rights of others'. Neither the November nor the October Manifesto really touched upon the true nature of Russia's social and political problems. The former made no concession to the peasants' desperate need for land and the latter set no real limitation upon the autocratic power of the Tsar. Russia faced the last nine years of peace with a liberal facade resting uneasily upon incompatible absolutist foundations. 'A constitution has been given,' remarked Trotsky, 'but the autocracy remains.'

Stolypin and repression

In another of his characteristically vivid phrases, Trotsky described the October Manifesto as 'the whip wrapped in the parchment of a constitution'. Indeed, the government had sufficiently recovered its nerve to set about the restoration of its authority by the dual policy of consistent repression and inconsistent reform. In November, the members of the St Petersburg Soviet and those of the Union of Peasants were arrested. In December, a last desperate rebellion in Moscow was crushed by regular troops with the loss of about 1,000 rebel lives, while loyal troops suppressed mutinous veterans of the eastern war along the route of the Trans-Siberian Railway. The efforts of the government were aided by the activities of extreme right-wing groups hostile to the liberalisation of 1905. A legal political party, the Union of the Russian People (October 1905), was supplemented by terrorist gangs known as the 'Black Hundreds' which attacked known reformists and specialised in anti-semitic pogroms.

In the course of the next few years, counter-terror became a longer-term government weapon in the hands of Pyotr Stolypin. A newcomer to the Council of Ministers in 1906, he was appointed its chairman in 1907. His credentials as a ruthless governor of the province of Saratov during the revolutionary year were perfect for his new task. He has been widely regarded as the second of the two men, after Sergei Witte, who might have saved the regime, had the Tsar had the wit to listen to his advice. Stolypin's plans for the regeneration of Russia were based on counter-terror and reform. He waged an unrelenting war against violent political opposition, a tactic made more necessary than ever by the resurgence of revolutionary violence in the summer of 1906. In 1907, an estimated 1,231 officials and 1,768 private citizens died in terrorist attacks. To this Stolypin replied with terror of his own. His 'field courts martial', operating under Article 87 of the Fundamental Laws, carried out 1,144 death sentences in the nine months preceding May 1907.

Alexander Guchkov (1862–1936)

Leading industrialist, prominent in the constitutional politics of the early 20th century. Chairman of Octobrist Party (1905). Speaker of Third Duma (1907–12). Guchkov became a leading member of 'Progressive Bloc' (1915), before promotion to Minister of War in Provisional Government (1917).

The bases of radical politics were also attacked through pressure upon unions and upon the press. Between 1906 and 1912, 600 unions closed and 1,000 newspapers ceased to publish. Seemingly, the policy was a success. In 1908 the number of political assassinations dropped to 365. From Alexander Guchkov, leader of the Octobrists in the Duma, came the grudging compliment that 'if we are now witnessing the last convulsions of the revolution, and it is undoubtedly coming to an end, then it is to this man that we owe it'.

Stolypin and reform

Stolypin was not such a reactionary as to imagine that counter-terror alone could stabilise the Tsarist regime. Reform, too, was essential and where Witte had set himself the task of modernising Russian industry, his successor turned to the more deep-rooted problem of the Russian peasantry. The key to Stolypin's agrarian policy was his belief that the surest basis for the regime was the support of a prosperous and contented peasantry. To achieve this without damaging the interests of the landlords he sought primarily to free the peasant from the communes created by the 1861 emancipation. Acting again through the government's emergency powers, he formulated a law (November 1906) whereby any peasant had the right to withdraw himself and his land from the commune. A further law (June 1910) dissolved all those communes where no redistribution of land had taken place since the emancipation. These laws were the culmination of a programme that had also granted equal civil rights in local administration (October 1906) to peasants and had transferred substantial amounts of state land to the Peasants' Bank (September 1906) in an attempt to satisfy 'land hunger'.

The subsequent growth of private peasant ownership was substantial. An estimated 20% of the peasantry enjoyed hereditary ownership of their land in 1905, while the proportion had risen to nearly 50% by 1915. Consolidation of scattered strips of land into viable farms was a slower process, and less than 10% of peasant holdings had been thus improved by 1915. Three million cases, however, were awaiting the attention of land officials when the advent of war slowed their work rate almost to a halt. The lowering of interest rates in the Land Bank and the offering of migration facilities to 3.5 million peasants in Siberia between 1905 and 1915, bear further witness to the concern of the Tsar's senior ministers with the agrarian problem.

The greatest weakness in Stolypin's reforms, like those of Witte, was that they did not enjoy the complete support of the Tsar. Strongly influenced by extreme right-wing factions resentful of any such changes, Nicholas II was probably on the verge of dismissing Stolypin when the latter was assassinated in Kiev (September 1911). The murderer, Dmitri Bogrov, had links with both the SRs and the secret police. The confusion that has always surrounded his motives for the crime is a measure of how Stolypin's 'enlightened conservatism' had attracted the hatred of both political extremes.

1. By what means did Stolypin attempt to solve the problems that were evident in the 1905 revolution?

2. To what extent did the Tsar actually surrender any of his power as a result of the 1905 revolution?

3. How true is it to claim that Tsarism survived the revolution of 1905 unscathed?

3.8 Did the Dumas represent a real constitutional advance in Russia?

The Russian constitution in 1906

Outwardly Russia entered 1906 with a radically revised and modernised constitution. In effect, this constitutionalism was limited in many respects. The revived Council of Ministers, presided over at first by Sergei Witte, had the appearance of a cabinet. In fact, the ministers were entirely depen-dent upon the Tsar for their appointment, direction and dismissal, and thus merely continued to serve the autocracy. The upper house of the assembly (Council of State), was half elected, by *zemstvo*, Church, noble and university bodies, but was also half appointed by the Tsar. The lower house, the State Duma, was wholly elective but from its birth in February 1906 it was tied hand and foot by a series of limitations upon its powers. It had no control over military expenditure, nor over the Tsar's household finances, and in any case an enormous French loan of 2,250 million gold francs (April 1906) rendered the Crown financially independent. The Duma had no means of controlling or even of censuring ministers. Most important of all, Article 87 of the Fundamental Laws (April 1906), drawn up without consultation with the Duma, left the Tsar with the power to govern by decree whenever the assembly was not in session.

The composition of the Duma

The representative nature of the Duma was further limited by the decision of all major left-wing groups to boycott the first set of elections. Thus the elections in early 1906 were mainly contested by the Kadets and two other groups:

- The Octobrists were moderate conservatives, taking their name from their acceptance of the October Manifesto.

- The Labour Group (*Trudoviki*) was a faction largely reflecting the views of the SRs, despite the fact that the SRs were not officially involved in the contest.

The relative fortunes of these and other groups in the elections to the four Dumas that met between 1906 and 1917 are reflected in the table.

Composition of the Dumas, 1906–17

	1st Duma	2nd Duma	3rd Duma	4th Duma
Social Democrats	–	65	14	4
Socialist Revolutionaries	–	34	–	–
Trudoviks	94	101	14	10
Progressives	–	–	39	47
Kadets (also known as the Party of the People's Liberty)	79	92	52	57
Non-Russian national group	121	–	26	21
Centre Party	–	–	–	33
Octobrists	17	32	120	99
Nationalists	–	–	76	88
Extreme Right	15	63	53	64

The changes in composition from Duma to Duma reflect two factors. One was the eventual decision of groups on both political extremes to participate in elections, if only to change the nature of the assembly. The more important factor was that election was by indirect 'college' voting, whereby communities of differing sizes nominated a delegate to exercise a single vote for them. This has been variously interpreted as an administra-tive necessity, given Russia's vast size, and as a cynical trick to rig election results. Certainly it gave the government the chance to limit or increase the influence of sections of the population by changing the size of the commu-nity exercising one 'college' vote.

The failure of the first and second Dumas

The task facing the Duma was nearly impossible. It faced, in historian Gerald Fischer's words, 'the dilemma of attaining complex, specifically western objectives in an illiberal, underdeveloped society'. Much compromise would have been needed if it were to reach these goals, and little was forthcoming. The Tsar was never more than coldly formal towards the Duma, but a number of historians have also laid blame upon the liberal majority in the early Dumas for their inflexibility and their insistence upon unrealistic demands.

The first Duma (April 1906) was unmistakably hostile to the government in its major demands – for land reform and for an amnesty for political prisoners – and it was dissolved after only 73 days. The second Duma (February 1907) suffered from a transfer of influence from the centre to the extremes. The number of Kadets was greatly reduced after their irresponsible and impulsive 'Vyborg Manifesto' (July 1906) in which 120 of their members broke the law and disqualified themselves from future elections by calling for civil disobedience against the government. On the other hand, groups from both the extreme right and the extreme left of Russian politics now decided to participate in the elections and to use the Duma for their own forms of propaganda. The second Duma, therefore, amounted to three and a half months of continuous uproar.

The third and fourth Dumas

The longer lives of the third and fourth Dumas (November 1907 and November 1912) resulted from Stolypin's dual decision to work with a suitably conservative assembly, and to revise the electoral laws to that end. While the electoral law of 1905 had blatantly favoured the conservative forces of landowners and peasants, the new one (June 1907) manipulated the electoral 'colleges' even further. In effect it left some 50% of the final votes in the hands of the landowners (up from 31%), 23% in the hands of the peasantry (down from 42%), while the growing urban proletariat exercised only 2% of the votes (down from 4%).

The result was the election of two assemblies that hovered between reform and reaction. Historians are divided as to whether or not these Dumas should be seen as successes. Certainly the third and fourth Dumas were thwarted on many important reformist issues. Bills for the extension of the *zemstvo* system into Poland and for religious toleration were defeated in the Council of State. When Stolypin used his emergency powers to pass the former measure it was a triumph for the Fundamental Laws rather than for the Duma. On the other hand, the hated Land Commandants (see Chapter 2) were replaced by reinstated Justices of the Peace, compulsory health insurance for industrial workers was introduced (June 1912) and, with local co-operation from the *zemstva*, much progress was made in Russian education. Universal primary education within ten years was adopted as an official policy (May 1908) and by 1914 it was 50% of the way towards completion, involving 7.2 million children. Figures for attendance at secondary schools (510,000) and at universities (40,000) in 1914 do not, unfortunately, reflect a uniform advance.

As historian Hugh Seton-Watson has pointed out, the achievement of the Dumas should not only be estimated in terms of the measures that they passed. It had not become a truly representative assembly because the government had never wanted such an assembly. However, by 1914 political parties were legally established and, while rebellion was punished, open political discussion was tolerated and was allowed to appear in the press. All of these factors represented advances scarcely dreamed of before 1905.

1. What powers did the Russian Duma have between 1906 and 1914, and what powers did it lack?

2. Why did the third and fourth Dumas last longer than the first and second Dumas?

3. In what ways, if any, had the work of Pyotr Stolypin strengthened the Tsarist regime in Russia by 1914?

3.9 What impression of Russian society is conveyed by scientific and cultural developments in the two decades before the outbreak of war?

The sciences

Émigré: One who has emigrated. In this case, a political refugee who has left his/her own country, usually for political reasons, to live and work abroad.

Those historians who take an optimistic view of Russia's development in the 20 years before the First World War have often emphasised the advances that were achieved in scientific and cultural terms. 'Not only the body of Russia but the soul as well,' commented the *émigré* M. Karpovich, 'was growing stronger in the decade that preceded the World War.' Indeed, considering how few Russians were highly educated and the limitations of its facilities for higher education, its contribution to science and technology in the 20 years before 1914 was quite remarkable. In most scientific fields, Russia produced men of genius. Ilya Mechnikov was a leading figure in the study of infection and immunisation, running the Pasteur Institute in Paris and winning a Nobel Prize in 1908. An earlier Nobel Prize (1904) went to perhaps the most famous of all Russian scientists, Ivan Pavlov, whose work on digestive enzymes and on conditioned reflexes in dogs makes him a household name today. In chemistry, Dmitri Mendeleyev evolved the Periodic Table and described a number of new elements, while in agricultural sciences K.A. Timiryazev was the foremost soil scientist of his day.

In applied technology, Russia suffered rather more from its material backwardness, but led the world in two important respects. Alexander Popov's work on radio communications ran parallel to, and sometimes ahead of, that of Guglielmo Marconi, while Russia's contribution to aerodynamics was of the greatest importance. The work of N.Y. Zhukovsky and S.A. Chaplygin on airflow, important as it was, gives precedence to that of K.E. Tsiolkovsky whose developments in the fields of design and fuel make him one of the most important figures in the history of rocket technology.

The arts

In most of the arts, a golden age had ended in Russia by 1914. The major exception to this rule was in the performing arts. In ballet, Sergei Diaghilev's *Ballets Russes* (1909) maintained its supremacy for decades. In its choreographer, Mikhail Fokine, its dancers, Vacheslav Nijinsky and Anna Pavlova, and in its primary composer, Igor Stravinsky, it boasted the world's best. The Moscow Arts Theatre, with Konstantin Stanislavsky as its major director, and Russian opera, with Feodor Chaliapin as its leading performer, also raised Russia to a level of unprecedented cultural brilliance. The greatest Russian writers of the age, however, were recently dead – Anton Chekhov in 1904 and Leo Tolstoy in 1910. Although not primarily political writers, both were obsessed in their last works – as in Chekhov's *The Cherry Orchard* (1904) and Tolstoy's *Resurrection* (1900) – with the stagnation and sterility of Russian society. Their successor was Maxim Peshkov who, writing under the pen-name 'Gorky' (meaning 'bitter'), had already produced a stream of novels and plays by 1914. These were more specifically political than those of his predecessors, exposing the squalor and hopelessness of society's 'lower depths'. Historian Lionel Kochan describes Gorky, in *The Making of Modern Russia* (1979), as 'the first consciously proletarian novelist', and these works were to make him the doyen of Soviet literature in the 1920s and early 1930s.

3.10 How stable and how strong was the Russian regime on the eve of world war?
A CASE STUDY IN HISTORICAL INTERPRETATION

Perhaps more than any previous period in Russian history, the 'Stolypin era' has provoked controversy among historians. This controversy has centred around the overall evaluation of Stolypin's work, but focuses upon the question of whether his reforms, with those of Witte, had created a viable basis for the survival of the Tsarist regime in Russia by 1914.

As is the case with many aspects of recent Russian history, such assessments have often followed partisan political lines. Soviet historians, following the Marxist–Leninist assumption that proletarian revolution was inevitable, naturally concluded that any attempt to reform or to save the Tsarist regime was doomed to failure. Such writers as Aron Avrekh, in *Stolypin and the Third Duma* (1968), concentrated upon the suppression of revolution, upon the 200,000 political prisoners of 1908, and the 5,000 death sentences passed in 1907–09. To Avrekh, the 'Stolypin course' was 'the inescapable situation of reaction, the historic destiny of the rotten regime', for revolution was still the only logical outcome of the social and economic forces at work.

In general, western historians have been less ready to accept this thesis of 'inevitable' revolution, but have viewed the period immediately before the war as one that was open to many possibilities. Their appraisals of Stolypin's work have usually been kinder, sometimes excusing his use of terror by reference to the revolutionary terrorism with which he was faced, and sometimes, like the American-Russian *émigré* Leonid Strakhovsky, viewing Stolypin as a most positive reformer and as the brightest hope of the Tsarist regime.

On the broader question of the adequacy of Russian modernisation, commentators have divided into 'optimistic' and 'pessimistic' schools, respectively confident and doubtful about Tsarist Russia's prospects had it avoided involvement in the European war. For the optimists, the economic historian A. Gerschenkron has been a prominent spokesman, especially in his book *Economic Backwardness in Historical Perspective* (1962). He saw the increasing economic maturity of Russia, based upon industrial development and sound agrarian reform, as a guarantee of peacetime stability. 'One might surmise,' Gerschenkron concludes, 'that in the absence of war Russia could have continued on the road of progressive westernisation.' Others have concluded that, even under the extraordinary pressures of war, the Russian economy performed impressively, and provided evidence that the 'Stolypin Era' had given the regime a strong economic foundation. This argument was first put forward by Norman Stone, in *The Eastern Front 1914–1917* (1974), who contended that Russia's wartime weaknesses arose from problems of distribution, rather than of production. More recently it has been forcefully stated by Dominic Lieven, who concludes that, at the height of its wartime operations, 'the Russian defence industry performed miracles'.

E.H. Carr provided a clear statement of the 'pessimistic' interpretation in his classic work, *The Bolshevik Revolution* (1950–53). He drew attention to the limitations of Stolypin's reforms over Russia in general and stressed the possibility that his sacrifice of the weaker peasant to 'the sober and the strong' would, in the end, only have added to the ranks of the revolutionary proletariat.

It is certainly not easy to assess the long-term prospects of Stolypin's agrarian reforms. His central aim, of course, was to establish a class of prosperous, conservative peasants, which would provide a basis of rural support for the Tsarist regime. It is clear that the majority of Russian peasants did not withdraw themselves and their land from the *mir*. About 20% had done so by 1916, yet it might reasonably be argued that such a proportion, amounting to some two million families, might have been sufficient to provide the conservative foundation that Stolypin sought. At the same time, another 3.5 million peasants were persuaded to migrate to virgin lands in Siberia.

The pessimists counter such figures with the fact that the Russian population increased by 21% between 1900 and 1910, adding nearly 30 million to the total population. Thus, they argue, a further imbalance was created between prosperous peasants and their poverty-stricken neighbours. The picture is also blurred by the fact that Russia enjoyed outstandingly good harvests between 1909 and 1913. Perhaps rural stability was the product of an ample food supply, rather than of Stolypin's reforms.

One way or another, the Russian countryside was peaceful on the eve of the First World War, and Lenin, in distant exile, expressed fears that Stolypin had taken an effective course. 'If Stolypin's agrarian policy was maintained for a very long period, and if it succeeded in transforming the whole structure of rural landholding, it could make us abandon any attempt at an agrarian policy in a bourgeois society.' It might be added that, a generation later, Stalin viewed the prosperous peasant class, the **kulaks**, as the greatest obstacle to the establishment of a communist economic system, and went to great lengths to destroy them (see Chapter 5).

> *Kulaks*: Richer, semi-capitalist peasants. The term literally means a 'fist', as a symbol for money-grabbing.

The years immediately before the First World War also provide some ambiguous indicators of the prosperity and stability of Russia's industrial towns. On the one hand, due in particular to the manufacture of armaments, industrial production grew at the rate of 6% per year between 1907 and 1914. The membership of trade unions and of the most radical political parties dropped considerably. Russia had only 40,000 union members in 1913, compared with 300,000 in 1907. Whether this was due to government reform or to government repression, it meant that the industrial working classes had less scope to express their discontent than they had enjoyed in 1905. Strike action, peaking in 1905–06, declined steadily over the next six years, only to explode once again in the last year of peace. It is no easy matter to predict what might have happened in the next decade, had Russia remained at peace. However, a simple observation of the facts leads to the conclusion that, as things stood in 1914, the Tsar's government was able to rely upon the army, and was able to control current levels of unrest among the urban workers.

Undoubtedly, political support for Tsarism was stronger in 1914 than it had been in 1905, in that Nicholas received grudging support from middle-class elements for whom proletarian revolt was the greatest fear. It is by no means clear, however, that the Tsar would have built upon that support in the long term, to create a genuine coalition of conservative interests. The decisive factor in this controversy may well be that which was stressed by historian Donald Treadgold in *Lenin and his Rivals* (1955). He emphasised the implacable hostility towards change of much of the Russian ruling class. This was especially true of the Tsar himself, who regarded good government not as 'an ideal to be sought, but [as] an irrelevance compared to the maintenance of the loyalty of the Russian people to his own person'.

It is also important to remember how completely, even at a time of political reform, Russian ministers remained the 'creatures' of the Tsar, with no significant scope for personal initiative. This is illustrated by the fact that Nicholas was served between 1905 and 1917 by eight different ministers for trade and industry and by 11 different ministers of the interior. Stolypin himself was succeeded in office by much less able men. His post was held in 1914 by Ivan Goremykin, 74 years of age, and almost certainly appointed by the Tsar in order to ensure that no disturbing programmes of further reform emerged from the Prime Minister's office. In *Russia in the Age of Modernisation and Revolution, 1881–1917* (1983), the historian Hans Rogger describes how Sergei Witte, 'perhaps the ablest man to serve the last two tsars, at times behaved in their presence like a junior officer – bowing excessively, his hands at the seams of his trousers, and displaying little of his bold and independent mind'. The same author reminds us that 'only an exceptional Tsar could long tolerate an exceptional minister,' and Nicholas, of course, was by no means an exceptional man. Perhaps, in the final analysis, progress towards a more modern Russia might still have been blocked by a narrow-minded and reactionary autocracy.

---

1. What different conclusions have been reached by historians about the potential, long-term success of Stolypin's reforms?

2. What arguments are there for and against the claim that by 1914 revolution in Russia was effectively inevitable?

Source-based questions: The political achievement of Pyotr Stolypin

Study the following source material and then answer the questions which follow.

SOURCE A

An analysis of Stolypin's policy, written by the contemporary British authority, Donald McKenzie Wallace, in 1912

Mr Stolypin formed two resolves, and he clung to them with marvellous tenacity: to suppress disorders relentlessly by every means at his disposal, and to preserve the Duma as long as hopes could be entertained of its doing useful work. Until the assembling of the third Duma he found no cordial support in any of the parties. All were leagued against him. For the conservative and reactionary Right, he was too liberal. For the revolutionary Left, he was a pillar of autocracy, an advocate of police repression and of drum-head courts martial.

SOURCE B

A judgement on Stolypin's policy by the Russian politician Alexander Izvolski, in his Memoirs, published in 1920

Mr Stolypin's agrarian reforms met with extraordinary success, surpassing the most optimistic expectations. The Russian peasant, prone as he is to listen to revolutionary propaganda when it appeals to his dominant passion for more land, is nevertheless possessed of a keen intelligence. He is not slow in going ahead of the measures decreed for facilitating the ownership of land which he farmed, and finding means of acquiring additional land by proper and legal methods. These results were so satisfactory that, on the eve of the revolution of 1917, it is safe to say that the entire agrarian problem was on the way to being solved definitively.

SOURCE C

Adapted from Imperial and Soviet Russia, David Christian, 1997

The reforms had least effect in the overcrowded central regions, where land shortage and peasant discontent were at their worst. In these areas the commune [*mir*] provided considerable protection for poorer peasants, and most households clung to it desperately. The agrarian reform did not create the politically conservative rural society that Stolypin hoped for, as the renewed peasant insurrections of 1917 proved. Nor had the constitutional reform helped to bridge the gap between the government and Russia's rapidly changing educated élite. As a result, the government remained as isolated as in 1905.

(a) Use Source A and your own knowledge.

Explain briefly the reference made in Source A to 'drum-head courts martial'. [3 marks]

(b) Use Sources B and C and your own knowledge.

Explain how Source B differs from Source C in the conclusions that it draws about the success of Stolypin's policies. [7 marks]

(c) Use Sources A, B and C and your own knowledge.

To what extent had the reforms carried out by the Russian government during Stolypin's period in office increased the stability of the Tsarist regime? [15 marks]

Source-based questions: How realistic were the prospects of liberal reform in the reign of Nicholas II?

Study the sources below and then answer questions (a) and (b) which follow.

SOURCE A

From Bernard Pares, *The Fall of the Russian Monarchy*, published in 1939

The third Duma, though its horizon was much more limited, did come to stay, and its membership was better qualified to take practical advantage of the education which it offered. Some seventy persons at least, forming the nucleus of the more important commissions, were learning in detail to understand the problems and difficulties of administration and therefore to understand both each other and the Government. One could see political competence growing day by day. And to a constant observer it was becoming more and more an open secret that the distinctions of party meant little, and that in the social warmth of their public work for Russia all these men were becoming friends.

The Duma was establishing itself as an indispensable part of the organisation of public life, and the Emperor himself took a certain pride in it as his own creation. Those surrounding him continued their attempts to prejudice it in his eyes, but having once rejected the occasion to abolish it in his *coup d'etat* of 1907, he was increasingly less likely to do so now. In 1912 he said to me: 'the Duma started too fast; now it is slower, but better'. That was the general judgement of others, and the result was a growing vigour of initiative not only in practical affairs, but also in thought and expression.

SOURCE B

From R.B. McKean, *The Russian Constitutional Monarchy 1907–17*, published in 1977

The Duma parties also suffered from severe defects of organisation. Although they claimed to represent the interests of social groups throughout the Empire, the Duma parties lacked truly national structures. Continual government restrictions upon political activities and the indifference of the educated public to party politics after 1907 promoted the decay of the parties' provincial branches. By 1913 the Octobrist party structure was almost defunct. The Kadets possessed a mere nine branches in the provinces and the Progressists none. In effect the Duma parties and politics were confined to the educated society of St Petersburg and Moscow. The nature of the electoral system and the class composition of the liberal parties meant that the opposition lacked any organic ties with the peasantry and the working class. As P.N. Durnovo observed, 'between the intelligentsia and the people there is a profound gulf of mutual misunderstanding and mistrust'.

SOURCE C

From Orlando Figes, *A People's Tragedy*, published in 1996

The 'zemstvo men' were unlikely pioneers of the revolution. Most of them were noble landowners, progressive and practical men like Prince Lvov, who simply wanted the monarchy to play a positive role in improving the life of its subjects. They sought to increase the influence of the zemstvos in the framing of government legislation, but the notion of leading a broad opposition movement was repugnant to them. Prince Lvov's mentor, D.N.Shipov, who organised the zemstvos at a national level, was himself a devoted monarchist and flatly opposed the demand for a constitution. The whole purpose of his work was to strengthen the autocracy by bringing the Tsar closer to his people, organised through the zemstvos and a consultative parliament.

There was plenty of ground, then, for the autocracy to reach an accommodation with the 'zemstvo men'. But, as so often in its inexorable downfall, the old regime chose repression instead of compromise and thus created the political hostility of the zemstvos. The chief architect of this suicidal policy was the all-powerful Ministry of the Interior, which regarded the zemstvos as a dangerous haven for revolutionaries and subjected them to a relentless campaign of persecution. Armed with the statute of 1890, the provincial governors capped the zemstvos' budgets, censored their publications and removed or arrested the elected members of their boards.

Source-based questions: How realistic were the prospects of liberal reform in the reign of Nicholas II?

SOURCE D

From Hans Rogger, *Russia in the Age of Modernisation and Revolution, 1881–1917*, published in 1983

The political contest between the government and its critics, which looked so menacing in 1914, was confined largely to the Duma. Since the death of Stolypin it had been growing more troublesome in face of the government's disregard. Ministers refused to appear before it for months on end; they tried to whittle away its rights of interpellation, of budgetary control, of legislative initiative, and of immunity for statements made from its rostrum. The reactionary Minister of the Interior, Nikolai Maklakov, even favoured the idea, taken up by Tsar Nicholas, that the legislature should be reduced to submitting minority and majority opinions for the Tsar's decision.

SOURCE E

Part of the speech of Nicholas II at the dissolution of the second Duma, June 1907

To our sorrow, a substantial portion of the representatives to the second Duma has not justified our expectations. Many of the delegates sent by the people approached their work, not with sincerity, not with a desire to strengthen Russia and to improve its organisation, but with an obvious desire to increase sedition and to further the disintegration of the state. The activity of these people in the State Duma has been an insuperable obstacle to fruitful work. A spirit of hostility has been brought into the Duma itself, preventing a sufficient number of its members, desirous of working for the good of their native land, from uniting for such work.

Answer both questions (a) and (b).

(a) Using your own knowledge and the evidence of Sources B, D and E, what do you consider to have been the main weaknesses in the Russian Duma between 1906 and 1914? [10 marks]

(b) 'The prime reason for the failure of liberal and democratic political movements in Russia before the First World War was the opposition of the Tsar and his government.' Using your own knowledge and the evidence of all five sources, explain how far you would agree with this interpretation. [20 marks]

Further Reading

Texts designed for AS and A2 Level students

Reaction and Revolution: Russia 1881–1924 by Michael Lynch (Hodder & Stoughton, Access to History series, 1992)

The Origins of the Russian Revolution by Alan Wood (Routledge, Lancaster Pamphlets, 1993)

Russia 1848–1917 by Jonathan Bromley (Heinemann Advanced History series, 2002)

More advanced reading

The Russian Empire, 1801–1917 by Hugh Seton-Watson (Oxford University Press, 1967)

Russia under the Old Regime by Richard Pipes (Weidenfeld & Nicolson, 1974)

Russia in the Age of Modernisation and Revolution, 1881–1917 by Hans Rogger (Longman, History of Russia series, 1983)

The Industrialisation of Russia, 1700–1914 by M.E. Falkus (Macmillan, 1972)

The Tsarist Economy 1850–1917 by P. Gatrell (Batsford, 1986)

Imperial and Soviet Russia: Power, Privilege and the Challenge of Modernity by David Christian (Macmillan, 1997) provides a good, concise summary of recent developments in the study of this period.

The Russian Peasantry 1600–1930 by David Moon (Longman, 1999)

4 The Russian Revolutions, 1914–1924

Key Issues

- What impact did the First World War have upon Russian politics and society?

- How did the Bolsheviks seize power in 1917?

- How did the Bolsheviks deal with the political and economic problems that beset them in 1918–1924?

4.1 What was the impact of the First World War upon Russia?

4.2 What triggered the February/March Revolution of 1917?

4.3 Why was the Provisional Government unable to solve the problems that confronted it in 1917?

4.4 What factors made the Bolsheviks such an important political force in 1917?

4.5 How did the Bolsheviks establish their power in Russia in 1917–19?

4.6 Why did civil war break out in Russia in 1918?

4.7 How and why were the White forces defeated in the Russian Civil War?

4.8 Why did Lenin launch the New Economic Policy in 1921?

4.9 Did the Bolsheviks launch a cultural revolution in Russia between 1917 and 1924?

4.10 Historical interpretation: Was the Russian Revolution the inevitable outcome of class struggle?

4.11 An in-depth study: Was the October Revolution a coup or mass uprising?

4.12 An in-depth study: Was Lenin a liberator or dictator? The Bolsheviks in power 1917–24

Framework of Events

1914	July: Germany and Austria-Hungary declare war on Russia
	August: Russian advance halted in East Prussia
1915	German advance into Poland and the Baltic provinces. Nicholas II assumes direct command of Russian forces
1916	Brusilov Offensive makes gains against Austro-Hungarian forces
1917	February/March: Strikes and army mutinies lead to abdication of Nicholas II. Formation of Provisional Government
	April: Arrival of Lenin in Petrograd
	August: Unsuccessful coup by General Kornilov
	October/November: Bolshevik seizure of power
1918	March: Treaty of Brest-Litovsk ends war with Germany. Beginning of foreign military intervention against the Bolsheviks
	July: Murder of the Imperial family
1919	July–October: Successful offensives by Red Army against White forces
1920	Conflict between Red Army and Polish forces
	November: Final withdrawal of White forces
1921	March: Kronstadt uprising. Introduction of New Economic Policy
	April: Stalin elected General Secretary of Russian Communist Party
	May: Conclusion of Treaty of Rapallo with Germany
1922	May: Lenin suffers stroke
1923	Beginning of contest between Stalin and Trotsky for party leadership
1924	January: Death of Lenin.

Overview

RUSSIA embarked upon the war against Germany and Austria-Hungary at a critical point in its history. To a greater extent than any of the other major combatants, Russia had faced daunting domestic problems in the course of the past decade. Industrialisation had given rise to urban poverty and unrest, and it remained unclear whether the reforms of Pyotr Stolypin had effectively pacified and stabilised the Russian peasantry, and broadened the basis of moderate conservative support for the Tsar's government. What is certain, however, is that Russia was as yet ill equipped to sustain a long war against so powerful an industrial state as Germany.

The duration of the First World War took all of the major combatants by surprise. Although all were greatly weakened by it, none suffered so severely as Russia. Heavy casualties and soaring food prices enhanced long-standing tensions in Russian society, and had a particular impact upon the industrial workers in the major cities. More important still was the succession of political errors committed by the Tsar and by other key members of the regime. The Tsar's decision to run the war as an autocrat, his refusal to co-operate with patriotic elements in the Duma and elsewhere, and his personal assumption of military responsibility all served to alienate elements which might otherwise have provided moderate conservative support for Nicholas. When the hardships of the war produced riots and strikes at the beginning of 1917, important elements in the army, in the Duma, and even within the Imperial family, could no longer see any reason to support a leader whose methods of government now appeared foolish and bankrupt. In many respects, the revolt of February/March 1917 was as spontaneous and leaderless as that of 1905. This time, however, there appeared to be an alternative form of government to that of the Tsar. Only 11 years after the formation of the Duma, some of its members sought to establish a government to fill the vacuum that Nicholas had left, substituting the legitimacy of popular election for the legitimacy of Divine Right. It was a remarkable step to take, as deserving of the title of 'revolution' as was the Bolshevik rising that followed later in the year.

The Provisional Government found itself in an impossible situation. In terms of the logic that had governed Russian politics before 1914, it had a degree of legitimacy, for its members represented several of the mainstream tendencies of Russian opposition politics. It had to deal, however, with a very different logic, born out of years of war, hunger and hardship. The Provisional Government failed because it could not reconcile the interests of its moderate members, and of its wartime allies, with the urgent demands of war-weary Russian troops, hungry Russian workers, and land-hungry peasants. Its failure was accelerated by the appearance on the scene of a new and powerful force, in the form of the Bolshevik Party. Its leader, Lenin, exploited the difficult circumstances of 1917 brilliantly, but ruthlessly. He promised the bulk of the population exactly what they desired: an immediate end to the war and a rapid resolution to the land question. By these promises, he had already formed a strong basis of support among Russian workers, before he cast aside electoral niceties and seized power by a daring *coup d'état* in October/November 1917.

By the early months of 1918, however, the Bolshevik coup appeared to be anything but a 'masterstroke'. Instead of calmly proceeding 'to build the socialist order', Lenin was confronted with a terrible array of obstacles to the maintenance of Bolshevik power. Instead of a universal revolution fuelled by the collapse of international capitalism, they faced resistance from a variety of Russian opponents, from liberals and radicals of rival tendencies, as well as Tsarists, often supported by foreign capitalist powers. It became necessary to introduce strict measures of recruitment and of procurement of food in order to be able to fight and to win a long civil war. Bolshevik success in this war resulted from the effectiveness of their organisation, and the committed support that they received from some portions of the population, as well as from the diversity of aims, the poor leadership and inadequate organisation of their 'White' opponents.

The years of civil war were of great importance in forming the nature of the communist state. On the most obvious level, these were the years in which the Bolsheviks imposed their authority over the greater part of the old Tsarist empire, and in which they eliminated most of their serious rivals. To do so, however, they had been forced to adopt many of the autocratic tools that Tsarist government had employed, and which socialist idealism had habitually rejected. A large, disciplined army was necessary to ensure military victory. An equally authoritarian and disciplined party structure, backed by ruthless political police, was necessary to ensure political discipline. Tight economic control was essential to feed the soldiers and workers, and to ensure that the new regime would not be subverted by its capitalist enemies. In international terms, the state was utterly isolated, surrounded by capitalist states that feared and mistrusted its ideology, and which had given the Soviet leadership, by their intervention in the civil war, good reason to expect further assaults in the future from the capitalist 'bloc'. By the time the civil war was won, pre-revolutionary communist theory had largely been discarded, and the foundations of the Stalinist state were clearly visible.

All this had been achieved at an appalling cost. The Russian economy had collapsed, with industrial production at the lowest level for decades, and millions starving as the agrarian economy failed even more spectacularly. Having eliminated so many elements of Tsarist Russia, the Bolsheviks continued to be threatened by one key element. They had to find an answer to the problem of the Russian peasantry, far less willing, now that the threat of the Whites had receded, to tolerate the demands of the Bolsheviks for the cheap sale or surrender of their crops. Incidents such as the Kronstadt rebellion (see page 102) made it clear that former supporters of the Bolsheviks, soldiers and urban workers, were equally alienated by the hardships that arose from this economic crisis. Under these pressures the Bolsheviks were forced to make concessions, and the last months of Lenin's life saw the introduction of the New Economic Policy.

The Russian calendar in 1917

In 1917 Russia was still using the Julian calendar, which originated in ancient Rome. In most of Europe this had been replaced by the Gregorian calendar, devised by Pope Gregory XIII in 1582. By 1917 the difference between the two calendars was approximately ten days. Thus the confusion as to whether the Russian Revolution is known as the 'October Revolution' (24–25 October) or the 'November Revolution' (7–8 November).

4.1 What was the impact of the First World War upon Russia?

1. Who or what do you regard as the most important reason for the October Revolution of 1917? Give reasons for your answer.

2. In order of priority, what do you regard as other important reasons for the October Revolution? Write a sentence next to each reason you have chosen, explaining your choice.

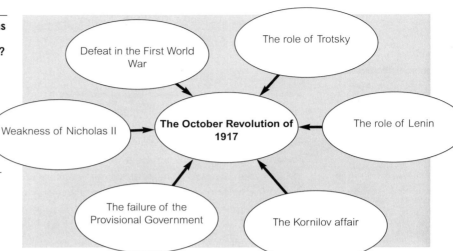

What was the impact upon the Tsarist regime?

The initial popularity of the war

Despite grim forebodings in some informed circles, the declaration of war in 1914 was undoubtedly popular in Russia. Although the former Minister of the Interior, P.N. Durnovo, accurately warned that the main burden of fighting would fall on Russia, voices such as his were drowned out in the swell of popular enthusiasm. The immediate voting of war credits by the Duma (8 August), the plundering of the German embassy by patriotic students and the general acceptance of the government's ban on the sale of vodka, all bore witness to the readiness at first to suspend old hostilities in defence of 'Mother Russia'. Even the capital city was renamed, the Germanic sound of St Petersburg giving way to the Slav Petrograd. Briefly, the Tsar enjoyed more popularity than at any other point in his reign. For once he could pose convincingly as the personification of all the Russians. Yet within three years he was Tsar no more, his prestige worn away in a succession of failures and miscalculations. Three interrelating factors stand out as contributing to this last collapse of Tsarist prestige.

War and the autocracy

Firstly, the patriotic formation of such bodies as the Union of Zemstva, to provide medical facilities, and the Congress of Representatives of Industry and Trade (August 1914), to co-ordinate production, raised an old, thorny question. How far could representative bodies, and the latter included representatives of the workers, be allowed to influence the conduct of the war? The attitude of the government was clearly that the autocracy should exercise sole control. A matter of particular controversy was the formation of 'military zones' (July 1914), comprising most of Finland, Poland, the Baltic provinces, the Caucasus and Petrograd. Within them all civil authority was subjected to that of the military, and every obstacle was put in the way of would-be civilian participation. To many it seemed that political ideology was becoming more important than the effective prosecution of the war. This impression grew stronger in the course of 1915 and in June of that year the existing *zemstvo* and municipal organisations merged to form the All-Russian Union of Zemstva and Cities (*ZemGor*). Although they continued to be denied any active role in the conduct of the war, such

Grigori Rasputin (1871–1916)
A Siberian *starets* or holy man, Rasputin had been known to the Imperial family since 1905. His influence over them dated from 1907 when it began to appear that he was able to control the haemophilia (a blood disease) from which the heir to the throne, Alexis, suffered. The means by which he did this have never been satisfactorily explained. There were damaging rumours of a sexual relationship between Tsarina Alexandra and Rasputin, though they were never proved. Rasputin's extravagant lifestyle and frequent bouts of drunkenness made him a public scandal. He was murdered in December 1916 by a young Russian noble.

bodies as *ZemGor* and the Duma acted as a focus for liberal discontent. The historian David Christian has even gone so far as to describe them as constituting 'the embryo of an alternative government'. The Tsar bitterly blamed 'disloyal' liberals for these tensions, but modern commentators are more inclined to blame the Tsar. 'The truth is,' states the historian Hugh Seton-Watson, 'that the insuperable obstacle was his dogmatic devotion to autocracy.'

Secondly, at this point came the decision of the Tsar to assume personal command as Commander-in-Chief of the armed forces (September 1915) and to take up residence at the front. However understandable in terms of royal duty and military morale, the decision directly identified the Tsar with all future military disasters. It left the government in Petrograd at the mercy of the Empress' infatuations and the schemes of political opportunists.

The role of Rasputin
Thirdly, the most famous, and perhaps the most damaging, of these factors was the increased influence over the Empress, and thus over government policy, of Grigori Rasputin. With the Tsar at the front, Rasputin became the main influence upon the deeply religious Empress.

What message does this cartoon give about the ability of Tsar Nicholas II to rule Russia?

Caricature by N. Ivanov. 'The Russian Royal Family' showing Tsar Nicholas II and Tsarina Alexandra as puppets in Rasputin's hands.

Mikhail Rodzianko (1859–1924)
Of aristocratic and military background, he became a leading advocate of liberal reform of the autocracy. A leader of the Octobrists, he served as a member of the third and fourth Dumas and led the Duma from March 1911. Strongly advocated a constitutional monarchy in 1917.

Treason: The crime of betraying your country, for example by helping its enemies or by trying to overthrow the government. Historically, treason was a crime punishable by death.

1. What factors undermined the political credibility of the Russian government between 1914 and 1917?

2. In what ways was the Russian war effort in 1914–17 hindered by the autocratic nature of its government?

The view of contemporary opponents such as the prominent Duma politician Mikhail Rodzianko that Rasputin was the supreme evil influence on the government is not always accepted today. Some have seen him rather as the tool of self-seeking schemers. At any rate, contemporaries saw his advice to the Empress as the main force behind the 'ministerial leapfrog' that occupied the year beginning in September 1915. Some ministries had as many as three or four chiefs within the year, most of them nonentities. Rasputin's murder in December 1916 came too late. The damage to the government and its reputation was irreparable and many contemporaries, remembering the German origins of the Empress, could not avoid the suspicion of **treason**.

What was the impact upon the Russian people?

In the end, the collapse of the Romanov dynasty in Russia was not triggered by ideological arguments, but by the suffering imposed by the war upon the Russian people.

The organisation and equipment of the army

The most immediate hardships, of course, were borne by those actually serving in the armed forces. Although Russia only mobilised a little less than 9% of its population during the war, compared with about 20% in both Germany and France, the size of the Russian population meant that a substantial number experienced the horrors of the front. The Russian army totalled 5.3 million men after the initial mobilisation (Germany and France mobilised 3.8 million at this point), and a total of 15.3 million Russians had seen military service by the end of hostilities. Numbers, however, were the Russian soldier's only advantage. Compared to his opposite numbers in other armies he was worse armed, worse treated and worse led. Shortcomings of armament and tactics exposed in the war of 1904–05 were being treated, but had not been overcome by the outbreak of war in 1914. It was still not unusual in 1915 for Russian artillery to be limited to two or three shells a day, and after mobilisation in 1914 the infantry had only two rifles for every three soldiers. Men were sent into battle with instructions to help themselves to the weapons of fallen comrades. Such factors made casualty levels that were, in any case, horrendous all the harder to bear. By early 1917, Russia had lost 1.6 million dead, 3.9 million wounded and 2.4 million taken prisoner.

The impact upon the civilian population

The civilian population also had increasingly daunting problems to face. The year 1916 was a comparatively good one for military production, with rifle production doubled and that of heavy artillery quadrupled, but these advances were made at the expense of civilian needs. Locomotive production, for example, was halved between 1913 and 1916 with only 67 new engines completed in 1916. This, together with constant military interference with the railway network for strategic purposes, contributed to the semi-breakdown of communication and distribution systems that was the main cause of urban food shortages.

There were other factors, too. Conscription caused a scarcity of both men and horses on the larger country estates, and town populations increased as war industries demanded extra labour. Generally, though, there was enough food. It simply was not getting to those who needed it. Indeed, historian Norman Stone shows, in *The Eastern Front, 1914–1917* (1975), that military shortages, too, were due less to failures of production than to inefficient distribution. Fuel shortages were another consistent problem. After the early loss of the Polish coalfields, total coal production in Russia never reached the same level as was achieved in the last year of

1. What hardships did the Russian people suffer as a result of the First World War?

2. How convincing is the argument that the sufferings imposed by the First World War were entirely responsible for the discontent felt by the Russian people in the years leading up to 1917?

peace, and an increasing proportion of what fuel there was was channelled towards military uses. Food prices rose dramatically. On average – and the figures were actually higher for major urban areas such as Petrograd – the price of flour rose by 99% between 1913 and 1916, meat by 232%, butter by 124% and salt by 483%. Money wages, it is true, rose by 133% over the same period, but this figure has to be set against a drop in the value of the rouble to only 56% of its pre-war value.

4.2 What triggered the February/March Revolution of 1917?

The growth of liberal opposition

Paul Miliukov (1859–1943)
Liberal politician and historian. Exiled for his political views (1895), he returned after the 1905 revolution. Founder member of the Kadet Party. Member of Third and Fourth Dumas, and headed the 'Progressive Bloc' during the First World War. As Minister for Foreign Affairs in the Provisional Government, he advocated continuation of the war and was forced to resign. Lived in exile in France from 1920.

Abdication: The act by which a monarch gives up his/her throne, usually in favour of a named successor.

If the First World War does not fully explain the collapse of the Tsarist regime, it did act as an accelerator in the process of alienating the Russian people from their rulers. By August 1915, the combination of the Kadets, Octobrists and Progressists in the Duma into the so-called 'Progressive Bloc', demanding a government 'possessing the confidence of the public', indicated that the old wounds were open once more. The government's answer was to suspend the sittings of the Duma (15 September 1915). Between that date and January 1916, when the Duma re-assembled, the dispute centred upon the conduct of the ministers including the premier, Ivan Goremykin, the Foreign Minister, S.D. Sazonov, and the War Minister, A.A. Polivanov. By mid-November 1916, the liberal politicians in the Duma had decided upon a more uncompromising attitude towards the government and its failures. On 15 November the assembly heard a famous charge of official incompetence by Paul Miliukov. Questioning whether government policy represented 'stupidity or treason', he concluded that 'we have lost faith in the ability of this government to achieve victory'. By January 1917 some leading members had even prepared provisional plans to force Nicholas' **abdication** in favour of his son.

The collapse of civilian and military morale

If some commentators have stressed the role of the liberals in the final discrediting of the monarchy, there is wide agreement that neither they, nor any other organised political groups, bear responsibility for the events that finally brought it down. 'The collapse of the Romanov autocracy,' stated the American commentator William H. Chamberlin, 'was one of the most leaderless, spontaneous, anonymous revolutions of all time.'

The initiative came primarily from the Petrograd workers whose patience with the deprivations of war was nearing exhaustion as 1917 opened. In January, some 150,000 of them had demonstrated on the anniversary of Bloody Sunday, and 80,000 had demonstrated support for the re-opened Duma in February. International Women's Day (8 March) brought tens of thousands of women, exasperated by months of food shortages, on to the streets. The coincidence of this with a wage strike at the Putilov works raised the number of demonstrators on that day to a new 'high' of perhaps 240,000.

The decisive anti-Tsarist factor, however, was the armed forces. The major difference between the events of 1917 and those of 1905 lay in the attitude of the Petrograd garrison. The shooting of 40 demonstrators on 11 March broke the morale of many of the conscript soldiers, and regiment after regiment associated with, and then actively supported, the strikers. Even the dreaded Cossack regiments refused to obey their officers. By the end of 12 March, Petrograd was in the hands of a revolution without recognised leaders, at a cost of an estimated 1,300 civilian and military lives. 'Not one party,' wrote the socialist observer N.N. Sukhanov in 1955, 'was preparing for the great overturn.'

The abdication of the Tsar

In the task of filling the power vacuum in Petrograd the liberal members of the Duma had the advantage of being on the spot, but their attitude was highly ambiguous. They half obeyed the Tsar's order to disperse, by transforming themselves into a Provisional Committee (12 March). Most of those members who supported Rodzianko's advice to Nicholas to abdicate did so only in the hope of salvaging something of the monarchy by crowning a more popular, constitutional Tsar. That these men ended as the Provisional Government of a republic was largely due to the indecision and fatalism of the Tsar himself.

Having originally dismissed the Duma's pleas for last-ditch reforms as 'some nonsense from that fatty Rodzianko', Nicholas then toyed with the idea of a military assault upon his own capital. He was dissuaded by the pleas of his generals, notably Brusilov and Ruzsky, who wanted constitutional reform. However, Nicholas was unable to compromise his own autocracy, and agreed to abdicate (15 March). The following day his brother, the Grand Duke Michael, refused the crown, leaving Russia a republic after 304 years of Romanov rule.

1. Which political and social groups opposed the Tsar's government at the beginning of 1917?

2. Why did the Tsar's government collapse in February/March 1917?

4.3 Why was the Provisional Government unable to solve the problems that confronted it in 1917?

Who were Russia's new leaders?

Georgi Lvov (1861–1925)
Aristocratic liberal whose earlier political involvement was with the *zemstvo* movement. President of the Provisional Government (1917). Sought co-operation with the Soviet and resigned (July 1917) when this proved impossible.

Trudoviks (Russian '*Trud*' – Labour): A non-Marxist socialist group, founded in April 1906 to participate in the First Duma. Its deputies were a mixture of peasant representatives and radical intellectuals.

The new republic was in the hands of two powers tolerating, but scarcely supporting each other. The Provisional Committee of the Duma formed itself into a Provisional Government (15 March) containing the most notable Kadet and Octobrist leaders. Georgi Lvov was the first premier, with Paul Miliukov as Foreign Minister and Alexander Guchkov as Minister of the Interior. Its rival for influence was the Petrograd Soviet, formed on 12 March, after the model of 1905, by the spontaneous action of workers and soldiers. It was at first an unwieldy body of up to 3,000 members, not dominated by any party, but by individuals of various persuasions. Among its leading orators, Alexander Kerensky was a **Trudovik** member of the Duma, while N. Chkeidze and M.I. Skobelev were Mensheviks (see insert on page 89).

Lenin was later to accuse the Soviet of a 'voluntary surrender of state power to the bourgeoisie and its Provisional Government'. The charge is not strictly fair in that, while the Duma politicians took on the responsibility of

Alexander Kerensky (1881–1970)
Elected to the Fourth Duma as a Trudovik member, and opposed the voting of war credits. Successively Minister of Justice, War Minister and Prime Minister in the Provisional Government in 1917. Subsequently lived in exile in France and in the USA. By a remarkable coincidence he was born in the same town as Lenin, and his father was headmaster of the school that Lenin attended.

government, the support of workers and of soldiers left the Soviet with most of the practical power. Such was its control over post, railway and telegraph services in Petrograd that virtually nothing could be done without its consent. Guchkov himself wrote that 'the Provisional Government possesses no real power and its orders are executed only as this is permitted by the Soviet of Workers' and Soldiers' Deputies.'

The Soviet's 'Order Number One' (14 March) decreed the establishment of soldiers' councils in each regiment of the armed forces, thus extending its influence to the military sector. From May 1917, the Soviet took part more directly in government when six Mensheviks and Trudoviks, including Skobelev (Minister of Labour) and Alexander Kerensky (Minister of War), became ministers in the Provisional Government. From July, Kerensky actually led the government as premier, but failed to bridge the gap of mistrust that separated the bourgeois body from that of the Petrograd workers, leading to an uneasy co-existence.

The land question

The first steps towards a policy that would be acceptable to both bodies were easily agreed. On its first day in office the Provisional Government decreed an eight-point programme that included a complete amnesty for all political prisoners, total political and religious freedom, and the promise of elections to a constituent assembly. Poland's right to independence was at last recognised (30 March) and capital punishment was abolished, even in the armed forces.

Thereafter, the problems of policy became more contentious. Two major tasks confronted the government, the more pressing of which was satisfying the peasants' age-old demand for land. Although the government quickly recognised their right to the great landed estates, an official policy of partition was impossible to implement without inviting mutiny and desertion by peasant soldiers 'trapped' at the front while their local estates were distributed among their neighbours. The peasants, however, were unwilling to wait. Thus disorder spread in the countryside as the peasants took the law into their own hands. The government received nearly 700 complaints about illegal attacks upon landed property in June 1917, and over 1,100 in July. It was the turn of the peasant now to pose as 'the autocrat of Russia'.

The maintenance of the war effort

Clearly, a solution to the land problem depended upon a solution to the second problem, that of the war in which Russia was engaged. The revolution raised the question of what war aims Russia should now pursue. The unanimous conviction of the Provisional Government was that the war should be pursued to a victorious conclusion. Miliukov, for one, saw no reason to abandon the original aims of annexations in eastern Europe and in the Turkish Empire, but was so far out of touch with popular opinion that he was forced to resign (15 May). The attitude of the Soviet was not for immediate peace either, for such a peace might merely put them at the mercy of a monarchist Germany. Instead, they rejected the 'policy of annexations' and refused 'to serve as an instrument of conquest and violence in the hands of kings, landowners and bankers'. Compromising between popular pressure and the need to honour obligations to Russia's allies, the Provisional Government accepted (8 April) the prime war aim of 'the establishment of a stable peace on the basis of the self-determination of nations'.

The collapse of the war effort, and the Kornilov Affair

The collapse of the war effort was the first major failure of the new government. Its July offensive in Galicia, aimed at proving the government's worth to allies and Russians alike, ended in the retreat of demoralised and under-equipped forces over a large area. In the same month came demands for the autonomy of the Ukraine, to which some ministers seemed ready to agree, while the left-wing 'July Rising' led by Bolshevik sympathisers from the Kronstadt naval base further illustrated the precariousness of the government's position.

In September, the threat came from the right. General Lavr Kornilov, appointed by the government to head the armed forces, marched on Petrograd. His main aim was probably to oust the Soviet which he saw as undermining military discipline, but his actions and pronouncements could be seen as attempting to impose a counter-revolutionary regime. His failure, largely due to the refusal of troops to obey his orders, left the prestige of the government at a new low ebb, and strengthened the hand of the Bolshevik extremists in the Soviet.

The attitude of historians to the events of June–September 1917 have been deeply influenced by their political sympathies. The role of the Bolshevik Party in the July Rising was played down by Soviet writers, who portrayed the events as spontaneous. Many western commentators, on the other hand, followed the line of historian Daniel Shub, in *Lenin* (1966), seeing the events as a planned 'coup' from which the Bolshevik leaders retreated at the last moment due to loss of nerve. More recently, Robert Service (*Lenin*, 2000) has directly contradicted this interpretation, asserting that the disturbances took Lenin by surprise, and that he played a leading role in restraining his Bolshevik followers. The truth of the Kornilov affair has been equally difficult to unravel. Most Soviet sources, and some non-Soviet writers, asserted that Kerensky was using Kornilov (who in Trotsky's phrase had 'the heart of a lion, but the brains of a lamb') for his own anti-Soviet ends. The charge has never been proven, and was strenuously denied in Kerensky's own writings.

What was Lenin's contribution to communist theory and organisation before 1917?

No individual made so radical and influential an impact upon the history of Russia between 1870 and 1991 as did Vladimir Ilyich Ulyanov, known as Lenin. The details of his early life appear below, but his impact as a revolutionary can be dated from 1902, when he published one of his most

---

1. What policies did the Provisional Government adopt towards the problems of land ownership and the continuation of the war?

2. Why was the Provisional Government in Russia unable to consolidate and maintain its power in 1917?

3. How convincing is the claim that, by October 1917, 'the Provisional Government was politically bankrupt, having failed in all its main policy aims'?

Vladimir Ilyich Lenin (1870–1924)

Originally V.I. Ulyanov. Born in Simbirsk (later renamed Ulyanovsk in his honour), the son of a teacher and school inspector. The key event of his early life seems to have been the execution of his elder brother, Alexander, in 1887 for his involvement in an attempt to assassinate the Tsar. The event appears to have triggered latent radical tendencies in the younger Ulyanov, and to have

marked him as a radical both in his own mind and in the view of the authorities. The years between 1887 and 1900 – with their mixture of expulsion from university, practice as a radical lawyer, imprisonment in Siberia, and eventual flight to western Europe – present a picture familiar from the biographies of many contemporary Russian radicals. During the second phase of his political life, Lenin distinguished himself

as a prolific writer and publicist, explaining Marxist theory and laying down his strong views on how the future struggle of Russian socialism should be organised. The most important development of these years was perhaps the foundation, with Julius Martov in Germany (1900), of the journal *The Spark* (*Iskra*). In 1903 Lenin brought about a split in the Russian Social Democratic Labour Party, between the Bolsheviks and the

Mensheviks (see insert opposite). He spent much of the next years of his life in exile in western Europe. He returned to Petrograd following the February 1917 revolution and urged an immediate seizure of power by the proletariat. In October 1917, Lenin led the Bolshevik revolution, and became the head of the first Soviet government until his death.

1. On what issues did Bolsheviks and Mensheviks disagree?

2. In what ways did Lenin add to, or alter, orthodox Marxist teaching?

3. In what ways were the Bolsheviks different from the Russian radicals who had previously tried to overthrow the Tsarist regime?

Lenin addresses the crowd in Red Square, Moscow, on the first anniversary of the Revolution, October/November 1918.

Proletariat: The working classes. Increasingly, in the late 19th century and 20th century the term was applied specifically to working-class people in industrial, urban areas.

influential works, entitled *What is to be Done?* In it, Lenin rejected the arguments of previous Russian socialists who wished to limit themselves to legal economic activities, or who continued to place their faith in the peasantry as a revolutionary force. Instead, Lenin stressed the need for a 'party of a new type'. He envisaged a disciplined and dedicated group of professional revolutionaries, which would act, in Lenin's famous phrase, as the 'vanguard of the **proletariat**'. By rejecting reliance upon the eventual

---

Political groups in Russia 1917–1921

Octobrists: Russian Liberals who regarded the 1905 October Manifesto as the limit for constitutional change within Russia.

Constitutional Democrats (Kadets): Russian Liberals who regarded the 1905 October Manifesto as a step on the road to full parliamentary government for Russia.

Social Revolutionaries: A radical group who wanted to transfer land to the Russian peasantry.

Left Social Revolutionaries: Those social revolutionaries who were willing to form a coalition with the Bolsheviks from October/November 1917. They left the coalition following the Treaty of Brest-Litovsk and attempted to overthrow the Bolshevik government in 1918.

Bolsheviks (known as Communists from 1918): Lenin's party. (See also page 68.)

Mensheviks: Those members of the Russian Social Democrat Party which supported the Provisional Government and wanted to see the establishment of a liberal democratic republic before Russia eventually became a socialist country.

Tsarists: Those who wanted to see the return of monarchic government under a member of the Romanov family.

Greens: A political grouping associated with the Ukraine anarchist Nestor Makno. They opposed both the Bolsheviks and the Whites during the Russian Civil War.

Nationalists: Groups who wanted to see the creation of their own national state from the old Russian Empire. Included Georgians, Ukrainians and people from the Baltic lands (Latvia, Lithuania and Estonia). By 1922 several areas had left the old Russian Empire to form new, independent states, such as Latvia. Lenin attempted to deal with the 'nationalities' issue with the creation of the Union of Soviet Socialist Republics (USSR) in 1922. This created 'socialist republics' in the Ukraine, **Transcaucasia** and White Russia (modern Belarus) as well as Russia.

Transcaucasia: The collective term for the territories of the Russian Empire, such as Georgia, Armenia and Azerbaijan, that lay beyond the Caucasus Mountains.

good sense of workers and peasants, by rejecting the aid of well-meaning but amateurish intellectuals, and by rejecting terrorism, *What is to be Done?* represented a substantial break with the past traditions of the Russian left. Such an organisation, however, was unacceptable to many who wished for a broader, more popular basis to the party, and who distrusted Lenin's tendency towards autocratic leadership.

At the second congress of the Russian Social Democratic Workers' Party (**RSDRP**) in London in 1903, the party split into the 'Men of the Majority' (*Bolsheviki*), favouring the views of Lenin, and the 'Men of the Minority' (*Mensheviki*), favouring the more democratic alternative now championed by Julius Martov. The terms are misleading, as Lenin's group had actually been outvoted by the end of the congress, but the names coined by him stuck firmly to the factions whose differences further weakened the short-term effectiveness of the RSDRP.

On the eve of the First World War, Lenin enjoyed a dual reputation within the narrow circles that constituted Russian Marxism. In addition to being one of the outstanding theorists and **revisionists** of the movement, he was also a determined political **pragmatist**, wholly convinced of the correctness of his own interpretation of events, and largely intolerant of opposition from within the movement.

RSDRP: The initials of the Russian Social Democratic Workers' Party, the formal name of the Russian Communist Party.

Revisionists: Socialists whose actions or opinions differ from orthodox Marxist theory, and who are therefore considered to be wrong and dangerous by orthodox Marxists.

Pragmatist: Person who deal with problems, or thinks about problems, in a practical way rather than in a theoretical way.

4.4 What factors made the Bolsheviks such an important political force in 1917?

Bolshevik strengths and weaknesses in early 1917

The major turning point in the destiny of the revolution was Lenin's arrival in Petrograd (16 April). He found the Bolsheviks in Russia in a sad state. They numbered only 26,000 members, were in a minority in the Petrograd Soviet and were divided on the issue of co-operation with the Provisional Government. On the other hand, they had so far 'kept their hands clean' by avoiding identification with the failures of that administration. The fact that Lenin and his comrades had their passage from exile in Switzerland arranged for them by the German government was of ambiguous value. It naturally laid the Bolsheviks open to the charge of being German agents. Although Lenin was, of course, serving Germany's purpose by further disruption of the Russia war effort, the charge has not been taken seriously by historians in its literal sense. However, the allegation that the Bolsheviks subsequently received large sums of German money to further their cause might have better foundation. Daniel Shub, for example, has produced evidence of transactions which, if genuine, would have given the Bolsheviks a substantial economic advantage over their revolutionary rivals.

It may be, however, that the real strength of the Bolsheviks lay less in the fact that they transformed events in 1917, than that they reflected important forces within Russian politics. A number of western historians, working in the 1970s and 1980s (see also section 4.10), focused their attention more upon the rank and file of the revolutionary movement than upon its leaders. Studying the development of trade unions and of civil rights among the urban workers, and social and economic development among the peasantry, they reached the conclusion that these constituted the real revolutionary force within Russia in 1917. The Bolsheviks, in their view, enjoyed success at this time, not because they converted the workers to their views, or had superior resources, but because they represented most accurately the aspirations of 'progressive' workers. Such a view has several important implications for the interpretation of Russian history. In this view, the great strength of the Bolshevik Party in 1917 was that it was flexible and open, rather than hierarchical and authoritarian – a genuine party of radical workers and peasants.

Lenin's programme in 1917

Pravda (Russian – Truth): The official newspaper of the Russian Communist Party.

A major advantage of the Bolsheviks was that, alone of the major participants in the events of 1917, they offered a political programme that was truly radical. The programme that Lenin pronounced upon his arrival, and published in *Pravda* in the so-called 'April Theses', was a complete rejection of the co-operation between the Soviet and the Provisional Government that was even advocated by a number of Bolsheviks. The ten points included:

- an appeal for an immediate end to the war;
- total withdrawal of support from the government;
- socialisation of the economy;
- the transfer of all state power to the Soviets.

The slogan 'All power to the Soviets' was not necessarily an immediate demand, for the Bolsheviks were far from controlling these bodies. What was immediate was the need for Lenin to impose his will upon his own party, and for constant propaganda to win the support of those alienated by the delays and failures of the Provisional Government. Lenin's contribution to this propaganda was *The State and Revolution* (published in 1918) in which he set forth in the Russian context the Marxist doctrine of the need completely to dismember the bourgeois state before a proletarian society could be constructed. This form of persuasion was less effective than the simple slogans ('End the War', or 'Bread, Peace, Land') aimed at less sophisticated political thinkers. 'If the peasants had not read Lenin,' Trotsky observed, 'Lenin had clearly read the thoughts of the peasants.'

Strengthening the Bolshevik position

1. What new policies and tactics did Lenin propose when he arrived in Russia in 1917?

2. How would you explain the increase in support for the Bolsheviks in Russia in the course of 1917?

3. 'The Bolsheviks did not seize power; they simply picked it up.' How accurate is this assessment of the October/November Revolution in 1917?

Meanwhile the Bolsheviks generally accepted Lenin's policy of opposition to and separation from the Provisional Government. At the first Congress of Soviets in June, where only 10% of representatives of 305 Soviets were Bolshevik, Lenin unsuccessfully advocated a break with the government. In July, complicity in the Petrograd rising led to an open attack upon the Bolsheviks, and a government attempt to arrest leaders such as Lenin, Zinoviev and Kamenev. Bolshevik support grew in these months for both negative and positive reasons. Among the negative reasons were the collapse of the government's military offensive, the reaction of Petrograd workers to the Kornilov Affair, and the suspicion that Kerensky might be willing to abandon Petrograd to the advancing Germans. More positive were the Bolshevik promises to tackle the questions of land and of peace and the growing support for the party among Petrograd factory Soviets.

By August, the party had 200,000 members, produced 41 different newspapers, and had recruited a striking force of 10,000 'Red Guards' in the factories, whose workers were often, in Lenin's words, 'more Bolshevik than the Bolsheviks'. When the Petrograd Soviet was re-elected in September, the Bolsheviks held a majority of seats for the first time – a success repeated in Moscow and elsewhere.

4.5 How did the Bolsheviks establish their power in Russia in 1917–19?

The circumstances under which the Provisional Government lost power during the 'second revolution' of October/November 1917 were in direct contrast to those that had brought them to power. True, major social and economic problems persisted. Industrial production was badly disrupted. Some industrial plants closed, causing unemployment, and inflation quickly cancelled out any benefit that the workers may have gained in terms of higher wages. The army came closer to disintegration, demoralised by continuing failure and by Bolshevik propaganda. 'The soldiers,' recalled N. Sukhanov, 'flowed through the countryside from the rear and the front, recalling a great migration of peoples.' An estimated two million desertions took place in the course of 1917.

The October/November coup

Unlike the events of February/March 1917, those of October/November owed little to spontaneous discontent, and almost everything to the deliberate actions of a tightly-knit group of revolutionary leaders. By late September, Lenin had decided that the circumstances were right for the Bolsheviks to bid for power. The decision had nothing to do with the feelings of the people. 'We cannot be guided by the mood of the masses,' he wrote at the time, 'that is changeable and unaccountable. The masses have given their confidence to the Bolsheviks and ask from them not words, but deeds.' It took over a month for Lenin to convince the party as a whole, and even then such notable members as Grigori Zinoviev and Lev Kamenev (see Chapter 5) stood out against him. His arguments in favour of an immediate rebellion were based not only upon the fear of a 'second Kornilov affair', or of a surrender of Petrograd to the Germans, but especially upon the hopeful signs of unrest in the German forces. This encouraged him to hope for international working-class support for a communist coup.

It was also essential to have practical control before the meeting of the next Congress of Soviets, which might be more difficult still to convince of the merits of such an adventure. The weapon for rebellion also presented itself with the formation (26 October) of the Military Revolutionary Committee by the Soviet, pledged to protect Petrograd against the Germans. With 48 Bolsheviks among its 66 members, it was capable of being turned against other enemies.

The 'revolution' of 24–25 October / 7–8 November was, in reality, an extremely skilful military *coup d'état* directed predominately by Trotsky. Key positions such as railway stations, telephone exchanges, banks and post offices were seized by 'Red Guards' with a distinct lack of opposition from their opponents. The body assembled at the Tauride Palace to discuss the formation of a Constituent Assembly was dismissed. Then late on 25 October / 8 November the half-hearted defence of the Winter Palace, now the headquarters of the Provisional Government, was overcome. The second Congress of Soviets, meeting that same day in Petrograd, now had 390 Bolshevik representatives, only too eager to accept Lenin's *fait accompli*. For Kerensky, there was no immediate alternative to flight, while the Mensheviks and the Social Revolutionaries, with only 80 and 180 seats respectively in the Congress, had little choice but to accept Trotsky's dismissal: 'You have played out your role. Go where you belong: to the dust heap of history.'

What judgement should be made on the Provisional Government that fell after eight months in office? The programme and theory of the government were admirable, as the most liberal constitution that the continent

Fait accompli: (French – accomplished fact): A political fact or event that cannot be changed or modified, and thus must be accepted.

had yet seen had been created out of Europe's strictest autocracy. However, 1917 was a time for action on pressing problems, not for theory. Although noble in intent, the programme was ill-defined and poorly enforced. Kerensky, in his memoirs, lays most of the blame for this upon those who 'betrayed' the government, most notably Kornilov and his supporters. Others are inclined to blame Kerensky himself, for whom, in the words of the historian Donald Treadgold, 'oratory became a substitute for action'.

The extension of Bolshevik power

Lenin's first speech to the Congress of Soviets consisted of a simple statement: 'We shall now proceed to construct the socialist order.' As the historian D. Mitchell has pointed out, however, the business of ruling Russia was not so simple. 'The Bolsheviks had not captured a Ship of State, they had boarded a derelict.' The priority of the first Soviet government was, therefore, the extension and consolidation of Bolshevik power. In early November, the authority of the administration elected by the Congress extended little beyond Petrograd. Lenin was chairman of the Council of **People's Commissars**, Alexei Rykov Commissar of the Interior, and Leon Trotsky Commissar for Foreign Affairs. In some places, as in Moscow, Kiev, Kazan and Smolensk, Bolsheviks had to overcome stern armed resistance. November, nevertheless, saw 15 main provincial towns fall into their hands, followed by 13 in December and a further 15 in January 1918.

Within the territory that the Bolsheviks controlled the main constitutional opposition to them came from the election of the long-awaited Constituent Assembly, which gathered in Petrograd with 380 Social Revolutionary (SR) representatives as against only 168 Bolsheviks. Lenin, however, was in no mood for constitutional games, and the body was dispersed by force after less than two days. It was, declared Lenin, 'a complete and frank liquidation of the idea of democracy by the idea of dictatorship'.

The CHEKA and the Red Army

The Marxist concept of the 'dictatorship of the proletariat' also involved the formation of two armed forces to destroy the remnants of aristocratic and bourgeois power. A secret police force known as the 'Extraordinary Commission' (but generally known as the CHEKA, from its Russian initials) was formed. In contrast to the leniency of the Provisional Government, its aim was quite openly to combat 'counter-revolution' by means of terror. One of its leaders claimed, 'The CHEKA does not judge, it strikes.' Its chief was Felix Dzerzhinsky, but contemporary evidence clearly indicates the role played by Lenin himself in enforcing the policy of terror. In July 1918, he urged that 'the energy and mass nature of the terror must be encouraged' and, a month later, called for it to be extended even 'to execute and exterminate hundreds of prostitutes, drunken soldiers, former officers, etc'. The Imperial family, under arrest at Ekaterinburg, were the most famous victims (July 1918). The official figure for executions in 1918 is 6,300, but this must be regarded as a conservative estimate.

The Bolshevik regime, having undermined and dispersed an army upon which it could not depend, now set about the formation of an army of its own. The Red Army was formed in January 1918, open to all 'class-conscious' workers of 18 years of age or more. The bourgeoisie was banned from membership, but 50,000 former Tsarist officers were retained to train the new force. To oversee them and the force as a whole, political commissars were attached to each unit, responsible for **indoctrination** and for

---

Alexei Rykov (1881–1938)
Joined the Bolsheviks in 1903, but mistrusted Lenin and supported plans for a coalition government in 1917. Commissar for the Interior (1917–18). Politburo member (1924–28). Opposed the leadership of Stalin, and was removed from office and eventually executed.

People's Commissars: Because the title of 'Minister' was discredited by its association with the Tsarist regime, ministers in the Soviet government officially bore the title 'People's Commissar'.

Felix Dzerzhinsky (1877–1926)
A dedicated Polish Bolshevik, Dzerzhinsky joined the Communist Party in Lithuania in 1895. Member of the Party's Central Committee (1917–26). Head of the CHEKA (December 1917). Commissar for Internal Affairs (March 1919). Member of the Politburo and Chairman of the Supreme Council of National Economy (1924). His honesty and devotion to the cause earned him the nickname 'Iron Felix'.

Indoctrination: The teaching of a particular belief or attitude with the aim that those being taught will not accept any other belief or attitude.

ensuring that the army remained under Bolshevik control. The reforms made since February/March 1917 were systematically cancelled to ensure reliable discipline.

- The powers of the regimental councils were curtailed.

- The practice of electing officers was abolished.

- The death penalty for deserters was reintroduced.

By August 1919 the Red Army numbered 300,000, and by January 1920 it boasted over 5,000,000 members, under the supreme command of Leon Trotsky.

What were the bases of Bolshevik policy in the early stages of Communist power?

The first Soviet constitution
Meanwhile, the constitution of the state took shape. A series of decrees in February 1918 attacked the Church, separating it from the state and banning religious teaching in schools. Another series, between April and June, nationalised banks, mineral resources, industrial concerns and foreign trade, and made the inheritance of property illegal. A formal constitution became law on 10 July 1918. The state was given the name of the Russian Soviet Federated Socialist Republic (RSFSR). It proclaimed itself a classless society, with freedom of worship, no private ownership of property, and based upon the economic principle of 'He who does not work, neither shall he eat'. The electoral system was based upon the unit of the village and city soviets, culminating in the All-Russian Congress of Soviets, the supreme authority in the state. Election was by universal suffrage, with the exception of former members or agents of the Tsarist government, those who profited from the labour of others, those with unearned income, priests, lunatics and criminals.

Ending the problem of the war: the Treaty of Brest-Litovsk (March 1918)
In the first days of Soviet power, the Bolsheviks produced a 'Decree on Peace' and a 'Decree on Land', as their earlier propaganda had obliged them to do. The former called upon all participants in the war to begin immediate peace negotiations, while the latter abolished all landed ownership, but encouraged the peasantry to continue the process of carving up the great estates themselves. The achievement of such ideals was not, however, such an easy matter.

The new regime formally opened peace negotiations with the Central Powers at Brest-Litovsk in late November, confident that the Bolshevik coup would trigger a general European revolution, thus ending the war. When, by early 1918, this had not materialised, and the impatient Germans had pushed deeper into Russian territory, Lenin was eventually able to convince his party that a separate peace was necessary. The Treaty of Brest-Litovsk was concluded on 3 March 1918. From a patriotic point of view, its terms were disastrous. Georgia, the Ukraine, Latvia, Lithuania and Poland came formally under German occupation. This meant that, of its pre-war resources, Russia lost 26% of its population, 32% of its arable land, 33% of its manufacturing industry, and 75% of its coal and iron resources. In explaining the decision of the Bolsheviks to make this sacrifice, it must be remembered that most of the lost territory was not actually under Bolshevik control in any case. Above all, the most pressing motive was that stated by Lenin himself in 1920: 'we gained a little time, and sacrificed a great deal of space for it'.

1. What tactics did the Bolsheviks use against their opponents within Russia in the course of 1917 and 1918?

2. Why did the Bolsheviks decide to seize power in November 1917?

Economic policy: War Communism

The succession of events of which the Treaty of Brest-Litovsk was part soon demonstrated the inadequacy of edicts such as the 'Decree on Land' and the 'Decree on Workers' Control'. The piecemeal division of land by peasant committees and the direction of factories by workers' committees proved wholly unsatisfactory as Russia was stripped of huge agricultural and industrial resources while faced simultaneously with the likelihood of a large-scale civil conflict. It was soon evident to Lenin that the intended slow progress towards nationalisation of the 'commanding heights' of the economy, such as fuel, transport and banking, was insufficient. The formation of a Supreme Economic Council (*Vesenkha*) in December 1917 can be seen as the first step towards the policy established by the 'Decree on Nationalisation' (June 1918), and now known as 'War Communism'. The main features of War Communism were:

- strict centralised control of all forms of economic production and distribution;

- virtual outlawing of all private trade;

- near destruction of the money economy by the printing of vast quantities of bank notes.

In January 1918, there were 27 billion roubles' worth of notes in circulation, backed by only 1.3 million roubles in gold. Three years later, the figures were 1,168 billion and 0.07 million.

In the countryside the main evidence of the new policy was the large-scale requisitioning of grain in order to feed the towns. In June 1918, the government formed 'Committees of Poor Peasants' to control the richer peasants, or *kulaks*, but soon had to resort to confiscation of supplies by military force. All food distribution was centralised into the hands of a Commissariat of Food and a Commissariat of Agriculture. These divided the population into four categories, the food ration of each depending upon its contribution to the economy. The highest category had roughly one-seventh of the calories received by German workers at the height of the allied blockade, while the lowest had rations insufficient to prevent starvation.

The disillusioned peasantry turned, as before, to disorder. In 1918, 249 rural risings were recorded, and 99 in Bolshevik-controlled territory the following year. In the towns the main feature was the wholesale nationalisation, which extended by December 1920 to all enterprises employing ten or more people, a total of about 37,000 enterprises. This was accompanied by:

- the forced mobilisation of unemployed labour to serve essential strategic industries;

- the outlawing of strikes;

- a large-scale desertion of the towns in favour of the countryside where food seemed more easily available.

Petrograd, with a population of 2.5 million in 1917, had only 0.6 million inhabitants three years later.

Kulaks: Richer, semi-capitalist peasants. The term literally means a 'fist', as a sign of money-grabbing.

---

1. What policies did the Bolsheviks use to tackle the economic problems that faced them after their seizure of power in 1917?

2. Did the Bolsheviks gain more than they lost by the Treaty of Brest-Litovsk?

3. To what extent, by the end of 1918, had the Bolsheviks solved the problems that faced them when they initially came to power?

4.6 Why did civil war break out in Russia in 1918?

Anton Denikin (1872–1947)
After service in the Russo-Japanese war and the First World War, Denikin supported Kornilov's coup against the Provisional Government in 1917. After the Bolshevik seizure of power, he formed and commanded the White army in south-east Russia. Relatively successful in military terms, he was politically clumsy and failed to co-operate effectively with civilian bodies or with national minorities.

Lavr Kornilov (1870–1918)
Of Cossack origins, he served with distinction in the Russo-Japanese war and in the First World War. Appointed to command the Petrograd garrison (1917) by the Provisional Government, he later led an unsuccessful coup against that government. Commanded White forces in southern Russia until killed in action.

Cossacks: Peoples of southern USSR, noted from early times as horsemen.

Who were the Whites, and what did they stand for?

By early 1918, the events of the 'second revolution' had alienated large sections of the Russian population from the Bolshevik government, but without uniting the aims or motives of these opponents. Whereas the Reds fought in the Civil War for very specific aims and Marxist-Leninist principles, albeit with a strong degree of compulsion at times, the Whites formed no such grouping. Broadly, the White forces consisted of three main parts:

● those attached to other revolutionary groups, hostile to or rejected by the Bolsheviks;

● former officers of the Imperial army, usually resentful of the 'betrayal' at Brest-Litovsk;

● nationalist groups seeking independence for their particular minority.

The administration that established itself in the Don region of southern Russia early in 1918 illustrates this diversity. Its military leaders were Tsarist generals, such as Anton Denikin, Lavr Kornilov and P.N. Krasnov, who had also held office under the Provisional Government and now claimed to fight 'until the Provisional Government and order in the nation are restored'. The politicians who joined them, however, were a mixture of Kadets such as Paul Miliukov, and SRs such as V. Chernov. Other SRs concentrated their forces further north, along the Volga, where they established an administration based at Samara (June 1918). In the Don region, the nationalist element was represented by the **Cossacks**, whose local ambitions clashed fundamentally with such White slogans as Alexeyev's 'Russia One and Indivisible'.

What kind of a war did this make for? The traditional interpretation among Soviet historians was that the Bolsheviks fought an essentially defensive war. Controlling a central zone of about one million square miles, with a population of about 60 million, they beat off various attempts by 'White' forces to penetrate this territory. In his recent work on the civil war, however, Evan Mawdsley (*The Russian Civil War*, 1987) paints a different picture. He prefers to see the war as a series of expeditions launched by the Red Army in an attempt to extend their control to more remote areas of the former Russian Empire, with the initiative lying in most cases with the Bolsheviks.

The disintegration of the Russian Empire

With the collapse of traditional authority in the Russian state, several regions were quick to declare themselves independent. Thus republics were proclaimed in Ukraine and in Transcaucasia (November 1917) and in Finland (December 1917). With the collapse of the German war effort in the next year, Estonia, Latvia, Lithuania and Poland all pressed their own claims to independence. The Polish claim was especially complicated. Both the Soviet government and the victorious allies assembled at Versailles (France) recognised Poland's right to independence. It was not clear, however, whether its eastern borders were to be fixed by the so-called Curzon Line, drawn by the allies around the main areas of Polish-speaking populations, or by the historic borders of the old Polish kingdom as it had existed before partition in 1772. The difference was considerable, and involved a Polish claim to much of Lithuania, the Ukraine and Byelorussia. The dispute raised tensions between Poland and its new communist neighbour that were to culminate in war in 1920.

The role of the Czechoslovak Legion

The great catalyst of civil conflict in Russia was the successful 'revolt' of the Czechoslovak Legion. The Legion had been formed in 1917 from Czechs and Slovaks resident in Russia, and from prisoners of war. It was dedicated to the fight for independence from the crumbling Austro-Hungarian Empire. After Brest-Litovsk it had placed itself at the disposal of the French, and begun a long journey via Siberia and the USA to continue the fight on the Western Front. In May 1918, a confrontation with Hungarian prisoners at Cheliabinsk led local Soviet officials to attempt to disarm the Legion. Instead they themselves were seized, and when Trotsky ordered military retaliation, the well-organised and well-equipped Czechs proceeded to seize and occupy all the main towns along the Trans-Siberian railway in the regions of Cheliabinsk, Omsk and Irkutsk. Although the Legion had no specifically anti-Bolshevik aims, its resounding success against Soviet forces provided enormous encouragement for the White cause. By June, representatives of the SRs had combined with the Czechs to form a third centre of White administration at Omsk.

Why did foreign powers intervene in the Russian Civil War?

The motives that led Russia's former allies to intervene in its internal conflicts have been the subject of considerable controversy. The standard interpretation among Soviet historians naturally reflected the contemporary view expressed by Lenin, who portrayed the allied missions as a concerted attempt to suppress communism. Some western commentators have accepted this view. For example, E.H. Carr, in *A History of Soviet Russia, 1917–1929* (1966), described the allies' declared intention of reopening the world war in the east against Germany as 'a pretext'. He speaks of 'the fear and hatred felt by the western governments for the revolutionary regime'.

Historian John Bradley (*Civil War in Russia*, 1975) has pointed to a number of factors that contradict this interpretation. A plan by Marshal Foch for a co-ordinated anti-Bolshevik campaign (January 1919) was rejected by allied leaders at Versailles. In February 1919, the Americans in particular were proposing negotiations between the Reds and Whites at Prinkipo Island, near Istanbul. It is also true that Britain and the USA had come close, before Brest-Litovsk, to aiding the Red Army, at Trotsky's request, against the Germans.

There is much evidence that, in its early stages, allied intervention in the Russian conflict should be viewed in the context of the world war. The separate peace made by the Bolsheviks at Brest-Litovsk released huge German forces and resources for use on the Western Front. It thus became imperative for the western allies to restart the war in the east, or at least, to prevent Germany from making free use of the Russian, Polish and Ukrainian raw materials available to them under the terms of Brest-Litovsk. German success in the east also seemed to threaten large concentrations of allied stores supplied earlier to Russia. It is no coincidence that British forces landed first in Murmansk (March 1918), and that British and Japanese forces also concentrated on the distant port of Vladivostok (April 1918) which was far from the Bolshevik 'heartland', but where substantial allied stores were housed. Britain's seizure of Baku was also motivated by the desire to keep local oil resources out of hostile hands.

Allied motives after 1918

Even after the end of the First World War, the allies still had pressing reasons for intervention. The French, for instance, continued to have a pressing motive in the form of the vast sum of 16 billion francs invested in Tsarist Russia between 1887 and 1917, in enterprises now nationalised without compensation by the Soviet State. Britain and the USA had lesser investments to defend. Japan, after the hard-won gains of 1904–05, found the prospect opening up of substantial territorial gains in eastern Asia at Russia's expense. That they failed to realise these ambitions was primarily due to the presence of American troops in Siberia, more concerned with checking Japanese annexations in the east than with combating Bolshevism further west. Nevertheless, by late 1918, as many as 70,000 Japanese troops had occupied Vladivostok, northern Sakhalin and much of Siberia east of Lake Baikal. Only when the Third **Communist International** ('*Comintern*') began, in mid-1919, to proclaim the 'overthrow of capitalism, the establishment of the dictatorship of the proletariat and of the International Soviet republic' did intervention become overtly ideological. By then allied efforts in Russia had become negligible.

Communist International ('*Comintern*'): The body established in the early years of the 20th century to co-ordinate the activities of communist parties in different states.

The scale and the achievement of intervention

The scale and scope of the intervention were, in any case, strictly limited. At the end of 1918 there were only about 150,000 troops in northern Russia and these were affected by war-weariness after four years of European conflict. The USA sent only about 6,000 to the Siberian theatre of war, and then with strictly limited objectives. More important were the substantial sums of money and the large quantities of military stores made available to the Whites. Britain and France both allocated the equivalent of £20 million for this purpose, although the historian R. Luckett stresses, in *The White Generals* (1971), that corruption and inefficiency often meant that relatively little of this aid actually reached the front.

The success achieved by the intervention was even more limited. The number of troops involved was small, and only in the north, around Murmansk and Arkhangelsk, did foreign troops really predominate in the White war effort. Aims and motives were all too often at odds, as in Siberia, where the political views of Admiral Kolchak's regime were so undemocratic that the Americans refused all co-operation with him, and the French could only co-operate with the greatest difficulty. In all, the intervention probably gave far greater assistance to the Soviet authorities who could now draw a veil over domestic disagreements by claiming that they were defending Russia against foreign imperialism. At the conclusion of British involvement, Lord Curzon described it as 'a totally discredited affair and a complete failure'. The same judgement could probably extend to the allied intervention as a whole.

1. For what reasons did the various factions oppose the Bolsheviks from 1918 onwards?

2. How convincing is the argument that allied forces intervened in the Russian Civil War because their governments were ideologically opposed to the Bolsheviks?

3. 'The intervention of the allies in the Russian Civil War was ill-judged, incoherent and achieved nothing.' What evidence can be given in support of this statement?

4.7 How and why were the White forces defeated in the Russian Civil War?

The White armies

In the summer of 1918, the combination of forces ranged against the Soviet government seemed to many observers to be overwhelming. To the south, the Volunteer Army under Anton Denikin, with French and British support, had cleared the Don and Kuban regions of Bolsheviks, and threatened the food and fuel supplies to Soviet-controlled areas. To the east, the varied forces occupying Siberia and controlling the Trans-Siberian Railway had at last agreed (September 1918) to the formation of a coalition government, the Directory. To the north, White forces under the Tsarist general E.K. Miller, with British support, controlled the ports of Murmansk and Arkhangelsk. To the west lay the Germans and a variety of hostile nationalists. Even in Russia, less-organised opposition, especially among the peasants and the SRs, led to risings in some 25 towns and cities. There was a rash of assassination attempts that killed M.S. Uritsky, chief of the Petrograd CHEKA, and the German ambassador, and saw Lenin himself seriously wounded.

The defeat of Kolchak, Yudenich and Denikin

The first concern of the Soviet government was to tackle the opposition forces centred upon Omsk. Their eventual success owed as much to the shortcomings of their opponents as to the efforts of the Red Army itself. Certainly Trotsky's organisation and the military leadership of commanders such as Mikhail Frunze were important factors. The Whites, nevertheless, were disunited and quarrelsome. The internal dispute that brought down the Directory (November 1918) resulted in the elevation of Alexander Kolchak, formerly Admiral of the Black Sea Fleet and a staunch political conservative, to the title of 'Supreme Ruler of All the Russias'. His failure to establish satisfactory understandings with the SRs, the Czechs, or even with some of the allies, contributed to a steady retreat after reaching Perm and Ufa in March 1919. By June, Kolchak's force had been pushed back beyond the Urals, and Soviet forces captured Omsk itself in November. Kolchak suffered the indignity of being handed over to the Red Army by the commander of the local French forces, and was duly shot (7 February 1920).

In the south and west, similarly, White forces under Denikin and under Nikolai Yudenich initially made rapid progress. In two months (August–October 1919), Denikin's forces advanced from Odessa to within 400 kilometres of Moscow, while Yudenich came within 50 kilometres of Petrograd in mid-October. In both cases, retreat was as rapid as the advance had been. Stubborn defence, organised by Trotsky, thwarted Yudenich before a counter-attack drove him back into Estonia. Between October and December, Bolshevik forces pushed Denikin back until most of the Ukraine had been recaptured from the Whites. From April 1920, only the force in the Crimea under Peter Wrangel stood between the Red Army and victory. Wrangel was probably the most able of the White commanders, but he came on the scene too late. His army won some notable victories while the Red Army was distracted by the Poles, but in mid-November 1920 he, too, with 135,000 soldiers and civilians, evacuated the Crimea, the last stronghold of the White cause.

What were the causes and the extent of the Bolshevik success?

Contemporaries tended to assume that the forces ranged against the Red Army, often consisting of professional soldiers commanded by experienced officers, constituted a formidable obstacle to Bolshevik success. Soviet historians, too, liked the version of events that cast the Red Army as brave fighters against overwhelming odds. In reality, the Bolshevik success, like that of the Japanese in Korea in 1905, was not as surprising as it might seem at first. In the south and in the east the White armies fought on wide fronts, often in areas with poor communications. Although they occupied large geographical areas, this often gave them control over relatively small populations, and few areas of major industrial production.

Assessing the quality of leadership of the White forces, Evan Mawdsley has concluded that 'the Whites possessed military talent in abundance, but very limited capacity for state-building or for the rallying of popular support.' With the exception of Wrangel, none of the military leaders could sympathise with, or even understand the hopes and wishes of the peasantry and the national minorities. These leaders became hopelessly

Alexander Kolchak (1873–1920)

After heroic service in the Russo-Japanese war and the First World War, Kolchak formed and commanded White forces in the Far East. He headed the Provisional All-Russian Government based in Omsk (1918), declaring himself 'Supreme Ruler'. Captured by Czech forces (1919), he was handed over to the Bolsheviks and executed.

Nikolai Yudenich (1862–1933)

A highly successful commander in the First World War, gaining notable victories against the Turks. Commanded White forces in north-western Russia (1919).

Mikhail Frunze (1885–1925)

Joined the Bolsheviks in 1904 and was active in the revolutionary events of 1905. Led communists in Byelorussia and Moscow in 1917. Commanded Red Army units in the Urals (1919), gaining successes against Kolchak, and defeated Wrangel in the Crimea (1920).

Peter Wrangel (1878–1928)

After cavalry service in the First World War, Wrangel commanded White forces in the Kuban and the Caucasus (1918–19), capturing Tsaritsyn. He served with Denikin and, after his defeat, organised the evacuation of White forces via the Crimea (1920). Probably the most able of the White commanders because he exercised strong discipline over his men and had an intelligent agrarian policy to appeal to the peasantry.

In Siberia:
British
Americans
Japanese

----- Russian boundaries before 1914

British Nationalist or interventionist groups opposing Bolsheviks

Furthest advance of anti-Bolshevik forces

Kolchak White commanders opposing Bolsheviks

The Civil War in European Russia, 1918–21

1. What elements are emphasised by the poster as those which Lenin was most concerned to defeat in 1920?

2. How accurate is the poster as a portrayal of Lenin's priorities in 1920?

'Comrade Lenin sweeps away the world's dirt', a propaganda poster produced in 1920

1. What were the main weaknesses of the White commanders during the Russian Civil War?

2. Was the weakness of the Whites the main cause of the Bolshevik victory in the Russian Civil War? Explain your answer fully.

identified with the restoration of the landlords and the old regime. In addition, the aims of the military leaders were sometimes at odds with those of the intervening allies. 'I think most of us were secretly in sympathy with the Bolsheviks,' wrote a British officer serving with Kolchak's forces, 'after our experiences with the corruption and cowardice of the other side.'

The political leaders who identified themselves with the White cause made almost no impact on policy or on international relations at all. 'They failed to recognise,' wrote the American historian, Anatole Mazour, 'that they were coping with a great revolution and not an isolated plot.'

The Communists, meanwhile, quite apart from the resources that they controlled, had the benefits of excellent leadership and coherent policy and propaganda. The historian Louis Fischer's description of Lenin as 'a one-man political-military staff' (*The Life of Lenin*, 1965) is inaccurate only insofar as it undervalues the dynamic role played by Trotsky. Appointed Commissar for War in March 1918, Trotsky made his main contribution to the revolution by his brilliant direction of the war on most of the major fronts. For all of these reasons, the traditional judgement about the likely outcome of the Russian Civil War has now been stood on its head, with the majority of historians echoing the judgement of Richard Pipes: 'the victory of the Red Army was a foregone conclusion.'

The only serious objection to Pipes' conclusion, perhaps, is that it does not apply evenly to all of the various theatres of war. In Poland, for instance, the Red Army had encountered a much more difficult opponent, an army of 740,000 men commanded by a government and leadership much more stable than those of the 'white' Russian regimes. In April 1920, Poland and Russia had finally resorted to arms to settle the question of the boundaries of the new Polish state. This was far more of a national war than an affair of Red versus White. It brought varying fortunes for the participants. In May 1920 the Poles, under Marshal Pilsudski, were in Kiev. Two months later the Red Army was within reach of Warsaw. Finally, by August 1920, with moral and material aid from the allies, Pilsudski's counter-attack had driven the Red Army almost back to Minsk. The Treaty of Riga (18 March 1921), like Brest-Litovsk, was accepted by Lenin because 'a bad peace seemed to me cheaper than the prolongation of the war'. It settled Russia's western borders until 1939 by granting Poland Galicia and parts of Byelorussia, and by confirming the independence of Estonia, Latvia and Lithuania.

4.8   Why did Lenin launch the New Economic Policy in 1921?

The failure of War Communism

By 1921, social and economic life in Russia had been brought to its knees by a series of disasters. The rigours and miscalculations of War Communism combined with the damage caused by the civil war. The number of deaths directly caused by the war has been estimated by the historian Robert Conquest (*The Great Terror: a Reassessment*, 1990) as 'no more than a million', but the economic collapse that accompanied war had far more drastic effects. Urban industry declined disastrously. The Russian coal industry in 1921 produced 27% of its pre-war output, a large proportion compared with steel (5.5%), pig iron (2.5%) or copper (1.7%). **Inflation** had effectively destroyed the rouble (Russian currency), and some 90% of all wages were '**paid in kind**'. This was made worse by disastrous famines. Especially serious in the Ukraine and in other parts of southern Russia, the famines probably caused some five million deaths. Taking into account associated diseases, the casualty figure for the years 1917–21 may be as high as 9 million.

Inflation: A general increase in the prices of goods and services in a country.

'**Paid in kind**': Payment is provided in the form of goods, rather than in money.

The Kronstadt rebellion

Probably as serious, from Lenin's point of view, was the evidence of political discontent from within the Communists' own ranks. The most spectacular example of widespread refusal to tolerate any further the deprivations of wartime came with the revolt at the Kronstadt naval base (February/March 1921), originally a major source of Bolshevik support. The demands of the sailors included freedom of the press, elections by secret ballot, and the release of political prisoners. The rising was brutally suppressed like similar, lesser peasant risings, but it could not be ignored. 'It illuminated reality,' stated Lenin, 'like a flash of lightning', and perhaps contributed more than any other factor to the government's decision to pursue a New Economic Policy (NEP).

Lenin made it very clear that the NEP was another in the series of temporary compromises that communist theory had to make when confronted with adverse circumstances. 'Life has exposed our error,' he told the Party. 'There was a need of a series of transitional stages to Communism.' The NEP was thus a sort of economic Brest-Litovsk and, like that treaty, had to be imposed against fierce criticism from communist purists.

The nature of the NEP

The major features of the new policy were concerned with agriculture. Above all, the government decided to abandon the requisitioning of grain supplies from peasants and to demand instead a tax paid in food, set at a lower level. The peasant retained some of his surplus which he was now permitted to sell for private profit, and was thus likely to be encouraged to grow more. Although the land remained the property of the state, the peasant was free to hire labour, machinery, and so forth.

In industry, freedom of enterprise was restored in a host of small factories and workshops, while the state continued to control the 'dominating heights' of the economy, such as heavy industry, transport and foreign trade. In 1922, 88.5% of all enterprises were privately run, although the smallness of their scale is indicated by the fact that they employed only 12.4% of the workforce.

The third main feature of the NEP was the restoration of a stable soviet currency. In October 1922, the reconstituted State Bank introduced the reconstituted rouble, backed by precious metals and foreign currency. Early in 1923, savings banks were reopened.

The achievement of the NEP

The path of the NEP was not always smooth. Bad harvests and drought in 1921 cancelled out most of the benefits to be gained by the peasants. In 1923, they had to contend with the so-called 'scissors crisis' when declining food prices and the soaring price of industrial goods minimised their gain from free enterprise. The government had to defend itself, right up to the launching of collectivisation in 1928, against the charge that it was defending this 'state capitalism' as a preparation for a return to private capitalism.

1. How useful is this data to a historian writing about Russian history in the period 1913–1926?

2. Does the data support the view that the NEP was a success? Explain your answer.

Indeed, in 1923 it was true that 75% of Russian retail trade was being handled by the 'Nepmen', the private traders who flourished under the NEP. Thus one of the by-products of the NEP was the strengthening of party discipline to eliminate internal friction. Over 30% of the party's membership was expelled between 1921 and 1924, a precedent that was to have grave implications in the 1930s. Eventually the aims of the policy – the restoration of production and of economic stability – were largely achieved. The table shows that, in most major industries, production figures by 1926 had nearly regained their pre-war levels.

Russian economic indicators, 1913–1926

	Factory output (million new roubles)	Coal (million tons)	Electricity (million kW)	Steel (thousand tons)	Grain (million tons)
1913	10,251	29.0	1,945	4,231	80.1
1920	1,410	8.7	–	–	46.1
1921	2,004	8.9	520	183	37.6
1922	2,619	9.5	775	392	50.3
1923	4,005	13.7	1,146	709	56.6
1924	4,660	16.1	1,562	1,140	51.4
1925	7,739	18.1	2,925	2,135	72.5
1926	11,083	27.6	3,508	3,141	76.8

From Alec Nove, *An Economic History of the USSR* (1982)

The death of Lenin

1. What evidence was there in 1921 of the failure of the policy of War Communism?

2. What were the main features of the New Economic Policy?

3. Was the introduction of the NEP in 1921 a success for the Soviet government?

Lenin did not live to see this recovery completed. A series of strokes that began in May 1922 finally killed him in January 1924. His organisational genius and unique blend of determination and flexibility played a greater role than anything else in the creation of soviet power. Public reaction to his death, represented by the millions who filed past his embalmed body in Moscow's Red Square, showed that the Communists now had a saint to respect, like the Orthodox Church before them. However, Lenin's insistence upon party power and party discipline, and his initiation of the policy of terror as a political weapon, also made him the creator of those elements in Russian Communism that were to dominate its history in the 1930s.

Source-based questions: The role of Lenin

Study the following FOUR passages – A, B, C and D –
about the role played by Lenin in the establishment of
Communism in Russia, and answer BOTH of the sub-
questions which follow.

SOURCE A

From *History of the Communist Party of the Soviet Union*
(Bolsheviks), published in the Soviet Union in 1938. This version
portrays Lenin as the guiding genius of the Revolution.

What would have happened to the Party, to
our revolution, to Marxism, if Lenin had
been overawed by the letter of Marxism and had
not had the courage to replace one of the old
propositions of Marxism, formulated by Engels, by
the new proposition regarding the republic of
Soviets, a proposition that corresponded to the
new historical conditions? The Party would have
groped in the dark, the Soviets would have been
disorganised, we should not have had a Soviet
power, and the Marxist theory would have
suffered a severe setback. The proletariat would
have lost, and the enemies of the proletariat would
have won.

SOURCE B

From: Robert Service writing in *Critical Companion to the
Russian Revolution* (ed. Acton, Chernaiev and Rosenberg),
published in 1997. This historian emphasises that a strong revolutionary tradition existed in Russia before Lenin came upon the
scene.

The influence of Lenin should not be
exaggerated. Lenin did not invent most of the
attitudes of Russian revolutionaries. They pre-
dated him. The populist terrorists in the
1860s–1880s had developed many of them; and
they were not entirely absent from certain trends
in European nineteenth-century socialism and
anarchism. Furthermore, several of the Russian
Marxists did not need Lenin to resuscitate this
tradition for them. It had not been Lenin but
Plekhanov who had first pleaded the case for
scientific, anti-sentimental and dictatorial policies.
And several of Lenin's contemporaries – Trotsky
comes immediately to mind – were developing the
tradition at the same time as him. Lenin had the
greatest but not the sole influence. Nor should we
overstate the scope of Lenin's influence in other
ways. It must always be taken into account that
Lenin had little direct regular contact with Russia
before April 1917. His influence was confined to
what he could achieve by his journalism and his
correspondence. Even in 1917 his contact with
Bolsheviks and the rest of society was not
uninterrupted. Arriving in Petrograd in early
April, he fled again in early July and returned to a
fitful, clandestine presence in the capital only in
mid-October. No photographs of him were
published, no film appeared. His appearances at
mass meetings were rare.

SOURCE C

From Martin McCauley, *The Soviet Union 1917–1991*, published
in 1993. This historian argues that Lenin's leadership was exercised in conjunction with a number of other influential
Bolsheviks.

Lenin was the natural leader of the party, but he
had to reaffirm his credentials repeatedly. Not
by nature a dictator, he never sought to silence his
critics by institutional means. He expected and
accepted opposition from his colleagues. Every
member of the Politburo during Lenin's active
political life (up to 1922) disagreed with him on a
major issue. How could it be otherwise with the
party attempting to build a new society on Russian
soil? However, this lack of consensus on many
major issues imposed a heavy burden on the
leader. Lenin, moreover, had very definite views
on which policies should be adopted and
implemented. Although factionalism was officially
banned after March 1921 he was a master
factionalist. If he was in a minority in the
Politburo he did not submit, he fought on. Since
the Politburo conferred enormous prestige and
privilege, its members could cultivate their own
constituencies. Zinoviev was party leader in
Petrograd and president of the Comintern;
Kamenev headed the Moscow party organisation;
Trotsky was Commissar for War; Rykov was
Lenin's deputy on *Sovnarkom*; Tomsky headed the
trade unions, and there was also Stalin.

SOURCE D

From: Richard Pipes, *Russia under the Bolshevik Regime
1919–1924*, published in 1994. This historian believes that Lenin
exercised a degree of control over the Bolsheviks that foreshadowed the regime of Stalin.

In Soviet Russia, the personal dictatorship of
Lenin over his party was camouflaged by such
formulas as 'democratic centralism' and the
custom of de-emphasising the role of individuals
in favour of impersonal historic forces. It is
nevertheless true that within a year after taking
power, Lenin became the unchallenged boss of the

Source-based questions: The role of Lenin

Communist Party, around whom emerged a veritable personality cult. Lenin never tolerated a view that conflicted with his own, even if it happened to be that of the majority. By 1920 it was a violation of Party regulations, punishable by expulsion, to form 'factions', a 'faction' being any group that acted in concert against first Lenin's and then Stalin's will: Lenin and Stalin were immune to the charge of 'factionalism'.

(i) Compare Passages A and B on the importance of Lenin in the establishment of Russian communism.
[15 marks]

(ii) Using these four passages and your own knowledge, explain how and why historians disagree about the role that Lenin played in the foundation and development of communist government in Russia.
[30 marks]

Source-based questions: The Kronstadt Rebellion

Study the following source material and then answer the questions which follow.

SOURCE A

From The Russian Tragedy by A. Berkman, published in 1922

The 'triumph' of the Bolsheviks over Kronstadt held within itself the defeat of Bolshevism. It exposed the true character of the Communist dictatorship. The whole Bolshevik economic system was changed as a result of the Kronstadt events. This 'triumph' sounded the death knell of Bolshevism with its Party dictatorship, mad centralisation, CHEKA terrorism and bureaucratic castes. It demonstrated that the Bolshevik regime is unmitigated tyranny and reaction. Kronstadt was the first popular and entirely independent attempt at liberation from the yoke of State Socialism, an attempt made directly by the people, by the workers, soldiers and sailors themselves.

SOURCE B

Declaration made by the Kronstadt Temporary Revolutionary Committee, 8 March 1921

The glorious arms of labour's state – the sickle and hammer – have actually been replaced by the Communist authorities with the bayonet and barred window. With the aid of militarised trade unions they have bound the workers to their benches. To the protests of the peasants, expressed in spontaneous uprisings, and of the workers, who are compelled to strike by the circumstances of their life, they answer with mass executions and bloodthirstiness, in which they are not surpassed by the Tsarist generals.

SOURCE C

Trotsky's view of the Kronstadt Rebellion, stated in a letter written from exile in Mexico, August 1937.

The best, most self-sacrificing sailors were completely withdrawn from Kronstadt. What remained was the grey mass without political education and unprepared for revolutionary sacrifice. The country was starving. The Kronstadters demanded privileges. The uprising was dictated by the desire to get privileged food rations. The victory of this uprising could bring nothing but the victory of the counter-revolution, regardless of what the sailors had in their heads. But the ideas themselves were deeply reactionary. They reflected the hostility of the backward peasantry toward the worker, the hatred of the petty bourgeois for revolutionary discipline.

(a) Use Source A and your own knowledge.

Explain briefly what the author means in Source A by his statement that 'the whole Bolshevik economic system was changed as a result of the Kronstadt events'.
[3 marks]

(b) Use Sources B and C and your own knowledge.

Explain how Source B differs from Source C in its interpretation of the motives behind the Kronstadt rebellion.
[7 marks]

(c) Use Sources A, B and C and your own knowledge.

Explain the relative importance of the different forms of opposition that the Bolshevik government encountered in establishing its authority in Russia between the October Revolution in 1917 and the death of Lenin in 1924.
[15 marks]

4.9 Did the Bolsheviks launch a cultural revolution in Russia between 1917 and 1924?

The period from 1917 to the end of the NEP experiment was one of unparalleled experimentation in Russian culture. Although a large number of artists and writers left the country at the outbreak of the revolution, those who remained revelled in the brief freedom from Tsarist censorship. They accepted the Soviet doctrine that they were now freer agents, released from the exploitation of bourgeois and aristocratic patrons.

The 'constructivists'

Immediately, the revolution raised new controversy, which was eventually resolved by the pressure of the state. Those artists who keenly supported the new regime, calling themselves 'constructivists', claimed that art should now serve an active social and political purpose. One of the greatest literary figures of the immediate post-revolutionary period was the poet Vladimir Mayakovsky, of whom T. Frankel has written, in *Revolution in Russia: Reassessment of 1917* (1992), 'his every effort was to unify art and life, to enlist art in the service of society'. His work in this period included slogans for political campaigns and posters as well as pro-Bolshevik poetry.

Theatre, too, rallied to the new atmosphere of revolution and liberation. The producer and designer Vsevolod Meyerhold teamed up with Mayakovsky and the artist Kasimir Malevich to produce the pageant 'Mystery Bouffe' (1918) which showed the proletariat defeating its exploiters. In 1920, Nikolai Yevreinov celebrated the third anniversary of the Revolution with a re-enactment of the storming of the Winter Palace, employing a cast of 8,000, and founding the tradition of May Day parades in Red Square. The group that formed itself around the journal *Proletarian Culture* (*Proletkult*) also enjoyed brief success between 1918 and 1922 in their efforts to found new literary and cultural forms by, and for, workers.

The 'fellow travellers'

A more lasting achievement was made by that group of writers and artists in Russia characterised by Trotsky as the 'fellow travellers'. In general, these men and women were not communists, but were broadly in sympathy with the ideals of the revolution. They found much fascinating human material in the great events of the revolution and the civil war. Some of the leading writers were D.A. Furmanov (*Chapaev*), V.V. Ivanov (*Armoured Train No. 14–69*), and Mikhail Sholokhov (*Quiet Flows the Don*). Another, E.I. Zamyatin, produced a political satire, *We* (1920), in which he showed a regimented socialist society whose inhabitants were identified only by numbers: the forerunner both of Aldous Huxley's *Brave New World* and George Orwell's *1984*. In poetry, Sergei Yesenin rivalled Mayakovsky's popularity with work that was highly personal, almost mystical.

'The cinema,' Lenin declared in 1921, 'is for us the most important of all the arts.' Naturally, therefore, the new art form found itself constrained at first to serve largely propagandistic purposes. Nevertheless, in the greater freedom of the NEP period, the Soviet cinema produced more than its fair share of the art's early classics, notable examples being Sergei Eisenstein's 'Battleship Potemkin', A.P. Dovzhenko's 'The Land', and V.I. Pudovkin's 'Mother', a film version of Gorky's novel. Music produced only one immediate heir to the great Russian traditions in Dmitri Shostakovich. He produced his First Symphony in 1926, and the subtitles given to the next two, the 'October' and the 'May Day' symphonies (1927 and 1929), demonstrated the tightrope that he, too, had to walk between artistic expression and official disapproval.

The growth of state control over the arts

The growth of collectivist policies under Stalin, however, also extended to the arts. Earlier means of artistic control employed during the civil war, such as the state's monopoly over publishing through the State Publishing Organisation (*Gosizdat*) were renewed. Also, new controls were introduced, such as the concentration of artists and writers into official unions. A policy aimed at constraining artists and writers strictly to serve the purposes of government policy saw the collapse of the best elements in the revived Russian culture. The artists Marc Chagall and Vasili Kandinsky had already chosen in the early 1920s to conduct their experiments in **Surrealist** painting in western Europe. Zamyatin followed them in 1931. In 1930 Mayakovsky, who had recently attacked the bureaucracy and narrow-mindedness of Soviet leadership in 'The Bedbug' (1929) and 'The Bathhouse' (1930), committed suicide. Even Maxim Gorky, the greatest of the Soviet writers, had protested against the 'disgraceful attitude' of the Soviet leaders 'towards the freedoms of speech and of person'. His own death in 1935 was surrounded by suspicious circumstances and rumours of poison.

The period 1928–1953 was to be the age of 'Socialist Realism' in art, under which Soviet artists and writers were to concentrate upon subjects helpful to the building of a socialist society. Such subjects were defined by Basil Dmytryshyn as including 'contented cows, dedicated milkmaids, devoted pig breeders, vigilant party members, and young lovers arguing by the light of the moon about the problems of industrial production'.

Surrealist: A term that fits both literature and painting, although Surrealist art has become better known. The Surrealist movement began in 1924. Surrealist paintings are of two main sorts: one where conventional techniques are used to depict a futuristic scene; the other is more inventive in technique.

---

1. In which areas of Russian culture did the Bolshevik revolution have its greatest impact?

2. To what extent were the arts in Russia turned to political purposes in the 15 years after 1917?

4.10 Was the Russian Revolution the inevitable outcome of class struggle?
A CASE STUDY IN HISTORICAL INTERPRETATION

However much historians claim that it is objective and unbiased, their work is frequently influenced by their political views or by the political environment in which they live. Sometimes, their work does not even aim at objectivity, but is planned and executed to serve a political purpose. No series of events in modern history has been so open to distortion, or been written about with so much partisan enthusiasm, as the Russian revolutions.

Soviet interpretations of 1917

For most of the 20th century the events of 1917 formed the basis of one of the most powerful political systems on earth. For Soviet writers, therefore, interpretations of the Bolsheviks' success were far from being abstract academic arguments. Instead, they provided the entire justification of the society and the political system in which they lived and worked, and the 'correct' interpretation of the Russian Revolution was as important as any other issue of political doctrine within the USSR. As the politics of the Soviet Union shifted, so did the historical explanations of its origins, producing not one Marxist interpretation, but a succession of subtly different versions.

As early as 1918, the Bolsheviks were justifying their actions of the previous year, eager to show that the October/November coup was not merely a piece of political opportunism. In *The Russian Revolution to Brest-Litovsk* (1918), Trotsky argued that the Bolsheviks enjoyed a broad basis of support among the Russian workers, arising from their correct interpretation of the class struggle. This would have led them to power by legitimate, democratic means had it not been for the counter-revolutionary conspiracies of Kornilov, Kerensky and others. In the short term, therefore, the October coup was forced upon the Bolsheviks by their opponents. Such a view received enthusiastic support from the American socialist writer, John Reed, whose eye-witness account – *Ten Days That Shook the World* (1919) – remained for many years one of the most influential accounts of the October Revolution.

Once firmly established in power, however, the Soviet leadership changed its tune. The Bolsheviks were now pictured in a more dominant role, moulding and directing the Russian working classes, rather than responding to their democratic will. Trotsky and Iakovlev, in *On the Historical Significance of October* (1922), now portrayed the October coup as a political masterstroke, splendidly orchestrated by the Bolshevik leadership. This was in sharp contrast to the spontaneous and chaotic events of the February revolution. The distinction was between a party that truly understood the inevitable logic of class struggle, and groupings that attempted to pervert the course of history for their selfish ends. In their success the Bolsheviks had enjoyed two great advantages: their clear understanding of Marxist principles and their centralised, disciplined organisation. Such organisational and ideological strengths, of course, owed an enormous debt to the genius of Lenin.

In the same way the Stalinist era produced a further very different version of the same events as it became politically unacceptable to attribute important roles in the revolution to men whom Stalin had declared to be 'enemies of the people'. This process culminated, in 1939, in the publication of the official *Short Course of the History of the Russian Communist Party (Bolsheviks)*. This new interpretation either minimised or ignored the roles played by Stalin's political rivals. Stalin himself emerged as a key figure, at the right hand of Lenin himself. This official version also made one other important change, attributing a leading role to the Bolsheviks in the February revolution and therefore enhancing their role in the events of 1917 as a whole. Throughout the events of 1917, it was now claimed, the Bolsheviks followed the inevitable logic of class struggle, acting as 'a revolutionary party of the proletariat, a party free from opportunism and revolutionary in its attitude towards the bourgeoisie and its state power'.

Western interpretations of 1917

Meanwhile, outside the Soviet Union, several groups wrote about the Russian revolutions with distinctly different agendas. One agenda was that of socialist commentators unsympathetic to Bolshevism, who claimed that Lenin's actions in and after 1917 were premature. Economic development and the class struggle in Russia had not yet reached the stage where proletarian revolution was viable. The revolution was rushed into a socialist phase before a mature bourgeois phase had been attained, in direct defiance of Marxist principles. This view was strongly argued, for instance, by exiled Mensheviks such as Viktor Chernov (*The Great Russian Revolution*, 1936) and T. Dan (*The Origins of Bolshevism*, 1964). Such interpretations naturally placed less emphasis upon impersonal economic and social forces, or upon the theoretical correctness of the Bolshevik Party as a whole. Instead, they place Lenin at the centre of the events of 1917. The British historian E.H. Carr, in *A History of the Soviet Union, 1917–1929* (1966), represents that view in writing that 'the triumph of the party seemed almost exclusively due to Lenin's consistent success in stamping his personality upon it and leading his often reluctant colleagues in his train'. Few western writers have questioned the greatness of Lenin, but many have tempered their praise with an awareness of his role in the formation of the subsequent communist dictatorship. Such an interpretation characterised the work of many American writers during the 'Cold War' period. It can be seen in the work of Daniel Shub (*Lenin: A Biography*, 1948), Adam Ulam (*Lenin and the Bolsheviks*, 1965) and Richard Pipes (*Revolutionary Russia*, 1968), all of whom see the revolution primarily as resulting from the cataclysmic disaster of the World War, brilliantly and cynically exploited by Lenin.

Such overall conclusions are very similar to those reached by those western historians who identified themselves with the 'liberal' school of interpretation. These writers see Russia's political history since the mid-19th century – through the emancipation of the serfs, the formation of the *zemstva*, and then of the Duma – as a promising progression towards liberal institutions. Those writers who have taken an optimistic view of Russia's economic development under Witte and Stolypin have also made an important contribution to this line of argument. This progress was then shattered by Russia's disastrous involvement in the First World War, which provided the extremists with their opportunity. In the beginning this view was put forward by disappointed Russian liberals, such as Paul Miliukov in *History of the Second Russian Revolution* (1921) and M. Florinski in *The End of the Russian Empire* (1931). The line was taken up later by Leonard Schapiro in *The Origins of Communist Autocracy* (1955) and by the English authority, Hugh Seton-Watson in *The Russian Empire, 1801–1917* (1967).

Western historical writing in the 'Cold War' era did produce, however, one school of thought which reached very different conclusions about the nature and origins of the Russian revolutions. This was developed in the 1970s and 1980s by historians who wished to study the revolution from 'below', rather than from the viewpoint of the leaders. These focused upon such issues as the development of trade unions and of civil rights among the urban workers, political developments within the armed forces, and social and economic development among the peasantry. Such work as that of Diane Koenker (*Moscow Workers and the 1917 Revolution*, 1981), Evan Mawdsley (*The Russian Revolution and the Baltic Fleet*, 1978), and Teodor Shanin (*The Awkward Class: Political Sociology of the Peasantry in a Developing Society, Russia 1910–1925*, 1972) returned working-class politics to the centre of events. The Bolsheviks, in their view, enjoyed success in 1917, not because they forced the workers into line, but because they represented most accurately the long-standing aspirations of such 'progressive' workers. Such a view has several important implications for the interpretation of Russian history. It portrays the Bolshevik Party in 1917 as flexible and open, rather than hierarchical and authoritarian, as a genuine party of radical workers and peasants, rather than a party dominated by intellectuals and émigrés. An associated conclusion would be that the Bolshevik Party, therefore, changed its nature in the years that followed, that it was the pressures of the civil war that made the party brutal and authoritarian.

The collapse of the Soviet Union in 1991 naturally had a very dramatic impact upon historical writing about the revolution. On a political level it undermined the orthodox Soviet interpretation of the revolution, and made it implausible to view the Bolshevik success in 1917 as part of a logical, world-wide progression towards communism. Conversely, it enabled 'Cold War' historians in the west to assume that they had been right all along, and that they had now won the argument. Such is certainly the spirit in which the conservative American historian Richard Pipes published *The Russian Revolution, 1899–1919* in 1990. Most important in the longer term, however, was the fact that the archives in Russia were no longer under strict government control, and that western historians may research in them more freely. Perhaps the most important work to result from these freer circumstances to date has been that of Orlando Figes (*A People's Tragedy: the Russian Revolution 1891–1924*, 1996). Figes takes a much less heroic view of these events, depicting a revolution that was really directed by no-one, neither by the Bolsheviks nor by abstract theories of class struggle. Instead, deeply rooted in Russia's past political and social history, it led to economic and social disaster in the early 1920s, and to an oppressive regime which alone could restore some form of order to Russia's chaotic society. Another leading researcher of recent years, Robert Service, also stresses the tensions that existed in an extremely complex society. In *A History of 20th Century Russia* (1997), he takes a more political approach than Figes. In emphasising, however, the range of social and ethnic tension that existed in Russia on the eve of war, and the inadequacy of the government's understanding of them, he too sees an increasing sense of chaos in Tsarist Russia. Revolution, in his conclusion, was the 'practically inevitable' outcome of such a situation. A decade of post-Soviet research, therefore, begins to suggest social and political tensions of a revolutionary nature, which were channelled and directed in the longer term by a highly organised and ruthless political party.

1. In what ways did Soviet historians differ at various times in their interpretation of the events of 1917?

2. Explain why the interpretations of the Russian revolutions has caused such debate and controversy between historians.

4.11 An in-depth study: Was the October Revolution a coup or mass uprising?

4.11.1 A Soviet view: history or propaganda?

4.11.2 Was the October Revolution really a coup by a small band of revolutionaries?

4.11.3 Did the Bolsheviks have popular support in October 1917?

Framework of Events

1917	February: February Revolution
	March: Tsar Nicholas II abdicated. End of monarchy
	Unofficial Committee of the Duma became Provisional Government
	Lenin wrote five Letters from Afar to Bolsheviks in Russia
	April: Lenin returned to Petrograd and delivered his April Theses
	Demonstrations in Petrograd against Russian War aims
	June: Demonstrations in Petrograd against June Offensive
	July: July Days in Petrograd (3–5 July)
	Lenin fled to Finland
	Sixth Party Congress in Petrograd. Slogan 'All Power to the Soviets' abandoned
	August: Kornilov Affair
	October: Lenin returned to Petrograd
	Central Committee Meeting on armed seizure of power
	October Revolution (24–5 October): Bolsheviks seizure of power in Petrograd
	Lenin addressed Second Congress of All Russia Soviet

4.11.1 A Soviet view: history or propaganda?

Winter Palace: built in St Petersburg (1754–62) as the winter residence of the Tsars. After the February Revolution it became the headquarters of the Provisional Government.

In the 1920s the Soviet film director Sergei Eisenstein produced the silent film *October*, which showed thousands of Red Guards attacking the **Winter Palace** in Petrograd. The film suggested that the October Revolution, which overthrew the Provisional Government, was a popular mass

A freeze-frame from the film October by Sergei Eisenstein (1927), which was made for the tenth anniversary celebrations of the October Revolution. Lenin is shown standing on top of an armoured car during the storming of the Winter Palace.

Deification: to personify someone as God.

Mausoleum: a large and stately tomb usually constructed for a deceased leader.

Kremlin: the twelfth- century citadel in Moscow containing the former Imperial Palace and offices of the Russian government. Also (formerly) the central government of the Soviet Union.

'Peace, Bread, Land': Bolshevik slogan from April 1917. Reflected Bolshevik opposition to the war; the resolution of the food crisis in the towns; and the redistribution of land to the peasants.

Propaganda: information circulated to assist the cause of a government or movement.

Cold War: a conflict of military tension and political hostility between the USA and the USSR and their respective allies from the end of WWII until the collapse of the USSR in 1991.

uprising. This belief – one that dominated the thinking of successive Soviet governments up to the fall of the USSR in 1991 – was promoted for a number of reasons.

At the time of Lenin's death, Josef Stalin (see page 134) and other communist leaders began to glorify Lenin as a great national leader. This **deification** of Lenin is apparent in the decision to preserve his body and put it on display in a large **mausoleum** in Red Square in Moscow, next to the **Kremlin**. In addition, Petrograd was renamed Leningrad in his honour. Lenin was portrayed as the god-like genius who had foretold Russia's recent history. His slogans 'All Power to the Soviets' and **'Peace, Bread, Land'** had been supported by the Russian masses, therefore by October 1917 the Bolsheviks' seizure of power merely reflected the popular mood of the country.

Propaganda portraying the October uprising as a popular revolution was also important in legitimising the Soviet regime, which from 1917 attempted to declare itself the government supported by the population. From 1917 to 1945 the Soviet regime saw itself as the model for any future socialist society. Consequently, it was essential to develop the idea that the Bolshevik seizure of power was popular. In 1945 the Soviet Union became involved in a **Cold War** with the USA and the West and, with both sides trying to prove their superiority, the use of such propaganda became even more important.

To support their claim that the October Revolution was a popular one, Soviet historians intersperse their interpretation of events with political propaganda. Primarily they draw attention to the fact that the Bolsheviks won in an almost bloodless transfer of power. Indeed, very little support was shown to the outgoing Provisional Government. The Bolsheviks won power across Russia relatively easily, and when they dissolved the Constituent Assembly on 5 January 1918 after only one day, there was very little open opposition.

4.11.2 Was the October Revolution really a coup by a small band of revolutionaries?

What if the opposite to the Soviet view is true? What if the October Revolution was merely a conspiracy by a small group of revolutionaries acting against the wishes of the Russian people? This alternative interpretation was popular in the USA and the West during the Cold War, as it was convenient for western governments to portray the USSR as a repressive regime ruling not with, but in spite of, popular support. The rapid collapse of communism in eastern Europe in 1989 and in the USSR in 1991 seemed to confirm this view.

A major adherent of this view is American historian, Richard Pipes. In *The Russian Revolution, 1899–1919* (1990) he states:

> 'Although it is common to speak of two Russian revolutions in 1917 only one merits the name. In February 1917, Russia experienced a genuine revolution ... that brought down the Tsarist regime. The Provisional Government that succeeded it gained immediate nation-wide acceptance. Neither was true of October 1917. The events which led to the overthrow of the Provisional Government were not spontaneous but plotted and executed by a tightly organised conspiracy. October was a classic coup d'etat.'

In both the 1905 Revolution and the February Revolution of 1917, Bolsheviks played only a minor role. In fact both revolutions caught Lenin by surprise. In 1916 he told supporters in Swizerland, where he was in exile, that revolution in Russia was decades away and that it would be the next generation's task to fulfil what he had begun. It would appear that Lenin had become out of touch with conditions within Russia as, apart from a few months in 1905/6, he had been in foreign exile since 1900.

Both of the revolutions were unplanned, spontaneous reactions by the Russian people against political oppression and economic hardship. In fact, if any revolution was in the planning in February 1917, it came from the right wing of Russian politics, who favoured the removal of an incompetent Tsar in order to save the Tsarist political system.

When Lenin returned to Russia he did so with the support and assistance of Russia's wartime enemy, Germany. As Lenin supported the idea of

---

The April Theses

Published in *Pravda* on 7 April 1917
- The war is a greedy war for territory and should be ended immediately.
- The revolution ... is to move to its second stage, which must place power in the hands of the proletariat and the poorest peasants.
- No support for the Provisional Government.
- The masses must be made to see that the Soviet is ... the only possible form of revolutionary government.
- Abolition of the police, the army and the bureaucracy. The salaries of all officials should not exceed the average wage of a worker.
- Confiscation of all landed estates from the landowners and aristocracy.
- Mass propaganda to win over peasants and workers.
- The immediate union of all banks in the country into a single national bank.
- All production of goods to come under Soviet control.
- An international organisation to be set up to spread revolution worldwide.

a revolutionary civil war in which Russian workers were encouraged to overthrow the government, the Germans believed that he would assist them in destabilising the Russian government and war effort.

Sealed train: a train where the occupants are not allowed to get off the train until it reaches its destination.

Lenin was transported from Switzerland in a **sealed train**, which travelled via Germany and neutral Sweden to Russian Finland. The welcome he received from all revolutionaries upon his arrival at Petrograd late on the night of 3 April soon turned to uproar. From the top of an armoured car parked outside the station Lenin delivered a 90–minute speech on what became known as his *April Theses*. Lenin denounced the Provisional Government as reactionary and demanded its overthrow, a view that ran counter to those held by the Russian Bolshevik leadership, headed by Kamenev and Stalin.

From the moment he returned to Russia Lenin planned to overthrow the Provisional Government, which he attempted on three occasions before his eventual seizure of power in October 1917.

What strategies did Lenin use to attempt the overthrow of the Provisional Government in 1917?

On 21 April Lenin attempted to topple the Provisional Government through mass demonstrations, using the catalyst of mass discontent over the government's commitment to continue in the war. The Bolshevik Central Committee even issued an order to send agitators to factories and barracks to persuade workers and soldiers to join in any demonstrations, but they were easily dispersed.

Again on 9 June, the Bolsheviks attempted to exploit the Provisional Government's lack of popularity in order to bring about its downfall. This time the pretext was disillusionment with a major Russian offensive on the Eastern Front. Yet all attempts to persuade the Petrograd Soviet and the Congress of Soviets to support such a move failed and a Bolshevik coup was averted.

The July Days

The events of the July Days have provoked harsh criticism of Lenin. To Richard Pipes:

'no event in the Russian Revolution has been more wilfully lied about ... the reason being that it was Lenin's worst blunder, a misjudgement

This photo of Lenin in disguise was taken for the false papers he used in order to return to Russia without fear of arrest. Lenin hid in friends' apartments throughout October.

that nearly caused the destruction of the Bolshevik Party: the equivalent of Hitler's 1923 beer-hall putsch. To absolve themselves of responsibility, the Bolsheviks have gone to unusual lengths to misrepresent the July putsch as a spontaneous demonstration which they sought to direct into peaceful channels.'

The pretext of the July Days had been to move some of the Petrograd garrison to the front. This was following the failure of the Russian June offensive, which had provoked fear of a German counter-offensive against the capital. On 4 July the pro-Bolshevik Machine Gun Regiment and the Red Guards occupied key points in the city. They were joined by 5000–6000 sailors from the Kronstadt naval base and later 10,000 workers from the Putilov factory. But just when it looked as though Lenin finally had Petrograd in his grasp, he lost his nerve and fled to Finland.

Opposition to Lenin further developed when the government claimed he was acting as an agent of the Germans and was receiving financial assistance from them. On 6 July Lenin and ten other Bolsheviks were charged with 'high treason and organising an armed uprising'. Altogether 800 were arrested and a few days later both Lenin and Zinoviev fled the city.

In her book, *Lenin* (1999), Beryl Williams cites the July Days as a turning point. Lenin and the Bolsheviks had attempted a takeover but had failed miserably and, after July, the initiative to threaten the government seemed to pass from Lenin's hands.

What led the Bolsheviks to call for an armed seizure of power?

In August, the Kornilov Affair raised the fear of a right-wing coup, which took pressure off the Bolsheviks. The Provisional Government armed the workers of Petrograd, and Bolshevik support increased dramatically. In Lenin's absence, power over the Red Guards fell to Leon Trotsky (see page 68), and it was he who engaged in the initial plan for an armed seizure of power.

Also of considerable significance in moving the Bolsheviks towards armed insurrection was an announcement by the Provisional Government on 9 August, proposing a timetable for national elections to a Constituent Assembly. The elections would be on 12 November with the opening session on 28 November. Lenin was well aware that in such an election the SRs would be the largest political force, so any armed seizure of power would have to take place before that date.

Lenin's tactics over the summer offered a way forward. Following his return to Russia he advocated the transferral of all political power to the All Russia Soviet. Lenin knew that the Bolsheviks did not have a chance to participate in and influence the Provisional Government, but they could, and did, rapidly increase their participation in regional soviets and the All Russia Soviet. Support for the Bolsheviks grew because they were the only major group in opposition to an increasingly unpopular Provisional Government. They were also popular for their call for 'Peace, Bread and Land', although some saw this slogan as a cynical attempt to win support.

The catalyst for the seizure of power on 24 October came not from Lenin but from the Provisional Government, which attempted to close down two Bolshevik newspapers. With the help of Trotsky, Lenin was able to persuade the Central Committee of the Party to accept the idea of an armed uprising. Using the Military Revolutionary Committee (MRC) of the Petrograd Soviet, the Bolsheviks planned to capture Petrograd on the eve of the Second Congress of the All Russia Soviet. Then, when they had seized power, they would announce they had done so on behalf of the Soviet. On the evenings of 24 and 25 October, MRC units and Red Guards occupied key areas of Petrograd, arrested the Provisional Government, and declared a new government the following day.

An interpretation of the storming of the Winter Palace by the Soviet artist Sokolov-Skaljal (1939).

How was a small conspiratorial group able to seize power in the world's largest country?

The answer lies in the chaotic conditions existing in Russia during 1917: economic hardship caused by the war; low levels of morale in the army, particularly after the failure of the June Offensive; and the breakdown of law and order in the countryside. The Bolsheviks were best placed to take advantage of this chaos as they were a centralised, disciplined party which had distanced itself from the Provisional Government. According to Orlando Figes in *A People's Tragedy* (1996), with their slogan of 'Peace, Bread, Land', the Bolsheviks deliberately undermined the authority of the Provisional Government, thus hastening its collapse.

Even though Bolsheviks were in the minority across the country as a whole, they gave the appearance of acting for the majority in the All Russia and Petrograd Soviet. In fact, at no time during 1917 did the Bolsheviks have majority support within Russia: their appeal was strongest amongst town dwellers and in sections of the armed forces. In the Constituent Assembly elections of November 1917 the Bolsheviks achieved only 24 per cent of the vote.

It has also been suggested that the very nature of the Bolshevik Party implied a conspiracy of a minority. In *What is to be Done?* Lenin recommended that the RSDLP should be restricted to a small group of professional revolutionaries, who would plan for the seizure of power in Russia on behalf of the industrial working class and peasantry.

Lenin deliberately used popular support for the All Russia Soviet to mask the Bolshevik plan to seize power. As historian, Leonard Schapiro states in *The Communist Party of the Soviet Union*, (1960):

> 'the soviets rather than the party attracted mass allegiance, which the Bolsheviks exploited.'

However, once in power Lenin had no desire to share power with the All Russia Soviet or with any other socialist party, except the Left SRs for a short period (December 1917 to March 1918). Support for the All Russia Soviet simply provided a smokescreen for a conspiracy.

Further evidence confirming this comes from a study of what the Bolsheviks did once they achieved power. Most representatives in the All Russia Soviet hoped that the Bolsheviks would form a coalition government, but Lenin planned to rule alone, and maintained power through the use of political terror and repression. The leading Bolsheviks Kamenev, Zinoviev and Alexei Rykov (see page 93) believed that if the Bolsheviks did not create a coalition socialist government, they would only be able to rule through terror.

4.11.3 Did the Bolsheviks have popular support in October 1917?

Richard Pipes's work has generated considerable historical debate about the nature of the October Revolution. However, whilst his study concentrates on the political history of the Revolution, it fails to take into account the social and economic conditions of the time. Critics of Pipes's perspective point out that, in the late summer and autumn of 1917, Russia was in a state of social turmoil: peasants were seizing land and individual nationalist groups were asserting their independence. Historians from John Keep in *Russian Revolution: A Study in Mass Mobilisation* (1976) to French historian Marc Ferro in *October 1917: A Social History of the Russian Revolution* (1980), who have concentrated on the social aspects of 1917, agree that disillusionment with the war and economic collapse meant that the Bolsheviks did indeed have widespread popular support.

The Constituent Assembly election results show the Bolsheviks polling 25 per cent of the popular vote. They achieved majority support amongst the urban working class and from over ten per cent of the peasantry. The SR vote is somewhat misleading as it does not differentiate between SRs and Left SRs, the latter of which formed a significant minority and joined the Bolsheviks in government in December 1917.

Many hoped that, once in power, the Bolsheviks would form a coalition government of socialist groups. Consequently, when this failed to materialise, support drifted away to the point that the Bolsheviks were forced to rule through terror.

Election Results for the Constituent Assembly, November 1917

	% of vote
Socialist Revolutionaries	40.4
Bolsheviks	24
Mensheviks	2.6
Left Socialist Revolutionaries	1
Other socialist parties	0.9
Kadets (Liberals)	4.7
Other liberal groups	2.8
National minority parties	13.4
Results not known	10.2

(From *The Russian Revolution 1899–1919* by Richard Pipes (1990)

Why did support for the Bolsheviks increase?
By October the Bolshevik Party was no longer a small, close-knit body of professional revolutionaries. According to historian Christopher Read, in *From Tsar to Soviets: Russian People and their Revolution, 1917–21* (1996), Bolshevik membership rose from 10,000 in February to over 200,000 in October. Similarly, in *Rethinking the Russian Revolution* (1990), Edward Acton claims that membership numbers climbed from 24,000 to 350,000.

By September 1917 the Bolsheviks were publishing 75 different newspapers and journals in eight different languages, and the print-run of the party newspaper *Pravda* (Truth) had increased from 90,000 in July to 200,000 in October.

Other reasons for the increased support for the Bolsheviks include the openness associated with the fall of the Tsar; the creation of the Provisional Government; and their demands for the end of the war and the distribution of land to the peasants. The Bolshevik slogan of 'Peace, Bread, Land' mirrored the views of the majority of the Russian people.

Bolshevik support rose most rapidly amongst the urban working class (proletariat), the social group around which Lenin had planned the socialist revolution. Bolshevik support also increased in factory committees as well as local soviets.

In *The Russian Revolution, 1917* (2000), Rex Wade states:

> 'The Russian Revolution of 1917 was a number of concurrent and overlapping revolutions: a popular revolt against the old regime; a workers' revolt against the hardships of the old industrial and social order; a revolt by soldiers against the old system of military service and then against the war; a peasants' evolution for land and control of their own lives; middle class elements and educated society for civil rights and parliamentary government and a revolt of most of the people against the war and slaughter.'

The Bolshevik's position seemed to attract many, if not all, of these groups.

What advantages did the Bolsheviks have over other political parties?

As 1917 progressed, the Bolsheviks developed a number of advantages over other parties and groups. They had a recognised leader, Lenin, who had made clear his implacable opposition to the Provisional Government and its policies, and they had a Central Committee, which offered a clear decision-making apparatus as well as a core of dedicated supporters forming the basis for growth.

There is also the issue of divisions in opposition groups. The Mensheviks were linked with the idea of **revolutionary defencism** – associated with their leader, Irakli Tsereteli – which became increasing unpopular after the failure of the June Offensive. Tsereteli had been in the Provisional Government from May, and this compromised his position with left-wing supporters, who looked to the founder of Menshevism, Yuli Martov, for alternative leadership.

Similarly, the SRs were compromised when their leader, Victor Chernov, also joined the Provisional Government in May. Growing opposition to the Provisional Government's agricultural policy was shown at the SR council, which took place between 6 and 10 August. Left SRs received 40 per cent of the vote and were eventually to join Lenin's government in December 1917.

Finally, with the creation of the Third Provisional Government, under Alexander Kerensky (see page 86), on 25 September, central authority within Russia had all but collapsed. Following the failure of the June Offensive, the Kornilov Affair, and the rapid economic collapse of the country, Russia simply lacked effective government. The Bolsheviks did not have to seize power, but merely fill a vacuum left by an inept and increasingly ignored Provisional Government.

Revolutionary defencism: policy associated with the Menshevik leadership of Tsereteli and Fedor Dan from February 1917. They opposed offensive operations in the war but were willing to fight if the Germans attacked the Russian army.

Irakli Tsereteli (1881–1960)
A Russian socialist who became a leading Menshevik after the 1903 RSDLP split and was editor of the Menshevik paper *Kvali* (Track). Minister of the Interior in the Provisional Government. After the October Revolution Lenin ordered Tsereteli's arrest so he remained in Georgia throughout the Civil War. When the Red Army captured the area he fled to France and later emigrated to the USA.

Was the October Revolution a coup or mass uprising?

Read the following extract and then answer the questions that follow.

The Bolshevik Revolution was anything but popular and democratic. The party was and remained a conspiratorial minority, whose active membership 'consisted in the main of intellectuals'. Their success can be explained in the first instance by their superior organisation. A highly centralised body of professional revolutionaries had been Lenin's ideal since he wrote 'What is to be Done?' in 1902. The tightly-knit, military style organisation he created stood in stark contrast to its feeble, fractured, ill-organized rivals.

Adapted from Edward Acton,
Rethinking the Russian Revolution Hodder Arnold, 1990

1. Using the information in the extract, and from this section, how far do you agree with the suggestion that the October Revolution was a coup by an unrepresentative minority?

2. 'The Bolsheviks did not gain power in October 1917, they merely filled a vacuum left by the disintegration of the Provisional Government'.

Assess the validity of this view.

4.12 An in-depth study: Was Lenin a liberator or dictator? The Bolsheviks in power 1917–24

4.12.1 How did he stay in power after October 1917?
4.12.2 How far did he change the Russian government, economy and society?
4.12.3 Was his attempt to export the revolution a complete failure?

Framework of Events

1917	Lenin addressed Second Congress of All Russia Soviet
	Bolshevik government (Sovnarkom) formed
	Elections to Constituent Assembly
	Bolsheviks called for armistice (ceasefire) on Eastern Front, which came into effect on 2 December
1918	Constituent Assembly dissolved by Bolsheviks
	Treaty of Brest-Litovsk
	Capital moved from Petrograd to Moscow
	Party name changed to Communist Party
	Introduction of War Communism
	Start of Left SR uprising
	Official creation of Russian Soviet Federative Soviet Republic
1919	First Comintern Congress
	Turning point in Civil War against the Whites
1920	Russo-Polish War
1921	End of Civil War
	Kronstadt Mutiny
	War Communism abandoned and NEP introduced
1922	Creation of USSR
	Lenin suffered two strokes
1924	Lenin died

I n *History of Russia: The Bolshevik Revolution, Part 1* (1960) the English historian, Edward H. Carr, declares that Lenin's greatest achievement was not in gaining political power, but in keeping it.

The problems facing Lenin were daunting. Alongside his promise to remove Russia from the First World War, Lenin also had to deal with a complete national breakdown in law and order. All of this was happening at a time of severe economic crisis when, to make matters worse, the old Russian Empire seemed to be disintegrating; minorities such as Finns, Ukrainians and Georgians were setting up their own governments.

In addition to these problems, Lenin was faced with the enormous task of creating a socialist society within Russia. Lenin hoped that social revolution in Russia would coincide with a worldwide socialist revolution. His lasting wish was to see socialist revolution take place in western Europe, in particular in Britain and Germany.

4.12.1 How did Lenin stay in power after October 1917?

According to Karl Marx, once a socialist revolution had taken place in an advanced industrial economy it would be followed by a 'dictatorship of the proletariat (industrial working class)', who would constitute the majority of the population. However, in the Russia of 1917 this was impossible as 80 per cent of the population were peasants. Also, Lenin believed that a Bolshevik dictatorship should act as the representative of the Russian working class.

How did Lenin remove opposition from within his own party?
From the moment that Lenin seized power he was determined to rule. In *A People's Tragedy: The Russian Revolution 1891–1924* (1996), Orlando Figes cites Lenin's determination to establish not only a Bolshevik dictatorship of Russia, but also a personal dictatorship over the Bolshevik Party itself. As Figes notes:

'Lenin's bullying tactics would soon lead to a situation where only one man would be left in the Party – the Dictator …. This was without doubt one of the most critical moments in the history of the Bolshevik Party.'

An example of Lenin's desire to establish supreme control came on 4 November 1917, when five moderate Bolsheviks – including Kamenev, Zinoviev and Rykov – resigned from the Party's Central Committee after being accused of holding talks with other socialist parties. Lenin also set about purging their supporters from the Central Committee.

Yet even this ruthless approach did not enable Lenin to totally eradicate internal dissent, or mean that he was completely unwilling to work with other parties for tactical reasons. In fact, from December 1917 to March 1918, Lenin agreed to a coalition with the Left SRs, although they were always treated as a minority.

Internal conflict was an important factor in leading Lenin to ban all factions within the Bolshevik/Communist Party at the Tenth Party Congress in March 1921. From 1921 the Party followed a policy of 'democratic centralism' whereby there was open discussion and debate on matters of policy but, once a decision had been made by the Party leadership, all members were expected to follow that decision unquestioningly. In this way Lenin had created a political dictatorship.

How did Lenin deal with external challenges?
The greatest external threat to Lenin's rule came from the Constituent Assembly elections, which were virtually a referendum on Bolshevik rule.

It was impossible for Lenin to cancel the elections without provoking widespread unrest. When the results were counted, the Bolsheviks had achieved only 24 per cent of the vote – amounting to approximately 10 million votes – mainly from workers and soldiers. Of vital importance however, was the Bolshevik majorities in Petrograd and Moscow, where they won 175 seats out of a total of 715.

When the Constituent Assembly met on 5 January 1918 in the Tauride Palace, Petrograd, the Bolsheviks demanded the subservience of the Assembly to decrees from the All Russia Soviet and Sovnarkom (the Russian Government). When this was rejected by 237 votes to 137 the Bolsheviks and Left SRs withdrew and Lenin dissolved the assembly. According to American historian, Richard Pipes, in *The Russian Revolution, 1899–1919* (1990):

> 'the dispersal of the Constituent Assembly was in many respects more important for the future of Russia than the October coup. There can be no doubt about Bolshevik intentions after January 5th, when they made it unmistakably clear they intended to pay no heed to public opinion.'

Fedor Dan (1871–1947)
A Russian writer and physician who became a Menshevik and a member of the Petrograd Soviet after the February Revolution, supporting the Provisional Government. Dan was an infamous opponent of Lenin and was expelled for inciting counter-revolution in 1922.

The main reason the Bolsheviks succeeded was that the opposition parties were struggling with their own internal conflicts. The SRs were split, the Left SRs having joined the Bolsheviks in government in December 1917. The leader of the majority SRs, Victor Chernov, called for a peaceful demonstration following dissolution, but this was easily handled by the Bolshevik Red Guards. The Mensheviks were also divided between followers of Fedor Dan and followers of Martov, and were only reunited in May 1918.

In the wake of the dissolution, opposition to the Bolsheviks within the civil service collapsed. It was indeed a major turning point in their creation of a dictatorship.

The Treaty of Brest-Litovsk, 3 March 1918
The greatest amount of dissent within the Party was caused by the signing of The Treaty of Brest-Litovsk: a peace treaty between Russia, Germany and Austria-Hungary. True to their demand for 'Peace', the Bolsheviks negotiated a ceasefire (armistice) on the Eastern Front two weeks after the October Revolution. The leading Bolshevik negotiator in this was Leon Trotsky, who used the peace talks to spread Bolshevik propaganda among German and Austro-Hungarian troops.

The Bolsheviks were forced to sign an extremely harsh peace, following the decision by the German High Command to renew their military operations on 18 February. Russia had to surrender Courland (Estonia), Latvia, Lithuania, Poland and the Ukraine, which amounted to 34 per cent of the population, 32 per cent of agricultural land and 54 per cent of industry.

Lenin supported the Treaty because he believed that without it the Bolsheviks would lose the Civil War that had broken out following their seizure of power. However, the decision to accept the Treaty was only carried by a single vote and, as an immediate consequence, the coalition with the Left SRs came to an end.

How did the Bolsheviks win the Civil War 1918–21?
Lenin's greatest triumph was to win the Civil War. Yet there is some dispute about when the Civil War actually began. It could be argued that it started with the defeat of **Cossack** forces outside Petrograd on 1 November 1917, but it was clearly underway by the signing of the Treaty of Brest Litovsk on 3 March 1918.

Traditionally, the Civil War has been seen as a conflict between the Reds (Bolsheviks) and the Whites (anti-Bolsheviks). However, the conflict was much more complex:

Cossack: cavalry troops from southern Russia. Usually supporters of the Whites in the Civil War.

Russian territory lost in the Treaty of Brest-Litovsk, March 1918.

- From 1918 to 1919 several foreign powers intervened in the Civil War: Britain, France, the USA, Japan and Italy, all of whom supported the anti-Bolshevik forces.

- The Czech Legion (Czech POWs from the Austro-Hungarian army), numbering 26,000, played an important part in fighting the Bolsheviks in Siberia in 1918.

- There were also conflicts with the Greens: peasant armies who fought both with and against the Bolsheviks at various times.

- National groups seeking independence. These included Finns, Estonians, Ukrainians and Georgians.

So there were several civil wars within the Russian Civil War. From November 1917 to 1920 the Bolsheviks fought the Whites, who were usually ex-Tsarists. From March to August 1918 the Bolsheviks fought the Left SRs. From 1920 to 1921 the Bolsheviks fought the Greens and the Poles.

The Bolsheviks won for a variety of reasons:

- They controlled the heartland of Russia from Petrograd to Moscow and Tsaritsyn (now Volgograd), which included most of the Russian population.

- Bolshevik propaganda portrayed Whites as anti-Russian and willing to return Russia to Tsarist rule.

- They had an effective centralised leadership, unlike the Whites, who lacked central coordination and clear policy aims, allowing the Reds to defeat them in turn.

- Leon Trotsky set up the Red Army using ex-Tsarist officers and conscription. The Red Army numbered five million by 1921.

- The Allied intervention was very limited and was reduced following the end of the First World War.

The use of political terror

Terror: the deliberate use of arrest, imprisonment and execution to enforce political control. The Red Terror began in earnest in the summer of 1918, at the height of the Civil War. Its most famous victims were the Russian royal family, who were murdered in July 1918 at Ekaterinburg in Siberia.

The most controversial aspect of Lenin's rule was his use of political **terror**. Apologists for Lenin claim that, confronted with massive economic crisis and counter-revolution, he had little alternative but to use terror against opponents and that, once the immediate crisis was over, political terror would subside. This is central to the official Soviet view put forward by works such as *A Short History of the Communist Party of the Soviet Union* (1970). Institutionalised, permanent terror is more associated with Stalin's regime (1924–53).

The Bolsheviks placed great emphasis on history. In the French Revolution (1792–4) political terror was used at times of political and economic crisis to ensure the survival of the revolution. Using this historical parallel, Lenin justified employing such tactics to guarantee the survival of the Bolshevik Revolution. This opinion is shared by Dmitri Volkogonov in *Lenin, Life and Legacy* (1994). A Colonel General in the Soviet armed forces, Volkogonov was also Director of the Institute of Military History in the 1980s and had access to its archives. He believes that 'Lenin cannot be accused of personal cruelty. The main argument for the terror was to protect the working class.' Faced with an acute crisis in

The Russian Civil War and foreign intervention 1918–21.

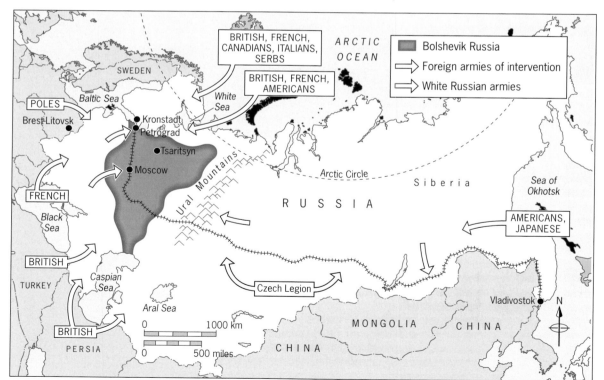

1918–21: famine, factories on strike, a breakdown in law and order, peasants hiding grain, and the army in disintegration, Lenin saw terror as the only thing that would save the country from collapse.

However, the British historian, Robert Service, takes the view that Lenin 'continued to lean in favour of dictatorship and terror'. Indeed Trotsky himself stated that Lenin believed in the use of terror 'at every suitable opportunity'. Richard Pipes goes further saying:

> 'the Red Terror constituted from the outset an essential element of the regime. It never disappeared hanging like a permanent cloud over Soviet Russia.'

The Cheka

The use of terror began early in Lenin's regime. The Military Revolutionary Committee (MRC) of the Petrograd Soviet had a specific section to tackle counter-revolution, headed by Felix Dzerzhinsky (see page 93). On 6 December 1917 Sovnarkom established the Cheka (The All Russia Extraordinary Commission for the Suppression of Counter Revolution and Sabotage). This was a major departure from the policies of the Provisional Government, who had abolished the Okhrana (Tsarist secret police) and the death penalty after the February Revolution.

The Cheka's main purpose was to arrest, imprison and execute political opponents but, in A *People's Tragedy; The Russian Revolution 1891–1924* (1996), Figes highlights a further motive for the creation of such a group. He sees it as part of a general war on privilege, the Orthodox Church and the wealthy. Figes also points out that the Red Terror actually intensified opposition to the Bolsheviks during the Civil War.

The Cheka existed from December 1917 to February 1922. At the US Senate Judiciary Committee hearings in 1971, British historian, Robert

Scene from 1921 in a Petrograd street showing the death toll of a morning's work by the Cheka. A dozen bodies lie on the ground while several people, including police, look on.

Conquest, claimed the Cheka had been responsible for 500,000 executions and deaths. In *Lenin, Terror and the Political Order* (1975), G. Leggat puts the figure closer to 140,000, but in either case these figures far exceed the reputed 14,000 killed by the Okhrana under the Tsars.

Defenders of Lenin stress the fact that he disbanded the Cheka in February 1922 as soon the crisis of Civil War was over. However, the abolition of the Cheka was simply a 'cosmetic exercise' according to Robert Service, as it was immediately replaced by the GPU (Main Political Administration), attached to the People's Commissariat of Internal Affairs. Whilst moderate Bolsheviks/Communists such as Lev Kamenev had attempted to limit the terror by this reform, in reality Lenin secured its continuance, laying the foundations for the terror regime of his successor, Stalin.

4.12.2 How far did Lenin change the Russian government, economy and society?

How Russia was governed under Lenin

Lenin created a completely new type of government following the October Revolution. Because of its association with the Tsarist regime, the term 'minister' was replaced by 'commissar'. With Lenin as chair, the Council of People's Commissars (Sovnarkom) formed the Russian government.

Sovnarkom shared political power with the All Russia Soviet but, following rigged elections to the Third Congress of the All Russia Soviet in January 1918, the Soviet and its regional counterparts lost political influence. In January 1918, and confirmed on July 1918, Russia received a **federal constitution**. However, this existed in name only. Real power lay with the Bolshevik/Communist Party. Soviet Russia was a centralised state with Lenin as its dictator.

At the Eighth Party Congress in March 1919, the Politburo was created. This committee acted on behalf of the Central Committee of the Communist Party. It replaced Sovnarkom as the main decision making body. It originally contained five members: Lenin, Trotsky, Kamenev, Stalin and Party Secretary, Krestinsky.

Social and economic policy changes

The creation of the Bolshevik regime was meant to usher in a completely new type of society: the world's first communist state. However, one major obstacle was that Russia was a country where 80 per cent of the population were peasants. According to Edward Acton in *Rethinking the Russian Revolution* (1990), another difficulty faced by Lenin was that:

> 'in the aftermath of the October Revolution the country suffered an economic collapse on the scale of a modern Black Death. 60 per cent of the workforce were unemployed by mid 1918. Petrograd lost 1 million inhabitants following the October Revolution.'

And all this was taking place with a background of Civil War from 1918 to 1921.

War Communism 1918

Lenin's first aim was to create a 'commune state', with decentralised control of factories and farms by workers and peasants respectively. This only lasted for a few months after the October Revolution, as in December 1917 it was replaced by a completely opposite approach: wholesale state nationalisation of factories. By 1921 economic conditions in Russia were so bad that famine was widespread. By the end of 1922 over three million had died of starvation and disease and outbreaks of cannibalism were even reported.

In June 1918 a further policy was introduced. Referred to at the time as

Federal constitution: a system of government where states are united and have a central government but considerable power and authority is given to the individual states.

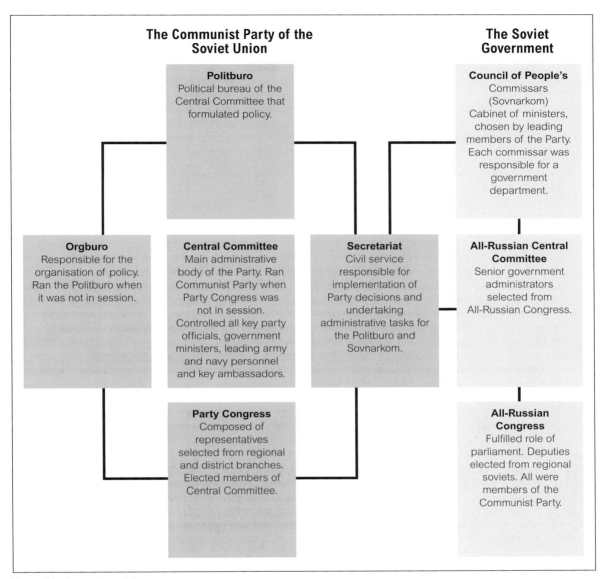

The political structure of the Soviet Union in the mid 1920s.

The Communist Party of the Soviet Union

Politburo
Political bureau of the Central Committee that formulated policy.

Orgburo
Responsible for the organisation of policy. Ran the Politburo when it was not in session.

Central Committee
Main administrative body of the Party. Ran Communist Party when Party Congress was not in session. Controlled all key party officials, government ministers, leading army and navy personnel and key ambassadors.

Secretariat
Civil service responsible for implementation of Party decisions and undertaking administrative tasks for the Politburo and Sovnarkom.

Party Congress
Composed of representatives selected from regional and district branches. Elected members of Central Committee.

The Soviet Government

Council of People's Commissars (Sovnarkom)
Cabinet of ministers, chosen by leading members of the Party. Each commissar was responsible for a government department.

All-Russian Central Committee
Senior government administrators selected from All-Russian Congress.

All-Russian Congress
Fulfilled role of parliament. Deputies elected from regional soviets. All were members of the Communist Party.

'Communism' it became known as War Communism. Soviet interpretations suggested that War Communism was a temporary policy brought about by the demands of the Civil War, but Lenin hoped it would form the basis of the Russian economy. Industrial production was planned through central planning offices run by the government. To control agriculture, Narkomprod (People's Commissariat for Foodstuffs) was created to organise local committees of poor peasants. These committees were to prove a failure, however. With cities short of food, Lenin resorted to using the Urals-Siberian method of grain procurement; gangs of Bolsheviks were sent to the countryside to forcibly take grain from the peasants. In factories industrial conscription was introduced and 'storm troops' of Bolsheviks were organised to boost industrial production.

The effects of War Communism were catastrophic. Peasant uprisings broke out across Russia. By 1920 iron production had dropped to one twelfth of what it had been in 1918 and, by October 1920, the Russian

---

Reforms passed by the Bolsheviks 1917–18

The Decree on Land, 26 October 1917

Abolished private ownership of land by wealthy landowners, merely recognising what had already taken place in the countryside. Lenin favoured the creation of collective farms rather than private peasant farms.

The Decree on Peace, 26 October 1917

Proposed a three-month armistice. Transmitted to Allied governments on 9 November.

The Decree on the Press, 27 October 1917

The 'counter-revolutionary press' (papers that criticised the Bolsheviks) was to be closed.

Declaration of the Rights of the Toiling and Exploited Masses, 8 January 1918

- abolished private property
- nationalised the banks
- founded Vesenka, the Supreme Economic Council
- introduced labour conscription.

The Creation of the Russian Soviet Federative Soviet Republic (RSFSR), January 1918

Declared Russia to be 'a republic of soviets of workers', soldiers' and peasants' deputies' and a 'free union of free nations, a federation of Soviet Republics'.

Black Market: illegal private trading.

currency – the rouble – was valued at just one per cent of its October 1917 value. The economy only seemed to function at all through the **Black Market**. By March 1921 Lenin's attempt to introduce a socialist-style economy was in ruins.

Lenin's New Economic Policy 1921

Lenin faced a major crisis in March 1921 with the economy on the verge of collapse. Large parts of the country were suffering peasant uprisings and, between 8 and 18 March the sailors of the Kronstadt naval base near Petrograd rose in rebellion against what they saw as the broken promises of Lenin's government. Trotsky only managed to suppress the mutiny with great ferocity.

Against this background the Tenth Party Congress met. Lenin announced the abandonment of War Communism, replacing it with a New Economic Policy (NEP). The NEP allowed private ownership of small firms (those employing fewer than 20 people) and, more importantly, it ended forcible grain requisitioning and allowed peasants to sell their grain on the private market. Large scale industry remained under state control, however. Lenin declared that 'only an agreement with the peasants will save the Russian Revolution until other revolutions break out somewhere else'. In social and economic terms this was a backwards step for communism. Lenin had

---

Industrial and agricultural production in millions of tons (except electricity)

	1913	1920	1921	1922	1923	1924	1925	1926
Grain	80.0	46.0	37.0	50.0	57.0	51.0	72.0	77.0
Coal	29.0	8.7	8.9	9.5	13.7	16.1	18.1	27.6
Steel	4.2	–	0.2	0.4	0.7	1.1	2.1	3.1
Iron	4.2	–	0.1	0.2	0.3	0.7	1.5	2.4
Electricity (mill KWhs)	1945	–	520	775	1146	1562	2925	3508

created a state of workers and peasants (represented by the state symbol of the hammer and sickle), but it was left to Stalin to accomplish a total social and economic revolution.

4.12.3 Was Lenin's attempt to export the revolution a complete failure?

To Lenin, socialist revolution was a worldwide phenomenon; the seizure of power in Russia was merely a prelude to the spread of revolution across the world. In line with his thinking in *Imperialism, the Highest Stage of Capitalism* (1916), revolution began in Russia as it was capitalism's weakest link. Like other Marxists, Lenin believed that socialism would only take permanent root in Russia with help from other advanced industrialised countries. The universal aim of world socialism was reflected in the name of the new state created in 1922. The Union of Soviet Socialist Republics had no geographical limitation in its title. Ultimately, the whole world would be in the USSR.

In 1918/9 the prospect of exporting the socialist revolution seemed promising but, as the severe strain of the First World War began to tell, riots and strikes affected many of the participants and, by November 1918 the Austro-Hungarian Empire was in the process of disintegration. In January 1919 the Spartacist Revolt took place in Berlin. In 1919 a Soviet-style republic was created in Bavaria, and Hungary became the Hungarian Socialist Republic. Yet these attempts at socialist revolution were short-lived and all had failed by the end of 1919. Elsewhere in Europe – in Britain and Italy – widespread industrial unrest occurred in the two years following the war.

The Third Communist International (Comintern)
To encourage a global socialist revolution Lenin set up Comintern in March 1919, under the presidency of Gregori Zinoviev, to replace the Second International, an international organisation of socialist parties. Comintern, or the Third International, aimed to co-ordinate the work of communist-style parties worldwide. However, instead of acting like an international body, Comintern aimed to subordinate all other communist parties to the direction of the Russian Communist Party.

The Russo-Polish War
The most controversial aspect of Lenin's policy was the Russo-Polish War of 1920/1. In April 1920, at the height of the Civil War, Polish forces invaded the western Ukraine and occupied Kiev (Kyiv), but were later repulsed by the Red Army. According to David Marples, in *Lenin's Revolution: Russia, 1917–21* (2000), the Red Army led a counter-offensive that took them to the outskirts of Warsaw, the Polish capital. However, Lenin did not order a mere counter-offensive but rather a full-scale westward export of the revolution. In *The Unknown Lenin: From the Secret Archive (1996)*, Richard Pipes cites a political report of the Central Committee of the Russian Communist Party, produced on 20 September 1920, which makes clear that Lenin aimed to turn Poland into a communist state as a prelude to spreading revolution to the West. Indeed, Lenin was particularly hopeful that Britain would succumb to socialist revolution.

Lenin's hopes were wildly over-optimistic. The Red Army was defeated outside Warsaw in September 1920, and this forced a retreat. In April 1921 Soviet Russia signed the Treaty of Riga with Poland, which forced Russia to give up a large part of western Belorussia to the new Polish state. The prospect of spreading revolution westward had been an abject failure.

Lenin was more successful elsewhere, however. In 1917 the Mensheviks had established a democratic socialist government in Georgia and, in 1921

Lenin used the Georgian, Stalin, to overthrow it by force. By 1922 Georgia was incorporated into the new Soviet republic of Transcaucasia, which joined the USSR in December of that year.

Summary

By the time of his first stroke on 26 May 1922, Lenin had firmly established communist rule in Russia and had prevented the complete disintegration of the old Russian Empire. Although Finland, the Baltic States and Poland had achieved independence, the vast bulk of the old state was reconstituted as the USSR.

Lenin had also led the Bolsheviks/Communists to victory in the Civil War and, in the process, set up a dictatorship of the party with himself as undisputed leader. In achieving this end, political repression and terror had become an integral part of his regime.

Lenin's attempts to create a socialist economy and society were not so successful. Various attempts at socialism, including the 'commune state', state nationalisation and War Communism, only helped speed up Russia's economic collapse. The NEP of March 1921 was an admission of failure. Instead of creating a workers' state, Lenin had created a state of both workers and peasants.

By the time of his death, the socialist revolution was limited to the old Russian Empire. Attempts at exporting revolution had failed. It would take Lenin's successor, Stalin, and the might of the Red Army, to export socialism to Eastern Europe in 1944–8.

Lenin: liberator or dictator? The Bolsheviks in power 1917–24

Read the following extract and then answer the questions that follow.

The changes made by the Bolsheviks in their policies after the October Revolution were drastic. They had promised a popularly-elected government but disbanded the Constituent Assembly in January 1918 when they got less than a quarter of the seats.

They had promised the least repressive revolutionary regime in history. And yet, the Cheka, their security police, became unprecedentedly violent and arbitrary. They had promised economic reconstruction. Yet both the collapse of industry and the disruption of trade between town and countryside continued. And Lenin and his comrades had promised peace across Europe. They had assumed that their October Revolution would be followed, within weeks, if not days by revolutions against the European capitalist order. Instead they had signed the Treaty of Brest Litovsk in March 1918, giving up sovereignty over the Ukraine and the entire Baltic region.'

Adapted from Robert Service, *Lenin, A Political Life, Volume 3: The Iron Ring*, Palgrave Macmillan, 1994

1. Using the information in the extract above, and from this section, to what extent did Lenin fail to meet his aims in the years 1917 to 1924?

2. 'Lenin's greatest achievement after the October Revolution was to remain in power.'

How far do you agree with this view?

Further Reading

Texts designed for AS and A2 Level students

The Russian Revolution by Anthony Wood (Longman, Seminar Studies series, 1979)

Reaction and Revolutions: Russia 1881–1924 by Michael Lynch (Hodder & Stoughton, Access to History series, 1992)

The Russian Revolution by Graham Darby (Longman, History in Depth series, 1998)

Lenin by Derrick Murphy (Collins Historymakers, 2005)

Lenin and the Russian Revolution by Steve Philips (Heinemann, 2000)

Communist Russia under Lenin and Stalin by Terry Fiehn and Chris Corin (John Murray, 2002)

More advanced reading

A People's Tragedy: the Russian Revolution 1891–1924 by Orlando Figes (Jonathan Cape, 1996) is probably the most influential re-interpretation of the subject written since the collapse of the Soviet Union.

Imperial and Soviet Russia: Power, Privilege and the Challenge of Modernity by David Christian (Macmillan, 1997) provides a more concise guide to recent work.

The Russian Revolution 1917–1921: a Short History by James D. White (Edward Arnold, 1994)

The Soviet Union 1917–1991 by Martin McCauley (Longman, History of Russia series, 1993)

The Russian Revolution 1917–1921 by Ronald Kowalski (Routledge, Sources in History, 1997) provides a good range of documents on this period.

A History of Soviet Russia 1917–1929 by E.H. Carr (Penguin, 1966) remains a classic study of the subject, written from a viewpoint relatively favourable to the revolution.

Lenin by Beryl Williams (Longman, Profiles in Power series, 1999)

Lenin by Robert Service (Macmillan, three volumes: 1985, 1991 and 1994)

5 The USSR in the age of Stalin and Khrushchev, 1924–1964

Key Issues

- How did Stalin become dictator of the Soviet Union?

- To what extent, and by what means, did the Soviet Union emerge as a major industrial power in the 1930s?

- How successful was Stalin in foreign affairs from 1924 to 1945?

- How effectively was the USSR governed during the period 1945 to 1964?

Framework of Events

1922	Stalin appointed General Secretary of Party's Central Committee.
	Lenin incapacitated by a stroke.
1924	Death of Lenin
1925	Dismissal of Trotsky as Commissar for War
1927	Procurement crisis
1928–32	First Five-Year Plan
1929	Beginning of agricultural collectivisation
1932–33	Major famine in the Ukraine
1933–37	Second Five-Year Plan
1934	Assassination of Sergei Kirov, and beginning of the political purges
	USSR admitted to League of Nations
1935	Beginning of 'Great Terror'
	Trials of Kamenev and Zinoviev
1936	Purge extended to the armed forces
	Trial of Marshal Tukhachevsky
1937–41	Third Five-Year Plan
1939	Nazi–Soviet Pact. Soviet forces occupy eastern Poland and the Baltic states.
1941	German attack on Soviet Union
1945	German surrender. Soviet occupation of much of eastern Europe. Fourth Five-Year Plan launched.
1953	Death of Stalin. Stalin replaced by Malenkov.

1954	Virgin Lands campaign begins
1955	Malenkov replaced by joint leadership of Bulganin and Khrushchev
1956	Twentieth Party Congress of the Soviet Communist Party. Khrushchev denounces Stalin.
1957	Sputnik I launched
1958	Khrushchev becomes Premier of USSR
1961	Yuri Gagarin is the first man in space
	Berlin Wall Crisis
1962	Cuban Missile Crisis
1964	Khrushchev deposed by a group led by Brezhnev and KGB boss, Semichastny

Overview

LENIN departed the political scene abruptly, leaving his successors a mixed inheritance. He had completed part of the task that the Bolsheviks had undertaken in 1917, for the regime had defeated its domestic enemies, and was firmly established in power. In terms of Soviet society and of the Soviet economy, however, he left an unfinished revolution, and a revolution in danger. The international revolt expected in the aftermath of the First World War had not materialised. Not only did the Soviet Union confront a hostile, capitalist world on its own, but it faced it with an economic system that lagged way behind those of the western powers. Levels of industrial production were generally lower than they had been before the war, and Russia's vast territories and resources were exploited inadequately, if at all. Perhaps the most pressing problem of all was that of securing from a suspicious and conservative peasantry a sufficient quantity of food to feed the industrial workers whose labour, in both ideological and practical terms, formed the foundation of the new Soviet society. Faced with such unforeseen problems, communist theorists proposed a variety of solutions, and Stalin's rise to power owed much to the fact that his solution was the most acceptable to a battered and war-weary society. It was his view that the Soviet Union should abandon any reliance upon foreign communists and international revolution, and should use its own substantial resources to achieve economic progress.

Stalin's system of government was characterised by two outstanding features. The first was the ruthless mobilisation of Russia's enormous economic resources in order to achieve industrial parity with the great capitalist economies. The second feature was the development of a powerful state system, capable of driving forward such a policy and of overcoming all opposition. By the end of the 1930s, the powers of the political police had expanded enormously and were backed by a system of prison and labour camps of unprecedented proportions. Stalin's pretence that he was using these powers against class enemies and the agents of foreign capitalism was largely untrue. Although the battle to compel the peasantry was real enough, more dangerous opposition came from within the Communist Party, and even from within the government itself. Stalin attacked this opposition by the crudest methods of power politics – in the 1920s to establish his leadership, and in the 1930s to consolidate his power and to drive forward his policies. Trumped-up and emotive charges were brought against his opponents, and they were eliminated from political life either by execution or distant imprisonment.

By the end of the 1930s, Stalin had achieved two goals. Firstly, he effectively created a new form of Soviet government, replacing the Bolsheviks who had followed Lenin in 1917 with a new brand of Soviet politician. From a younger generation, these men and women were usually from distinctly proletarian backgrounds, far removed from the intellectuals who had planned the early theories of Bolshevism and the 1917 revolution. More radical still, Stalin overrode the authority of the Party, and created an extremely powerful and remarkably successful system of personal rule. Secondly, he had turned the Soviet Union into a major industrial power, capable of surviving the enormous demands of the '**Great Patriotic War**', and of emerging after 1945 as one of the two great world powers. On the other hand, a high price had been paid for these achievements. The social and humanitarian idealism that had accompanied the 1917 revolution had been abandoned. It had given way to new forms of political and economic brutality that eventually undermined the claims of the Soviet Union to provide a new and superior social pattern.

It was perhaps in the area of foreign policy that Stalin inherited the most complex and insoluble problems. When Stalin first established his authority in the Soviet Union it was already clear that Lenin's initial assumptions about foreign policy were naïve and inaccurate. The Russian Revolution did not trigger the collapse of world capitalism, and it would be necessary for the Soviet Union to define its stance towards its capitalist neighbours. Unfortunately, between the mid-1920s and the mid-1930s, Soviet politicians adopted two different and contradictory stances. Working through *Comintern*, some sought Soviet security through the promotion of communism within the capitalist states. At the same time, the Soviet Foreign Ministry sought orthodox diplomatic relations with many of the European states. Such relations assumed much greater importance in the 1930s, as powerful enemies began to emerge to the west and to the east of the Soviet Union, in Germany and in Japan. From the mid-1930s onwards, the Soviet Union conducted its foreign policy in an orthodox fashion, seeking allies against those forces that threatened its security. Yet its position among the European powers remained unorthodox. Conservative politicians in France, Britain and Eastern Europe could not trust a power that had recently supported the principle of international revolution. Nor could Stalin feel confident that these politicians would not in the end prefer Hitler's ideology to his own. In some cases, he had good grounds for his suspicions. Perhaps the best bet for the security of the Soviet Union was to imitate the capitalist powers and to do a deal with Hitler. That option, too, proved unsuccessful in the long run. When Nazi Germany repudiated the 1939 pact, and launched its attack upon the Soviet Union in 1941, Stalin was left in isolation, his foreign policy a failure in all important respects.

Desperate as the plight of the Soviet Union appeared in late 1941, the power of the state and the prestige of its leader were transformed in the course of the next four years. The cost to the Soviet Union of the Great Patriotic War was huge, and its human and material losses were by far the worst of any of the combatants. The fruits of victory, on the other hand, were immense: the USSR gained control over the territories and economies of most of the states of eastern Europe, and emerged as the greatest power on the European and Asian continents, matched in global terms only by the USA. Perhaps the greatest benefits went to Stalin himself. He emerged with his domestic power and reputation enhanced to the extent that he appeared as the infallible father of the state, without a domestic political rival.

'Great Patriotic War': The name by which the Second World War is usually referred to in Russia. It helps to show how Stalin wished to present the conflict to the Soviet people, as a defence of the motherland, akin to the war of 1812, rather than as a part of a wider struggle.

Comintern: Shortened term for the (third) Communist International. Between 1919 and 1943 this was nominally the organisation responsible for the co-ordination of international communist activity.

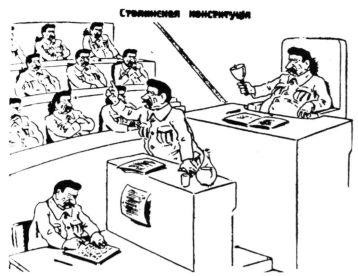

A more cynical view of Soviet government. This cartoon, entitled 'The Stalin Constitution' shows Stalin occupying every position and playing every role. It was published by Russian exiles in 1936.

In the last eight years of his life, Stalin used this vast power to restore and to consolidate the political and economic system that he had established in the 1930s. The reconstruction of the Soviet economy once again went hand in hand with the subordination of the peasantry to the requirements of the urban workers, and the imposition of political terror.

If such policies could be justified in the 1930s as necessary steps in the creation of a communist society, it does not seem that they were as readily accepted by Soviet politicians in the post-war years. Although they did not dare to oppose Stalin during his lifetime, they were very quick indeed to reform his system after his death. Reforms were quickly applied to the secret police and to the system of prison camps, and the Soviet economy moved in directions more favourable to the peasantry and to the production of consumer goods. In 1956, indeed, Nikita Khrushchev felt strong enough to condemn Stalin's methods and to abandon his 'cult of the personality'. Soviet foreign policy was to demonstrate in the next 15 years that some of Stalin's principles and priorities lived on. In terms of domestic policy, however, an era of ruthless economic planning and of political terror was indeed at an end.

1. Which of the factors in the mind map was the most successful aspect of Stalin's rule? Give reasons for your answer.

2. What do you regard as Stalin's greatest failures in (a) foreign affairs and (b) domestic affairs?

3. Was Stalin both brutal and effective throughout his rule? Explain your answer.

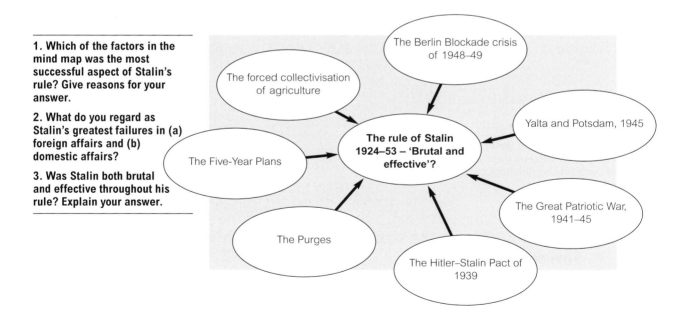

5.1 Who was Josef Stalin?

Josef Stalin (1879–1953)
Adopted name of Josef Djugashvili. Became a leading member of the Bolshevik Party in its early stages and was active in the October Revolution in 1917. Stalin became People's Commissar for Nationalities in the first Soviet government, and General Secretary of the Bolshevik Party's Central Committee (1922–53). After Lenin's death, he took over the leadership of the Soviet Union, and launched the Five-Year Plans for the industrialisation of the Soviet Union and the collectivisation of Soviet agriculture. Signed the Nazi–Soviet Pact (1939) but failed to prevent the German invasion of the Soviet Union two years later. It was largely Soviet military strength which led to the collapse of the Nazi regime in 1945.

1. What roles had Stalin played within the Bolshevik Party by the time it seized power in 1917?

2. In what ways was Stalin's background different from those of other leading Bolsheviks of 1917?

Political formation

Born Josef Djugashvili (21 January 1879), the future dictator of the Soviet Union was not Russian by birth. He came from the small town of Gori, in Georgia, and was the son of a shoemaker, and the grandson of serfs. As such, he was one of the few true proletarians in the leading ranks of the Bolshevik Party. The most significant features of his early life were the harshness and occasional brutality of his father and the unusual ambition and devotion of his mother, which secured for him the rare privilege of 11 years of education (1888–99). It is significant that the theological college in Tbilisi – that Djugashvili attended from 1894 until his expulsion five years later – had a history of student unrest and political disloyalty. 'I became a Marxist,' its most famous student later recalled, 'because of my social position, but also because of the harsh intolerance and discipline that crushed me so mercilessly at the seminary.'

Stalin's political stance seems to have developed steadily between 1898, when he joined a social democratic underground group in Tbilisi, and 1904 when he clearly identified himself with the Bolshevik faction of the communists. Unlike those of the intellectual Marxists in exile, Stalin's subsequent career followed a practical path of strike organisation, agitation and armed robberies for the benefit of party funds, interspersed with periods of imprisonment and Siberian exile. He used the name 'Koba' from 1902, and signed himself 'Stalin' ('man of steel') for the first time in 1913. The leading traits of his character – distrust, alertness, dissimulation, endurance and, above all, an intense sense of class hatred – can all be traced from his childhood and early career. For Stalin this hatred was never merely a matter of Marxist theory. The historian Isaac Deutscher wrote in *Stalin: A Political Biography* (1966), 'In Djugashvili, class hatred was not his second nature – it was his first.'

Stalin's reputation in local revolutionary circles expanded to a wider stage between 1905 (when he travelled abroad for the first time to attend a Bolshevik conference in Finland) and 1912 (when he was appointed by Lenin to the Central Committee of the party). Perhaps Lenin's choice was determined by his desire to shake up the assembly of theoretical Marxists with a rougher breed of revolutionary. In exile in Siberia at the beginning of 1917, Stalin quickly assumed a number of unobtrusive but influential roles in the revolution. He was editor of the Bolshevik journal *Pravda*, leader of the Petrograd Soviet, and temporary director of Bolshevik strategy until the return of the exiles from abroad. If not a familiar public figure, he was a man of substantial internal political influence, as the events of the next decade were to demonstrate.

5.2 How did Stalin win the struggle to succeed Lenin as leader of the Soviet state?

The strokes that removed Lenin from active politics (26 May 1922), and which finally killed him (21 January 1924), destroyed the undisputed source of leadership in Russia. 'The impact of Lenin's illness on the Bolshevik leadership can hardly be exaggerated,' wrote Isaac Deutscher. 'The whole constellation ceased, almost at once, to shine with the reflected light of its master mind.'

Nikolai Bukharin (1888–1938)	Grigori Zinoviev (1883–1936)	Lev Kamenev (1883–1936)
Intellectual Bolshevik. Opposed Lenin over the Treaty of Brest-Litovsk (1918). Supported Stalin against Trotsky, but later opposed his policies on the planned economy and authoritarian government. Arrested and executed.	Joined Lenin in exile in 1903. Editor of *Pravda* and Chairman of *Comintern*. Supported Stalin against Trotsky, but subsequently switched allegiance. Dismissed from office and expelled from Party (1927). Arrested and executed.	Moderate Bolshevik who opposed Lenin's 'adventurism' in the course of 1917. Head of Moscow Soviet (1918–25). Dismissed from Politburo (1925) and subsequently from Party. Accused of Kirov's murder in 1936, and executed.

The main candidates for the succession

There could be no adequate replacement for Lenin's genius, and the short-comings of the various candidates had already been aptly summarised in his Testament, composed during his last illness. Leon Trotsky, for all his great intellectual qualities, was guilty of a 'too far-reaching self-confidence and a disposition to be too much attracted by the purely administrative side of affairs'. Grigori Zinoviev and Lev Kamenev had shown a disturbing hesitancy in the months before the seizure of power in October 1917, and Nikolai Bukharin's grasp of theoretical Marxism was regarded as faulty. Josef Stalin, lastly, offset his great practical abilities with an excessive roughness, impatience and lack of caution and of consideration for his colleagues.

The main feature of the struggle for the succession during the last weeks of Lenin's life was the isolation of Trotsky from the other candidates. In part this was due to his personal arrogance, and in part because he never lived down the lateness of his conversion to Bolshevism. Furthermore, his achievements at the head of the Red Army were offset by the widespread fear that this military leader might turn against the Russian Revolution, as General Bonaparte had turned against the French Revolution. The failure of his campaign between October 1923 and January 1924 for greater democracy in the upper reaches of the party stressed the narrowness of his support, and his absence through illness from Lenin's funeral badly undermined his credibility as a successor in the popular view.

On the other hand, the coalition that opposed him – Zinoviev, Kamenev and Stalin – exerted immense influence. Zinoviev dominated the party organisation in Petrograd (renamed Leningrad in honour of the dead leader in 1924), and was head of the *Comintern*. Kamenev exercised similar influence in Moscow. Stalin, while occupying the unglamorous post of Commissar for Nationalities, had spent the past years insinuating himself into a strong position in the party bureaucracy. Not only was he a member of the party's inner cabinet (**Politburo**) but, like Zinoviev and Kamenev, he was also prominent in the executive bureau (**Orgburo**) and in the Commissariat of Workers' and Peasants' Inspection, which was responsible for the elimination of economic inefficiency and corruption. Above all, since 1922, Stalin had held the post of general secretary of the party's Central Committee. This enabled him to exert considerable control over party membership. In terms of the range of political weapons available to him, no other Bolshevik was the rival of Stalin.

Stalin's control over the party machinery

In 1924 it was widely assumed that the death of Lenin would result in a collective leadership of the Soviet Union. The reasons for the steady

Politburo: Officially a sub-committee of the Central Committee of the Communist Party of the USSR responsible for the definition and execution of government policy. In effect, under Stalin, the main executive body of Soviet government.

Orgburo: The body designed by the Central Committee to oversee the organisation and resourcing of government policies.

Anastas Mikoyan (1895–1978)
Joined the Bolsheviks in 1915. Central Committee member (1923), and consistent supporter of Stalin. Member of Politburo (1935–52). Subsequently supported Khrushchev (see page 160) and remained leading 'elder statesman' in USSR to the time of his death.

Lazar Kaganovich (1893–1991)
Supporter of Stalin in the struggle for the succession to Lenin. Secretary of the Central Committee (1924–25 and 1928–29). Active in the implementation of forced collectivisation (1929 onwards), and as a 'trouble-shooter' in various Soviet ministries (1935 onwards). Dismissed by Khrushchev (1957) and sent to manage a cement factory.

Mikhail Kalinin (1875–1946)
Close associate of Lenin from 1913, and supporter of Stalin in succession struggle. Member of the Politburo (1925–46). Titular head of state (1938–46).

Sergei Kirov (1886–1934)
Bolshevik activist from 1904. Central Committee member (1923). Head of Party in Leningrad (1925). Member of the Politburo (1930). Secretary of Central Committee (1934). Assassinated 1 December 1934.

Kliment Voroshilov (1881–1970)
Bolshevik from 1903, and played military role in Civil War. Helped Dzerzhinsky to form CHEKA. Commissar for Defence (1934–41). Marshal of the Soviet Union (1935), and thus a leading figure in the Soviet war effort between 1940–45. Chairman of the Presidium of the Supreme Soviet (1953–60), but subsequently lost influence.

decline of that form of political authority, and the emergence of Stalin's undisputed leadership, are complex. Neither the Stalinist explanation, that he offered the only correct analysis of the future course of the Soviet Union, nor Trotsky's bitter reflection that Stalin rode to power on a wave of war-weariness and reaction, is fully satisfactory. In large part the phenomenon must be explained by Stalin's political skill, and by his shrewd handling of the weapons at his disposal.

Foremost among these was the party machinery over which he exercised such control, and which he could use to assign supporters of his opponents to remote posts, while admitting to high office those upon whose support he could rely. The promotion to the Central Committee of Anastas Mikoyan (1923) and Lazar Kaganovich (1924), and to the Politburo of Vyacheslav Molotov and Mikhail Kalinin (1926), marked the emergence of a new school of 'Stalinist' Bolsheviks. The appointment of Sergei Kirov as head of the party in Leningrad (1926), formerly Zinoviev's stronghold, and of Kliment Voroshilov in Trotsky's former military office (1925), marked the extension of this tactic to key political areas. At this crucial point in the struggle, the Stalinists also enjoyed the support of the 'Rightist' wing of the party, headed by Nikolai Bukharin, Mikhail Tomsky and Alexei Rykov.

Creating the cult of Lenin

Secondly, Stalin showed great skill, both in the creation of a cult of 'Leninism', and in the formation of his own image as 'the best, the staunchest, the truest comrade-in-arms of Lenin'. His stage-management of Lenin's funeral was, according to historian Isaac Deutscher, in *Stalin: A Political Biography* (1966), 'calculated to stir the mind of a primitive, semi-oriental people into a mood of exaltation for the new Leninist cult'. The effect was compounded by Stalin's foundation of the Lenin Institute (January 1924), and by a series of calculated lectures on 'The Foundations of Leninism' delivered at the Communist University in Moscow (April 1924). Given his late conversion to Bolshevism, Trotsky was at a particular disadvantage in terms of Leninist orthodoxy.

Stalin's third great advantage lay in the blameless simplicity of his former private and political life. His image as the uncomplicated and dedicated peasant, married to the daughter of an old Bolshevik (1918), contrasted favourably with those of his more sophisticated rivals. As Commissar for Nationalities, moreover, he could claim the successful merging of the national republics into the Union of Soviet Socialist Republics (1922) as one of the greatest achievements of the revolution to date.

Lastly, Stalin benefited from a string of tactical errors by his most prominent opponents. Trotsky's attack upon such elements of Lenin's policy as the New Economic Policy, in his essays 'Lessons of October' (1924), was a miscalculation in the prevailing atmosphere of 'Lenin worship'. The refusal of both Trotsky and Zinoviev to publish Lenin's Testament, with its damaging verdict upon Stalin, saved Stalin from the most dangerous threat to his position. Indeed, the historian Roy Medvedev, in *On Stalin and Stalinism* (1983), has stressed that in the crucial early stages of the contest, 'Trotsky considered it beneath his dignity to engage actively in a struggle for power'. The belated union of Trotsky, Zinoviev and Kamenev (1926) in the so-called 'United Opposition' to Stalin, was unlikely to increase their credibility in the light of their mutual hostility a few months earlier.

It is important to remember how ill-equipped most members of the Politburo were to cope with a political opponent of Stalin's talents. As the historian Martin McCauley explains, in *Stalin and Stalinism* (1995), 'the Politburo opponents of Stalin had had little practical experience of politics before 1917. They had not mounted the party ladder step by step and had not had to claw their way up; 1917 made them, at a stroke, key political figures. They were singularly ill-equipped to recognise a party climber when they saw one.' From 1926 onwards, the position of this opposition became more and more hopeless. Isolated and outnumbered, Zinoviev lost his leadership of the Communist International, and all three leaders of the 'United Opposition' were voted off the Politburo by the end of the year. In October 1927, Trotsky and Zinoviev lost their places on the Central Committee, and were expelled altogether from the Party a month later, followed by 75 of their supporters. In January 1928, Trotsky began a period of internal exile in Soviet Asia, and was taking the first steps upon a road to banishment from the USSR that was only to end with his assassination in Mexico City in 1940.

1. Who were Stalin's rivals for the leadership of the USSR after the death of Lenin?

2. How convincing is the argument that Stalin's success in securing power in the 1920s owed more to the weaknesses and mistakes of his rivals than to his own strengths?

5.3 What were the main features of 'Stalinism'?

'Socialism in one country'

The leadership struggle of the late 1920s was certainly in part a clash of powerful personalities. Yet it was also a genuine dispute about the future path of Soviet Communism. The candidates, for instance, differed over the issue of democratic decision making within the party, over the pace at which the economic backwardness of the Soviet Union should be tackled, and over the roles allowed to independent merchants, manufacturers and peasants under the New Economic Policy. Above all, the dispute centred upon two alternative views of the future of Bolshevism.

Trotsky and his followers held fast to the theory of the 'permanency of revolution'. The revolution in Russia, they claimed, could not be regarded as an end in itself, but only as a vital link in the wider process of European and even world revolution. By its example, and with the continued assistance of the Soviet Union, the revolution would eventually lead to the general destruction of capitalism. Only then could the future of the Soviet system be secure. It was a view closely in accord with the expectations of Lenin right up to his death, but offered a prospect of further struggle that was profoundly unattractive after recent Russian sufferings. It was most discouraging in the light of recent socialist failures in Germany, Hungary and elsewhere.

Although Stalin seems to have subscribed to this view until late 1924, he then began to formulate an alternative usually known as the theory of 'socialism in one country'. By this he stressed that, despite the Soviet Union's present state of ruin and exhaustion, its immense resources would be sufficient for the construction of a stable socialist society, without external aid. Within two years, 'Trotskyism' was being officially condemned as 'a lack of faith in the strength and capabilities of the Russian revolution and a negation and repudiation of Lenin's theory of proletarian revolution'. While Stalin left open the possibility of future Soviet participation in a wider revolution, he made consolidation of the Russian achievement an unalterable priority.

The appeal of 'socialism in one country'

By the last two years of the decade, Stalin's thesis had won complete dominance over that of Trotsky as the official view of the Soviet government. Some writers have explained this as the natural consequence of Stalin's political victory within the party. It is now, however, more usual to reverse this reasoning and to see Stalin's political supremacy as the result, rather than the cause, of the wide acceptance of the theory of 'socialism in one country'. The American historian S.F. Cohen argues strongly in *The Soviet Union since Stalin* (1980) that Stalin's rise depended in large part upon his acceptance by the 'influentials' within the Party, and that a majority of them supported him 'less because of his bureaucratic power than because they preferred his leadership and policies. To some extent their choice doubtless expressed their identification with the General Secretary as a forceful practical politician.'

Why was the principle so widely accepted? Firstly, however unorthodox it was in pure Leninist terms, it was hard to dispute the practical logic of Stalin's approach in the light of contemporary European developments. Secondly, it offered the prospect of a future that lay wholly in Soviet hands, and involved little dependence upon forces beyond Soviet control. Lastly, it offered to the Soviet people as a whole the prospect of relief from the enormous suffering and perpetual struggle of the decade 1914–24. There was probably much justification in Trotsky's later conviction that the unreadiness of the people to undertake a further era of struggle contributed largely to his defeat in the leadership contest.

The 'Stalinist' state

Important as this all-embracing strategy was, the control of Stalin and his supporters depended upon effective and ruthless implementation of their policies. By the end of the 1920s, a complex system of state machinery had been established for this purpose.

● *The constitution of 1924*

The theoretical heart of Soviet political organisation in 1928 was the constitution introduced in 1924. It confirmed the merger of the component national units of the old Empire into the Union of Soviet Socialist Republics (USSR), and left each republic with the theoretical right to leave the Union if its 'non-Russian working class' so wished. In reality, any such wish would invariably be treated as the counter-revolutionary agitation of nationalist, bourgeois elements. At the head of the constitutional structure stood the All-Russian Congress of Soviets, with its executive Central Committee, and its élite **Presidium**, in which all major decisions were made. Below stretched a hierarchy of Soviets – at republican, provincial, district and local levels. All adults had the right to vote, except those deprived of citizenship. That right extended only to the election of local soviet members who, in turn, selected members for each higher soviet. The system thus constituted a complex filter to test the orthodoxy of each aspiring politician.

Presidium: A permanent administrative committee, especially in communist countries.

● *The Communist Party of the Soviet Union*

The articles of the constitution veiled the three main driving forces behind Soviet politics. The first of these was the Communist Party of the Soviet Union (Bolshevik), membership of which was an essential qualification for every potential political candidate. It was a body that had undergone great changes since the heady days of 1917. By 1922 a series of purges had rid the party of any serious ideological diversity, eliminating the last traces of Menshevik or Social Revolutionary opinion. In the later 1920s two more changes took place. The party grew steadily in size, from 1.3 million members in early 1928 to 3.5 million in January 1933. It also changed its composition – becoming less of a party of the workers, who constituted 48.6% of membership in the 1930s, and more a party of a new, Soviet-educated **intelligentsia**.

Intelligentsia: The most educated people in a country or community, especially those interested in the arts, philosophy and politics.

● *The political police*

The constitution also failed to indicate the growing importance of the government agencies for internal security. The State Political Administration

Genrikh Yagoda (1891–1938)
Prominent member and leader of Soviet security police. Joined CHEKA in 1920, becoming deputy head of GPU (1924) and chief of NKVD (1934), in which capacity he was responsible for initiating the purges. Dismissed in 1936, and arrested and executed two years later.

Nikolai Yezhov (1895–1939)
Commissar for Internal Affairs (1936), and thus responsible for the most brutal stages of the purges. Dismissed and appointed Commissar for Water Transport (1938), but soon arrested and executed as a scapegoat for the excesses of the purges.

Lavrenti Beria (1899–1953)
Of Georgian origin. Commissar for Internal Affairs (1938) and thus responsible for state security, and head of KGB. Politburo member (1939). Prominent in the Soviet war effort, and in the post-war establishment of Soviet control over eastern Europe. Arrested and executed after the death of Stalin.

(GPU or OGPU) was the successor of the CHEKA, the first communist secret police. Until his death in 1926, it was headed by the CHEKA's founder, Felix Dzerzhinsky. Its duties were vaguely defined but, as the historian Leonard Schapiro notes, in *The Communist Party of the Soviet Union* (1970), 'in practice, it never lacked the power to do whatever it was required to do by the party'. In July 1934, the OGPU was merged into a wider body, the People's Commissariat of Internal Affairs (NKVD). Under the leadership of Genrikh Yagoda (1934–36), Nikolai Yezhov (1936–38) and Lavrenti Beria (1938–53), the NKVD was the main tool for the internal policy of the Soviet state. It supervised many of the most important and dangerous projects of the Five-Year Plans, including the Pechora railway and the White Sea ('Belamor') Ship Canal, played a central role in the purging of the Party, and controlled a labour force perhaps as large as 10 million in the state's prison camps.

● *The army*

Another element in the practical government of the USSR – the army – was also brought under close party control by the end of the 1920s. Trotsky's hopes of a citizen militia, under direct proletarian control, were killed off by the necessities of the Civil War. In 1925 Trotsky himself was replaced as Commissar for War by Mikhail Frunze. A series of reforms in 1924–25 placed the political supervision of the army firmly in the hands of the Party's Central Committee. This confirmed the system of dual command whereby the military commanders worked alongside political commissars who took precedence over them in all political decisions. By 1933, all senior commanders and 93% of divisional commanders were party members. The degree of authority enjoyed by the Party was illustrated in October 1925 when Frunze was ordered by his political superiors to undergo a medical operation from which he died. This authority was, of course, to be confirmed spectacularly during the course of the political purges of the 1930s.

1. In what ways did Stalin and Trotsky disagree about the path that should be taken by Russian Communism after 1924?

2. What were the main agencies by which the Soviet state was controlled in the early years of Stalin's power?

3. Why was the principle of 'socialism in one country' popular with Soviet politicians in the late 1920s?

5.4 Why was the NEP abandoned in favour of a planned economy?

The most dramatic policy decision taken by the Stalinist establishment was the abandonment of Lenin's New Economic Policy, and of Bukharin's policy of 'the creep at a snail's pace' towards socialism. Apart from the obvious ideological hostility within the party to the NEP, it is also true that it had, by 1926, largely achieved its industrial purpose. The toleration of a degree of private economic activity had restored output in most major areas of the economy to pre-1914 levels, and the level of private trading outside agriculture dropped steadily from 42.5% of the total (1924–25) to 22.5% (1928). The alternative of rapid, forced industrial growth through centralised planning and control had been advanced by

Trotsky, Kamenev and Zinoviev in the mid-1920s, but had been resisted by Stalin as too great a departure from Leninism. Predictably, he now changed his view and broke with his former 'rightist' allies. Tomsky's leadership of the Soviet Trade Unions, Bukharin's post at the head of the *Comintern*, and Rykov's chairmanship of the Council of Commissars (*Sovnarkom*), all passed to Stalinists in June 1929. The public admission by the 'rightists' that their views were faulty (November 1929) marks the beginning of Stalin's undisputed power in the USSR which was to last until his death in 1953.

Why did Stalin now change course so abruptly to embrace the policies of his conquered opponents?

Although this has sometimes been seen as a cynical expression of his new-found political security, it is more likely that Stalin's change of course was a pragmatic response to the risk of substantial food shortages resulting from the so-called '**procurement** crisis' of 1927–28. Despite the decline in private industrial trade, in 1928 the independent peasant continued to cultivate 97.3% of the farmland of the Soviet Union. The difficulty in procuring sufficient grain supplies for the industrial towns arose in part from the inefficiency of many small, private farms, but also from the peasants' reluctance to deliver grain at the artificially low prices offered by the state. The result was a shortfall of 2 million tons of grain by 1927. This was potentially disastrous in view of the role played by urban hunger in the events of 1917. Under such circumstances, the policy of 'socialism in one country' risked falling at the first hurdle thanks, it was felt, to the greed of the richer peasants, the *kulaks*.

Procurement: The act of obtaining something, such as supplies, for an army or other organisation.

The principle of the Five-Year Plans

The introduction of the first Five-Year Plan, to run from 1928 to 1933, committed the USSR to the path of planned and centralised economic policy. A second Five-Year Plan followed (1933–37), while a third (1937–42) was disrupted by the outbreak of war. The overall aim of these plans was to match and to overhaul the economies of the advanced capitalist states in the shortest possible time. 'We are fifty or a hundred years

What is the value of such a photograph as a historical source?

A 'spontaneous' demonstration by peasants against the *kulaks*, 1930. Their banner declares 'We demand collectivisation and the extermination of the *kulaks* as a class'.

Collectivisation: The bringing of farms and factories under state ownership and control. The usual method is to combine a number of small farms or factories into one large one.

1. What were the main differences between the NEP and the policy of economic planning that Stalin introduced at the end of the 1920s?

2. Why did Stalin's government find it necessary in the late 1920s (a) to undertake a policy of rapid industrialisation and (b) to collectivise agriculture?

behind the advanced countries,' Stalin declared in 1931. 'We must make good this distance in ten years. Either we do it, or we shall be crushed.' In view of the fate that befell the USSR in 1941, the prediction proved to be uncannily accurate.

The main tool of the government in these tasks was the Central Planning Committee (*Gosplan*). In industry, the planned economy meant an expansion of output, an improvement of communications, and the discovery and exploitation of new resources – all carried out in accordance with predetermined production quotas. In agriculture it meant not only the forced grain procurements of 1928–29, but also a fundamental change in the agrarian life of the USSR. The way out of Russia's agrarian backwardness, Stalin declared to the party in December 1927, 'is to turn the small and scattered peasant farms into large united farms based upon cultivation of the land in common'. Although it was stressed that the party should proceed with caution, the statement spelled the end of the brief decade of liberation for the Russian peasant, and marked the beginning of the era of **collectivisation**.

5.5 What were the achievements of the planned economy?

Agriculture: the elimination of the kulaks

No branch of the Soviet economy was as sensationally affected by the policy of centralisation as agriculture. In the short term, the 'evils' of small-scale farming, inadequate equipment, and low proportions of the harvest reaching the market, were combated by rigorous and often brutal searches for, and confiscation of, grain stocks by local officials. In the longer term, under the Five-Year Plan, they were combated by the forcible collectivisation of peasant production. Some historians, such as Roy Medvedev, have seen this as a 'war against the peasant', as a logical extension of Bolshevik class struggle, eliminating the last class grouping in the Soviet Union that still earned its living from the ownership of property. Others have preferred to view it as a 'war between peasants', in which the government's main weapon against the prosperous *kulaks*, just under a million of the total peasantry, was the jealousy of the seven million poor peasants (*Bedniaks*), those without livestock or modern implements of any kind.

With the aid of party officials, police and army, a class war was waged in

'Sacking grain', an oil painting by the Soviet artist Tatyana Yablonskaya

At roughly what date, and for what purpose, would this picture have been painted?

the countryside between late 1928 and March 1930, involving the dispossession, deportation and often the murder of those designated as *kulaks*. By 1930, it was announced that 58% of peasant holdings were 'collectivised', although the term usually only meant that the land, livestock and equipment of the *kulaks* was handed over for communal use by the *Bedniaks*. The middle peasants (*Seredniaks*) were not only scared into the collectives by the fate of the *kulaks*, but left with no alternative form of livelihood.

In 1930, even Stalin seems to have taken fright at the 'pandemonium' reigning in rural Russia. By blaming local officials for over-zealousness, and authorising withdrawal from collectives, the government produced the sharp drop indicated in the table below. In reality, policy remained unchanged. The ruthless elimination of the private farmer continued until, in 1938, the Soviet Union boasted 242,000 collective farms. These farms subdivided into two basic types:

● The state farm (*Sovkhoz*) was entirely state property, on which peasants worked for wages.

● The collective farm (*Kolkhoz*) was a 'voluntary' co-operative, on which land and equipment were collectively owned by the peasantry. Until 1958, no collective farm possessed its own heavy machinery. Instead, they were served by 'machine tractor stations', whose state-owned machinery and state-controlled specialists were at the disposal of the peasantry.

Each *Kolkhoz* was committed to deliver a substantial proportion of its produce to the state, while on a *Sovkhoz* the produce was, in any case, state property.

Collectivisation

Year	Percentage of rural household collectivised
December 1928	1.7
October 1929	4.1
March 1930	58.0
September 1930	21.0
1931	52.7
1932	61.5
1933	65.6
1934	71.4
1935	83.2
1936	90.5

The cost of collectivisation

It is certain that, as the Soviet commentator Dmitri Volkogonov wrote in *Stalin, Triumph and Tragedy* (1991), 'Stalin's forced agrarian revolution condemned Soviet agriculture to decades of stagnation. The bloody experiment, costing millions of lives, brought the country no relief.' Destruction by rebellious peasants, the loss of *kulak* expertise, and the inexperience of many collective farm managers resulted in a sharp decline in many areas of production. Between 1928 and 1934 the cattle population of the USSR declined from 66.8 million to 33.5 million, the number of sheep and goats fell from 114.6 million to 36.5 million, and the number of horses from 34 million to 16.5 million. The historian David Christian notes in *Imperial and Soviet Russia: Power, Privilege and the Challenge of Modernity* (1997) that these policies 'condemned a whole generation of Russians to a meat-less diet', but in many rural areas the overall impact was far more serious than that. Grain shortages, combined with continued forced procurements, led to catastrophic rural famine. This was especially severe in the Ukraine and northern Caucasus region, where successive census figures between 1933 and 1938 suggest a death toll of around five million people.

Only slowly, as a government confident of victory showed more tolerance towards small-scale private enterprise among the peasantry, did livestock populations and rural living standards rise. Not until 1940 did figures for grain production match those of 1914. What short-term gains there were from collectivisation were enjoyed by Soviet industry, which benefited from a flow of surplus peasant labour into more attractive factory occupations, and by industrial workers, who gained a reliable, if not always plentiful, supply of cheap grain. A crucial part of the basis of Soviet industrial power was thus laid, at the cost of the peasantry. Stalin himself would later privately compare this battle with the later struggle for survival against the Germans, and there are important similarities between the two. In both cases, the Soviet state paid an enormous and terrifying price, even if it achieved an outstanding victory. The proportion of the harvest procured to feed urban workers in 1940 was nearly twice that procured in 1929; 40% compared with 22%. Alone among Russian governments in the 19th and early 20th centuries, Stalin's regime had truly broken the will and resistance of the Russian peasantry and subjected it to the wider purposes of the state.

Industry: the first Five-Year Plan

The task of the first Five-Year Plan, commenced in 1928, was nothing less than to lay the foundations for the transformation of Soviet society into an industrial force comparable to the United States of America. Its main emphasis fell upon the production of energy and of construction materials: coal, oil, electricity, iron, steel and cement. The rate of increase envisaged, averaging an annual rate of 20%, was hugely unrealistic, and the declaration (31 December 1932) that the plan had been completed in four years, was a propaganda exercise. Detractors might point to significant shortfalls, as in steel production (where only 62% of the quota was completed), in iron (59%), in heavy metallurgy (67.7%) and in consumer goods (73.5%).

A friendlier observer might still conclude that the achievement of 1928–32 was substantial:

● Machinery output increased four times, oil production doubled and electrical output in 1932 was 250% of the 1928 figure.

● 17 new blast furnaces were completed and 20 others modernised.

● 15 new rolling mills came into operation, with 12 others reconstructed.

The plan also produced some notable 'show pieces', such as the new centres of iron and steel production at Magnitogorsk in the Urals, and Kuznetsk in central Siberia. Also there was the building of the Dnieprostroi

The Five-Year Plans

	1927	1932	(goal)	1937	(goal)
Electricity (million kWh)	505	1,340	(2,200)	3,620	(3,800)
Coal (million tons)	35.4	64.3	(75)	128	(152.5)
Oil (million tons)	11.7	21.4	(22)	28.5	(46.8)
Iron ore (million tons)	5.7	12.1	(19)	?	?
Pig iron (million tons)	3.3	6.2	(10)	14.5	(16)
Steel (million tons)	4.0	5.9	(10.4)	17.7	(17)
Labour force (millions)	11.3	22.8	(15.8)	26.9	(28.9)

Dam, the biggest in Europe. Stalin's own criticism of the Dnieprostroi project in the mid-1920s – that it was like a poor peasant spending money on a gramophone instead of buying a cow – remained true, but he was now far more appreciative of the propaganda value of such achievements.

The second Five-Year Plan

The second Five-Year Plan, which ran its full course from 1933 to 1937, avoided some of the mistakes of the first. Its average annual target was a rather more reasonable 14% increase, and by virtue of a more experienced and better-trained workforce avoided at least some of the waste and poor quality of 1928–32. Priority continued to be given to heavy industry, but greater emphasis was now placed upon newer metallurgical resources, such as lead, zinc, nickel and tin. The second plan also concentrated more upon the improvement of Soviet communications. Railways were largely double-tracked, and this sphere of activity produced many of the plan's 'show pieces', such as the Moscow–Volga and Volga–Don Canals and the palatial Moscow Metro.

Before the end of the second Five-Year Plan, the deteriorating international situation called for more and more state investment to be diverted to rearmament and began to interfere with the projections of the planners. Whereas armaments had consumed only 3.4% of total expenditure in 1933, the figure had swollen to 16.1% in 1936, and in 1940, the third year of the third plan, accounted for 32.6% of government investment.

Nevertheless, there can be little doubt that the pre-war Five-Year Plans achieved their primary aims. By 1940, Soviet society and the Soviet economy had been transformed, especially in the following respects.

- Production of industrial goods was roughly 2.6 times greater than in 1928.

- Some key industrial sectors, such as iron, oil and electricity, had grown at an even faster rate.

- The size of the urban work force (32% of the total working population), relative to the peasantry (47%), had increased rapidly.

- The gross national product of the Soviet Union had increased by nearly 12% between 1928 and 1937, far more rapidly than those of Britain (2.5%), Germany (2.6%) or the USA (1.3%).

- Unemployment had dwindled from about 1.7 million in 1929 to virtually zero.

The plans may be criticised for lack of realism, for administrative inefficiency, and for the human cost they entailed, yet the goal of making the Soviet Union an industrial power was undoubtedly achieved.

1. In which main respects did Russian industry advance during the first and second Five-Year Plans?

2. How convincing is the argument that the collectivisation of agriculture was an 'ideological triumph, but an economic disaster'?

3. 'On balance, the first two Five-Year Plans were successful.' Do you agree with this statement?

5.6 What was the impact of Soviet economic policy upon the industrial workers?

The regimentation of industrial labour

Quite apart from the obvious deprivations suffered by much of the peasantry in the course of collectivisation, the Five-Year Plans also involved considerable sacrifice for many industrial workers. The initial stage of industrialisation rode roughshod over the individual freedom of the Soviet worker. The government's more ambitious projects might involve the mobilisation of labour to remote areas, working with inadequate equipment and without facilities and comforts of their own, closely supervised by NKVD 'shock brigades'. Unrealistic production quotas usually meant the neglect of safety precautions and the risk of prosecution as a 'saboteur' or 'wrecker', if the targets were not met.

The replacement of Tomsky by N.M. Shvernik as head of Soviet Trade Unions (June 1929) turned these bodies into virtual government departments unresponsive to the interests of the individual workers. Similarly, the worker found him or herself hedged in by a whole new body of Soviet law. Absenteeism from work without due cause became an offence punishable by loss of job, food rations and housing (November 1932). The internal passport system of Tsarist days was reintroduced (December 1932) to prevent the drift of labour from areas of greatest need. It must be doubtful whether the gradual and irregular introduction of such facilities as subsidised canteen meals and free medical attention fully offset these losses.

Prices and wages

Tremendous difficulties confront the historian who tries to make precise judgements about industrial standards of living in this period. The task, writes Alec Nove in *An Economic History of the USSR* (1969), 'is rendered almost impossible not only by the existence of rationing, price differences and shortages, but also queues, declines in quality and neglect of consumer requirements'. There can be little doubt, however, that the first years of collectivisation were accompanied by a wave of rises in food prices. In 1933 alone, official Soviet figures showed rises of 80% in the cost of bread and eggs, and of 55% in the cost of butter. Alec Nove is uncompromising in his description of the years 1928–33 as witnessing 'the most precipitous decline in living standards known in recorded history'.

Subsequent years saw a steady improvement in levels of wages and of consumer goods production. Nevertheless, western and Soviet research has agreed that 'real' wages in 1937 were not more than 85% of the 1928 level, an indication of how low the level was in 1933. Such statistics, of course, often hide more immediate problems. While the number of industrial workers doubled in 1927–32, the living space created for them increased by only 16%. Thus 'overcrowding, shared kitchens, frayed nerves, limited sanitation and poorly maintained buildings became a way of life for a whole generation of Soviet people' (Martin McCauley, *The Soviet Union 1917–1991*, 1993).

The worsening international situation after 1938 ended the temporary trend towards better living standards. Once again, the production of consumer goods was limited and government control over the workforce was tightened. Renewed labour legislation in 1940 lengthened the working week from five days to six, and made absenteeism, which came to include lateness for work by more than 20 minutes, a criminal offence punishable now by imprisonment.

The Stakhanovites

For a select few, the industrial drive could bring recognition and rewards. The abandonment in 1931 of earlier attempts to level wages paved the way for the privileged treatment of the most skilled and productive workers. This culminated in the '**Stakhanovite**' movement. For the average worker the 'Stakhanovites' were the cause of greater government pressure for increased production. Thus government decrees of 1936, 1938 and 1939 all demanded the raising of shift production quotas by as much as 50%. In general, it was not until the later 1950s, when the scars of war had been partly erased, that the Soviet government ceased to sacrifice the interests of the individual workers to those of the state.

'**Stakhanovite' movement**: This took its name from a Donbas miner, Alexei Stakhanov. In September 1935 he achieved the (probably contrived) feat of cutting 14 times his quota of coal. Such workers stood to gain rewards in many forms, such as higher salaries, access to better housing and to scarce consumer goods.

---

1. **In what ways did the living conditions of workers in Soviet industry change as a result of the Five-Year Plans?**

2. **'The Soviet state gained but the Soviet people lost as a consequence of the economic policies pursued by Stalin in the period 1928–1945.' Discuss this statement.**

5.7 Why did Stalin carry out far-reaching political purges in the 1930s?

Precedents for the purges

Having initiated an economic transformation of revolutionary proportions, Stalin set about the transformation of the Soviet Communist Party by a series of murderous and far-reaching purges (1934–38). In seeking to establish his motives we must first realise that purges in themselves were common in Soviet government. In addition to the purges carried out during Lenin's lifetime, 116,000 members had been expelled from the party in April 1929 on charges of 'passivity', 'lack of discipline', or as 'alien elements'. They were followed by another 800,000 in 1933. The Five-Year Plan also brought **'show trials'** in its wake, such as the Shakhti trial (1928) in which bourgeois mining specialists and foreign technicians were accused of sabotage. It is with some justification, therefore, that some historians refer to Soviet government between the wars as the 'permanent purge'. The 'Great Purge', like London's 'Great Plague', was merely an extreme example of a well-known phenomenon. It was striking in its extent, and in that its victims were not Whites or *kulaks*, but respected Communists and comrades of Lenin himself.

'Show trials': Trials held by the government for political purposes. They serve, not to establish the guilt or innocence of the accused, but to convey a propaganda message to the public and to foreign observers.

Motives for the purges

Stalin's precise motivation is not easy to establish. The official contemporary claim, that the party was infiltrated by 'Trotskyites', 'Zinovievites' and 'Bukharinites' who were all agents of international capitalism, can no longer be taken seriously. Nor does the claim that Stalin sought scapegoats for domestic economic problems explain the eventual scale of the purges. The most important factor was probably the growth of opposition within the party to Stalin's ruthless and divisive policies, especially to the pace and consequences of collectivisation. Trotsky wrote from exile in March 1933 that 'within the party and beyond, the slogan "Down with Stalin" is heard more and more widely'. N.M. Riutin was more explicit in 1932: 'The rights of the Party have been usurped by a tiny gang of unprincipled political intriguers. Stalin and his clique are destroying the communist cause.'

Stalin's political opponents still retained some influence. Bukharin for instance was now editor of *Isvestya*. Without doubt the emergence of Sergei Kirov, head of the party organisation in Leningrad, seemed to many to offer a capable and popular alternative to Stalin. The fact that five members of the ten-man Politburo in 1934 (Kirov, Kossyar, Kuibyshev, Ordzhonikidze and Rudzutak) died in various circumstances in the years of the purge, suggests that resistance to Stalin may even have been widespread in the top ranks of government. Nikita Khrushchev was probably close to the truth when he stated in his 'Secret Speech' of 1956 that Stalin had committed his excesses to boost and guarantee his own security, the continuation of his supremacy, and the supremacy of his policies within the Soviet Union.

Isvestya (Russian – 'News'): Daily newspaper founded in 1918 as the official organ of the Soviet government.

The murder of Kirov

The course of the Great Purge may be divided into three stages. The first stage can be dated from 1 December 1934, when the leader of the Leningrad administration, Sergei Kirov, was assassinated at his office. Historians remain uncertain as to whether or not Kirov died at Stalin's orders. Official Soviet sources successively blamed the crime on foreign capitalists, on Soviet 'rightists', and on Trotskyites, while many western writers conclude that Stalin was directly responsible for the murder of a potential rival. The historian Isaac Deutscher, on the other hand, suggests in *Stalin: a Political Biography* (1966) that Stalin may have been genuinely shocked by the event, but

Andrei Zhdanov (1896–1948)
Bolshevik from 1915 and member of the Central Committee in 1930. Secretary of Central Committee (1934). Head of Party in Leningrad (1934–44) after murder of Kirov. Politburo member (1939). Prominent in establishment of Cominform (1947). Died in mysterious circumstance (31 August 1948).

Andrei Vyshinsky (1883–1954)
Jurist and diplomat. Despite his initial sympathy for the Mensheviks, Vyshinsky enjoyed a brilliant judicial career under Stalin. Procurator of the RSFSR (1931–33); Procurator of the USSR (1935–39). Thus conducted many of the 'show trials' during the purges. Commissar for Internal Affairs (1949–52).

---

1. Who were the victims of Stalin's political purges?

2. What reasons were given at the time, and what explanations have been given by later historians, for the political purges that Stalin carried out in the 1930s?

3. In what ways did the nature of Stalin's purges change as the 1930s progressed?

---

turned it to his own purposes – much as the German Nazis had recently exploited the lucky stroke of the Reichstag fire.

A feature of this first stage was that the senior ranks of the party remained untouched. The 14 men executed for Kirov's murder were all minor figures and, although Kamenev and Zinoviev were imprisoned for 'opposition', they were not directly accused of the assassination. Nevertheless, the deaths at this time of Politburo member Valerian Kuibyshev (1935) and of the writer Maxim Gorky (1936) have never been satisfactorily explained, and may mark the beginning of the elimination of those who opposed Stalin's chosen path. In retrospect, this early stage also saw the establishment of the machinery and personnel necessary for the succeeding waves of purges. By appointing Andrei Zhdanov in Kirov's place in Leningrad, by placing Nikita Khrushchev at the head of the party in Moscow, and by subjecting the law courts to the influence of Andrei Vyshinsky as Chief Procurator, Stalin ensured reliable implementation of his orders in several vital areas of the administration.

The second stage was triggered in August 1936 by the arrest and execution of Kamenev, Zinoviev and 14 others. They were charged with plotting terrorist activities, including the death of Kirov, on behalf of the 'Trotskyite-Zinovievite Counter-Revolutionary Bloc'. Their trials produced several features soon to become familiar, notably the confessions of the accused and the implication in those confessions of other prominent figures. Why did these men confess? The application of torture, and of threats to their families, undoubtedly explains much. It has also been argued that many of the victims of the purges saw their deaths as a last service to a party to which they had dedicated their lives, and which they genuinely believed to be under attack. 'The loyalty of these men to the idea of The Party', writes historian Leonard Schapiro, 'was in the last resort the main reason for Stalin's victory.' The same writer also stresses the number of accused who refused to confess, and who therefore met their fate under more obscure circumstances.

Nevertheless, Stalin's control of events was not yet complete, as was demonstrated by the acquittal (September 1936) of Bukharin and Rykov on charges arising out of the earlier trials. This acquittal is often seen as the trigger of the third and greatest wave of purges. Among its first victims was Yagoda, head of the NKVD. One of the first tasks of his successor, Yezhov, was the preparation of renewed charges of treason and espionage against Bukharin and Rykov. The fact that the Commander-in-Chief of the Red Army, Marshal Tukhachevsky, and several other senior officers, were also tried and shot (June 1937) for plotting with Japan and Germany, indicated that the armed forces too were about to be 'cleansed'.

The last series of 'show trials' ran into 1938, involving the condemnation of 21 prominent Bolsheviks including Bukharin and Rykov. These, however, were merely the tip of the iceberg of suspicion and implication that involved the friends, families and subordinates of the accused. Suspicion reached into every area of Soviet life. No reliable figures as to the extent of the purges are possible, of course. It is extremely unlikely that the total number of deaths can be estimated at less than hundreds of thousands, while the total population of the USSR's penal camps (prisons) by 1940 has sometimes been set as high as 10 million.

Did the political purges of the 1930s strengthen or weaken Stalin's regime?

The establishment of a Stalinist élite
When the great tide of political persecution receded in 1938, ending with the execution of Yezhov and other NKVD functionaries, two major

changes in Soviet government were noticeable. Firstly, the political position of Stalin himself was almost unchallengeable. All possible sources of opposition, in the party, in the armed forces, among economic and political theorists, had been crushed. 'Every man in the Politburo,' wrote Leonard Schapiro, 'was a tried and proved follower of the leader, who could be relied upon to support him through every twist and turn of policy. Below the Politburo nothing counted.'

Secondly, the Soviet Communist Party, which had borne the brunt of the purges, was transformed. It was not just a matter of personnel, a substitution of Zhdanov, Khrushchev, Voroshilov and Molotov for Zinoviev, Kamenev, Bukharin and Rykov. Stalin had effectively destroyed the revolutionary generation of Russian communists. Of the 139 Central Committee members in 1934, over 90 had been shot. Of 1,961 delegates to the 17th Party Congress in the same year, 1,108 were arrested in the purges.

Foreign communists living in Russia also suffered heavily. The Hungarian revolutionary leader Béla Kun was among the NVKD's victims. Of Lenin's Politburo, only Stalin and Trotsky remained alive, the latter under sentence of death passed in his absence. Stalin knew, as Isaac Deutscher has explained, 'that the older generation of revolutionaries would always look upon him as a falsifier of first truths, and usurper. He now appealed to the young generation which knew little or nothing about the pristine ideas of Bolshevism and was unwilling to be bothered about them.'

In short, a generation of officials replaced a generation of revolutionaries. One should not overlook the fact, however, that this new generation supported their leader with enthusiasm and affection. Stalin did not rule the Soviet Union in the last 15 years of his life through terror alone, but enjoyed, as the historian David Christian stresses, 'the support, in particular, of younger party members, industrial managers, and government and police officials who benefited from the changes of the 1930s'.

The impact of the purges upon Soviet security
Apart from the human cost, the whole security of the Soviet Union was nearly undermined as the price of this transformation. The Red Army, in particular, paid a terrible price for arousing Stalin's mistrust. Three marshals out of five, and 13 army commanders out of 15 died. Ninety per cent of all Soviet generals, 80% of all colonels, and an estimated 30,000 officers below the rank of colonel lost their posts and often their lives. The difficulties experienced in the 'Winter War' with Finland in 1939–40 may be traced directly to the loss of so much military expertise in the purges.

The foreign relations of the Soviet Union were also bound to be adversely affected. Foreign powers were offered the alternatives of viewing the Soviet Union as a state riddled with treason, if the charges against purge victims were accurate, or as a power led by a madman if the charges were false. Lastly, the less tangible legacy of the purges may be traced in the insularity and siege mentality that characterised Soviet society for the next two generations. Such responses were natural in a society led to believe that it was under assault from **capitalists**, **fascists**, **imperialists** and **renegade communists** alike. This legacy also survived for years in 'a grotesque fear of initiative and responsibility in all grades of the administration' (Deutscher). This was a direct result of the personal peril that accompanied any position of responsibility during the years of Stalin's purges.

Capitalists: Supporters of the economic system of capitalism, which is based on the theory that possession of capital or money leads to the making of profits through the power of investment.

Fascists: Supporters of a highly nationalistic political ideology, aiming to overthrow democracy and set up a dictatorship. Central to such groups is the heroic leader and the extensive use of propaganda.

Imperialists: Supporters of the belief that one nation should take over other areas as colonies or dependent territories.

Renegade communists: Supporters of communism who abandon the political beliefs that they used to have, and accept opposing or different beliefs.

1. What were the results of Stalin's purges for the government of the USSR?

2. 'There was no purpose behind the political purges of the 1930s other than the consolidation of Stalin's personal authority.' To what extent to you agree with this statement?

5.8 Did Stalinism achieve a social revolution within the USSR?

Historian Isaac Deutscher writes that 'Stalin offered the people a mixed diet of terror and illusion.' Alongside the terror of the purges, Stalin created the illusion of a true dawn of socialism represented by the formulation of a new Soviet constitution in 1936. The theoretical basis of the document was the assumption that victory over the *kulaks* had ended the decade and a half of class struggle in Russia and that a truly socialist order had now been constructed.

Government and the rights of the individual

By comparison with its predecessor, the 'Stalin Constitution' extended the jurisdiction of the central, federal government. Moscow now exercised control, through All-Union ministries, over all important areas of administration, such as defence and foreign affairs. This left responsibility for such relatively minor matters as elementary education to the constituent republics. This dominance was confirmed by Moscow's overall control of the budget, and by the pervasive influence of the Party. The chief legislative body of the USSR continued to be the Supreme Soviet, whose Presidium continued to exercise all major executive functions of the state.

As a further indication of the end of class warfare, clergymen, former Tsarist officials, and other 'class enemies', now enjoyed full civil rights again. Among the rights now guaranteed to Soviet citizens were:

- freedom of speech
- freedom of the press
- the rights to work, to rest and leisure
- the right to education
- the right to maintenance in old age and in sickness.

The constitution stated quite clearly that these rights existed only if exercised 'in conformity with the interests of the working people and in order to strengthen the socialist system'.

Soviet educational achievements

Overall, the educational achievement of the Soviet government between the wars was impressive. The introduction of compulsory primary education (July 1930) resulted in the doubling of the Soviet Union's primary school population, from nine million to 18 million, between 1920 and 1933. Meanwhile, the number of secondary pupils rose from 0.5 million (1922) to 3.5 million (1933). In 1941, the total school population of the USSR was around 35 million. The greatest achievement was the victory over the traditional peasant curse of illiteracy. This afflicted 75% of the population in 1917, but was rare by the outbreak of the Second World War, by which time 70,000 public libraries had opened in the Soviet Union.

Who received this education?
The drive to educate children of working-class origin to the exclusion of others was abandoned in the early 1930s to meet the demands of the Five-Year Plan. The proportion of women in higher education rose sharply, and by 1940, 58% of all higher education places (40% in engineering and 46% in agriculture) were held by females. The nationalities of the USSR, on the other hand, were not evenly represented. In the course of the 1930s, Russians, Ukrainians and Jews accounted for 80% of all the places in higher education.

The family

As social stability became the government's priority, the family began to revert to its traditional role. As an institution it had been under severe

Komsomol: Shortened form of Russian words meaning 'Communist League of Youth'. Youth organisation founded in 1917 (although the name only dates from 1926) with the aim of preparing youth for active membership of the Soviet Communist Party.

pressure in the 1920s, from revolutionary notions such as free love, free divorce and legalised abortions. It was also under pressure from the efforts of such party organisations as the Communist League of Youth (*Komsomol*), to divert the allegiance of the young. A fall in the official birth rate and a rise in crime figures prompted an official change of course. Decrees, such as that which established parental responsibility for the misdemeanours of their children (May 1935), and that which made abortion illegal except upon medical grounds (June 1936), reinstated the family as the basis of society. The role of the mother was also traditionalised by a system of rewards for child bearing. A mother of five children received the 'medal of motherhood', while the mother of ten became a 'mother heroine'.

Religion and the state

The most serious opposition to the Bolsheviks in their attempts to create a new society had come from established religions, especially from the Orthodox Church. Marxists could not easily tolerate a philosophy that stressed the importance of the next world at the expense of material conditions in this one. On the other hand, the creation of martyrs was counter-productive. It was assumed that religious belief, being a feature of the old society, would lose all purpose as the new society took shape. The Soviet compromise was thus to strip the churches of all material possessions and of all state power, but to enshrine in successive constitutions the right to freedom of worship, alongside the right to have no religious beliefs at all.

Thus, in 1918, Church and state were formally separated. This involved the confiscation of all Church property, but allowed congregations to lease back buildings from the state, and to maintain priests for their worship. In 1921 public religious instruction was declared illegal for all citizens under 18 years of age, and churchmen were deprived of civil rights as 'non-productive workers'. After an initial period of resistance, which saw the imprisonment of religious leaders for anti-communist utterances, and for refusal to surrender Church property, the Orthodox Church and most other religious communities settled into a period of uneasy co-existence with the Soviet regime. Undoubtedly, the political influence of the Orthodox Church was destroyed. There is much evidence to suggest, however, that its spiritual influence survived, diminished but unbroken. The Orthodox Church received its reward for its patience during the war years of 1941–45, when the need for national unity caused the government to restore some of its former autonomy.

1. In what areas of Soviet life had Stalin's regime brought about the most important changes by the end of the 1930s?

2. The 'Stalin Constitution' of 1936 suggested that all Soviet citizens were now equal in a classless society. How true was this?

5.9 What factors guided Soviet foreign policy between the two world wars?

The theory of Communist foreign policy

In the immediate aftermath of the October/November Revolution, many Soviet theorists did not anticipate any problems in the formulation of foreign policy. In their view the Russian revolution was the forerunner of the general collapse of capitalism, and heralded the end of international tensions and disputes, which were the product of capitalist rivalries. Instead, in the next three years they witnessed the traumas of civil war and of foreign intervention. To this was added the total failure of those Communists who, in Germany and in Hungary, attempted to follow the Russian example. By the conclusion of the peace treaties in Paris, Russia's international situation was precarious. It was isolated, surrounded by hostile powers, and in great economic difficulties. Thus, the central aim of Soviet foreign policy between the wars was simple and singular: it was survival.

Two principal routes to survival suggested themselves in the 1920s. For Trotsky, and for many others on the left of the Bolshevik Party, the favoured foreign policy was collaboration with foreign revolutionaries to undermine the strength of the capitalist regimes. The consolidation of Stalin's power, however, saw an irreversible drift away from this internationalism. In foreign, as in domestic, policies, Stalin saw the best hope for Soviet survival in the development of material strength. Where normal co-existence with capitalist states served Soviet interests, he was quite willing to accept it.

Communist foreign policy in practice, 1921–1929

The fact remained that the Soviet Union had no natural allies among the European powers, no states with whom it had an overall community of interests. They remained capitalist powers and, according to the historian George Kennan in *Soviet Foreign Policy, 1917–1941* (1978), 'the enmity Stalin bore towards the western bourgeois world was no less fierce than that of Lenin'. Thus, Soviet contacts with Britain and with France remained ambiguous. The declaration of G.V. Chicherin, Commissar for Foreign Affairs (October 1921), that Russia was willing to recognise and honour Tsarist debts to other powers, helped to counteract initial hostility. In the years that followed, the Soviet government secured several important benefits from the victorious powers. A trade agreement was secured with Britain in March 1921, and Britain, France and Italy officially recognised the Soviet regime in 1924. Mutual suspicion about long-term motives, however, made closer relations impossible. The incident of the so-called 'Zinoviev Letter', purporting to contain instructions to British agitators for political and economic disruption (October 1924), showed the fragility of Soviet credibility. Although it was never proved genuine, many conservatives remained convinced that Russia still harboured ambitions for international revolution. Indeed, between 1927 and 1929, all official relations between Britain and the Soviet Union were severed.

The Treaty of Rapallo

Superficially, the greatest successes for Soviet diplomacy were scored in dealings with Germany. In the short term, the signature of the Treaty of Rapallo (April 1922) seemed a triumph. The establishment of full diplomatic relations with Germany ended Soviet isolation and ensured that Germany would drop claims for the repayment of Tsarist debts. The military and economic advice gained from Germany was invaluable in the post-revolutionary chaos. In the longer term, however, the appearance of triumph was deceptive. The Treaty of Rapallo provided a sharp shock to the allies, and their assumption that it concealed a deeper relationship between Germany and the Soviet Union soured Soviet relations with the west until 1941. Furthermore, Rapallo was not an alliance, but merely an arrangement useful to two isolated and apprehensive states. Russian relations with Germany continued to seesaw for a decade afterwards. Germany's apparent integration into the Versailles 'system', through the Locarno Pact and the Dawes Plan, could be interpreted in Moscow as evidence of growing capitalist solidarity. Conversely, incidents such as the failed communist rising in Germany in October 1923 served to renew fears of revolutionary internationalism.

Stalin's reaction to Nazism

Although, in retrospect, the rise of Adolf Hitler was a turning point in Soviet–German relations, it does not seem that Stalin was immediately aware of the fact. Contemporary Japanese expansion in China probably

Nazism: Shortened form of the German *Nationalsozialist*. The National Socialist Party in Germany, led by Adolf Hilter from 1920 and in power 1933–45. The ideology and practice of Nazism includes racist nationalism and state control of the economy.

League of Nations: Association of self-governing states and dominions created as part of the 1919 Peace Treaty, 'in order to promote international co-operation and to achieve international peace and security'. The USA did not join, and the association's failure to deal effectively with outbreaks in Japan, Italy and Germany in the 1930s meant that it has lost its relevance by the outbreak of the Second World War. It was subsequently replaced by the United Nations.

1. What different ideas did Soviet leaders put forward in the 1920s about preserving the security of the Soviet Union?

2. How serious was the foreign threat to the Soviet Union in the 1920s and 1930s?

3. In what ways, if any, was Soviet foreign policy changed by the rise of Nazism in the 1930s?

made it unclear whether the greater threat to Soviet territory lay in the west or in the east. **Nazism**, in the view of Soviet theorists, was not a new phenomenon. It was the inevitable death agony of capitalism caused by the recent economic crisis. To seek allies among the capitalist powers against a purely capitalist threat would thus be absurd. It is not clear at what point Stalin changed his view of Nazism. Several commentators have attached great importance to the non-aggression pact between Germany and Poland in January 1934. This suggested that, whatever the nature of Nazism, it was making common cause with Russia's enemies to threaten the domestic security of the Soviet Union.

Certainly 1934 saw a major change in the tactics of Soviet diplomacy. Firstly, the Soviet Union showed great interest once more in understandings with western states. It concluded mutual assistance pacts with Czechoslovakia and France (May 1935). In the course of these negotiations the USSR also undertook to enter the **League of Nations** (September 1934). Such moves probably had the dual motive of scaring Hitler into a revision of aggressive plans and ensuring that, if he did start a conflict, it would be fought on several fronts, and not concentrated against the USSR.

Lastly, the nature of Moscow's advice to foreign communist parties changed radically. For a decade they had been consistently instructed that socialists and social democrats were capitalist allies and false friends. Now they were advised and instructed to form 'popular front' alliances with those parties, in order to present more effective opposition to the real enemy, Fascism.

There can be little doubt that by 1935 the Soviet government had clearly identified the threat posed by Nazism. They had not, however, identified any reliable ally against that threat. It is hard to resist the conclusion, that Stalin sought international security without any real conviction that it could be found anywhere other than in the industrial and military strength of the Soviet Union itself.

5.10 By what means did the Soviet government re-establish political control and economic stability after the Second World War?

The enormous triumph of the Soviet Union in defeating the Nazi invaders was obviously achieved at a huge cost. Nevertheless, it left the Soviet government stronger than it had ever been before. The prestige of the regime, and especially the personal prestige of Stalin himself, was at an unprecedented level. In effect, there was no challenge within the Soviet Union to Stalin's authority, or to the policies that he put forward. In addition, the advance of Soviet troops deep into the states of eastern Europe broke the ring of hostile powers that had surrounded the Soviet Union before the war, and gave it greater territorial security than it had ever enjoyed hitherto. To many, this seemed to provide the perfect opportunity for the liberalisation of Soviet politics, now that the regime was no longer under such direct threat. Instead of devising new policies, however, Stalin reacted to this victory by implementing the old ones with renewed energy and determination. The years between 1945 and 1953 came to constitute what the historian Martin McCauley has called the period of 'High Stalinism'.

In general, historians have viewed these final years of Stalin's rule in one of two ways. Contemporary commentators, and many since, have seen this as the high point of his career, as a period of 'mature dictatorship' in which Stalin at last exercised the kind of power to which he had always aspired.

More recently, others have seen these final years as the ultimate proof of Stalin's failure. In pursuing the same policies as before the war, despite the strengths of his personal position, Stalin demonstrated the misconceptions upon which his government was based. He continued to be driven by the same mistrust, by the same neurotic fears of enemies at home and abroad, as had haunted him in the 1930s. Such commentators see this as the main explanation for the rapid abandonment of so much of the structure of Stalinism in the weeks and months immediately after his death. The historian Chris Ward, in *Stalin's Russia* (1993), paints just such a picture of the final years of Stalinism. 'This was no self-confident tyrant in charge of a smoothly functioning totalitarian machine, but a sick old man, unpredictable, dangerous, lied to by terrified subordinates [and] presiding over a ramshackle bureaucracy.'

How effectively did the Soviet Union overcome the economic damage of the war?

The greatest and most immediate challenge facing the Soviet government was to overcome the material and economic damage that the war had inflicted upon the Soviet Union. The scale of the task can hardly be overstated.

- 70,000 villages in the occupied regions of the Soviet Union had been completely destroyed.

- 17 million head of cattle had been lost.

- 65,000 kilometres of railway track had been destroyed.

- 50% of all urban living space available in the pre-war years had now ceased to exist.

- An estimated 25 million Soviet citizens were homeless.

Labour shortages, of course, were acute. An estimated nine million Soviet citizens had died in combat or in prisoner of war camps. Many, many more had died at the hands of the occupying forces, so many that the Soviet commentator Dmitri Volkogonov (*Stalin, Triumph and Tragedy*, 1991) has put the total Soviet death roll as high as 26 million. With combat losses taking such a heavy toll upon the male population, women constituted 47% of the Soviet labour force in 1950. On the other hand, military victory provided some compensations for these disadvantages. The creation of a block of client states in eastern Europe, for instance, not only provided territorial security, but also created enormous opportunities for economic plunder. Alone among the victorious powers, the Soviet Union demanded huge **reparation payments** from Germany, amounting to $10,000 million (at 1938 values), and collected much of this by stripping industrial installations in Germany to transfer the materials to the USSR. Similar tactics were applied in Hungary, Romania and Bulgaria. In addition, the domestic labour force was enhanced by the contribution of two million German prisoners of war.

The challenge of reconstruction was confronted by the Fourth Five-Year Plan, running from 1946 to 1950. A further Five-Year Plan operated from 1951 to 1955 to consolidate the process of recovery. Naturally the priority of these plans was to rectify the damage suffered by the Soviet economy during the war years and, in industrial terms, the plans achieved an enormous degree of success. In all major areas of the industrial economy, 1940 levels of production had not only been restored by 1950, but had been surpassed by some margin.

- Steel production stood at 27.3 million tons, compared to 18.3 million.

Reparation payments: Payments made by a defeated state to compensate the victorious state(s) for damage or expenses caused by the war.

- Oil production was 37.9 million tons, compared to 31.1 million.

- National income was 61% higher than the pre-war level.

- Industrial wages were nearly twice the 1940 level.

These impressive statistics did not extend to the agrarian economy. Indeed, in terms of Soviet agriculture, the Fourth Five-Year Plan has been viewed by some historians as a missed opportunity. Martin McCauley emphasises, for example, in *The Soviet Union 1917–1991* (1993), that in the atmosphere of post-war euphoria, the opportunity existed to relax some of the pressures that had been applied to the Russian peasantry to force them into collectivisation in the first place. There was no need to return to the 1930s. Nevertheless, the Soviet government after 1945 did largely maintain the policy of building high industrial productivity upon the hardship of the peasants. Much of this pressure was exerted in order to rebuild the system of collective farms ravaged by the war. A decree of September 1946 ordered the return to the collective system of large quantities of livestock and of land that had slipped out of the control of the collective farms during the disruption caused by the fighting. Machinery, of course, was also in short supply and, with the Plan's primary emphasis placed upon the reconstruction of industry, the grain harvest of 1946 was less than half that of 1940. Even by 1950, grain production had still not reached the levels achieved immediately before the war.

Agricultural recovery was further handicapped by the adoption of some bizarre biological theories. Radical Soviet biologists – of whom T.D. Lysenko and V.R. Vilyams were the most notable – rejected orthodox theories of genetics. They replaced them with theories of their own which seemed to be more in line with socialist ideology. This new 'agrobiology' was also in line with the government's preference for 'Russian' thinking, free from humiliating intellectual reliance upon the West. The problem was that the theories did not work. Despite dangerous falls in production levels, Lysenko's theories remained in fashion until the 1960s and were also employed in communist China where, between 1959 and 1961, they contributed to a catastrophic famine.

The re-establishment of political authoritarianism

Several factors combined to ensure that the domestic political atmosphere would be as tense as it had been immediately before the war. In the first place, the armed conflict with Germany quickly gave way to the diplomatic confrontation with the western powers that became known as the Cold War. Once again the Soviet government had reason to regard with suspicion anyone who had recently been in contact with foreign political influences. This was particularly tragic for those who had been taken prisoner, or who had been compelled to perform forced labour in Germany during the war. Instead of liberation and a welcome return to their homeland, many of these found that they were regarded with extreme suspicion. Many were marched straight from their POW camps into the labour camps of the NKVD and about two million prisoners of war, aware of the fate that awaited them, had to be forcibly returned to the Soviet Union by the British and Americans who had 'liberated' them in Germany.

In addition, Stalin was as determined as ever to eliminate any threats to his personal authority which may have survived the war, or which might actually have been generated by the war. One such threat emanated from the army, which had covered itself with glory in the course of the conflict. Many men and women had been admitted to the ranks of the Party solely on the basis of wartime acts of bravery, and the need was felt now to restore the ideological integrity that had been diluted by this policy. An average of

100,000 expulsions from the Party took place each year between 1945 and Stalin's death in 1953. A greater potential threat to Stalin's position was posed by some of the military commanders who had played the most prominent roles in achieving victory. Stalin quickly tackled the direct political influence of such men by dissolving (September 1945) the State Defence Committee, predominantly staffed by leading military figures. The greatest of them all, Marshal Zhukov, defender of Leningrad and victor of Stalingrad, was severely criticised for 'awarding himself the laurels of principal victor'. There is even some evidence that plans were made to bring trumped-up treason charges against him but, in a rare example of restraint, Stalin was content to reduce Zhukov to a less prestigious military position.

In the final years of Stalin's life, nevertheless, there were clear signs that he was planning a further round of political purges, similar to those of the 1930s. The death of Andrei Zhdanov, the Party chief in Leningrad, was closely followed by the mysterious 'Leningrad Affair'. In 1949, all five Party secretaries in Leningrad, along with many other local officials, were arrested and subsequently executed. Recalling that the purges of the 1930s had begun with the murder of the Party chief in Leningrad, some historians have speculated that Zhdanov himself may have been a victim of Stalin's habitual mistrust. Elsewhere many prominent and established 'Stalinists', such as Molotov, Mikoyan and Khrushchev, were removed from office, although they returned to positions of influence shortly afterwards. The most ominous signs came in early 1953, with the announcement in the Soviet press that a plot had been discovered within the **Kremlin** itself. It was announced that doctors within the Kremlin medical centre were plotting, in the pay of the western powers, to murder leading Soviet politicians. Indeed, they were already responsible for the deaths of two such leaders: Zhdanov (died in 1948) and A.S. Shcherbakov, who had died suddenly in 1945. A new purge seemed to be in the offing but, within days, Stalin himself was dead. Almost immediately, it was admitted by his successors that the so-called 'Doctors' Plot' was a fabrication.

More serious and practical problems faced the Soviet government in imposing its authority upon the territories that had been added to the USSR in eastern Europe. This was particularly true in the Baltic territories of Estonia, Latvia and Lithuania – independent states from 1918 to 1939 and then, after a very brief Soviet occupation, subjected to German occupation until 1944. Now designated as republics of the Soviet Union, these territories scarcely welcomed their new status. To overcome their reluctance, the Soviet government pursued policies that were far harsher than the policies of 'russification' undertaken by the Tsarist government here and elsewhere 50 years earlier (see Chapter 2). Over 200,000 inhabitants of the three former states were deported and imprisoned immediately for the roles that they had played during the German occupation, and another wave of deportations in 1949 removed a further 150,000. What amounted to a partisan war of resistance took place in the territories between 1945 and 1952, with casualties running into thousands. To replace those who were deported, and to correct the political balance, Russian immigration took place on a similar scale. 180,000 Russians were settled in Estonia (1944–47) and 400,000 in Latvia (1945–59). By 1953 the proportion of native Latvians in the population of the Soviet republic stood at a mere 60%.

Kremlin: Location of the Soviet central government in Moscow.

The control of Soviet culture

The third major feature of Soviet policy during these years is perhaps a little more difficult to understand. In the course of the war the Soviet Union had been involved to an unprecedented degree in the politics of western Europe and of the USA. Its leaders, its intellectuals, and even many of the ordinary soldiers had come into contact with westerners more closely than at any stage in the 1920s and 1930s. Rather than creating a bridge between the USSR and the West, however, Stalin was determined to reverse this process, and to ensure that his own vision of Soviet ideology and culture would not be polluted by ideas imported from the West. Those who appeared to favour such ideas were branded 'cosmopolitan', and the government launched an unswerving programme of 'anti-cosmopolitanism'.

A key figure in the enforcement of this policy was Andrei Zhdanov, an increasingly powerful figure after the war until his death in 1948. In the view of Zhdanov and his accomplices 'servility towards everything foreign' became a prime cultural, and therefore political, crime. Writers, musicians and artists were strongly discouraged from taking a favourable attitude towards western culture, and from implying that major figures in Russian culture owed any great debt to the culture of western Europe. Conversely, the official line insisted upon the superiority of Russian culture, and upon its independence from outside influences. Magazines were closed down because of their editorial policies, and the careers of writers were wrecked, notably that of the poet Anna Akhmatova. Even established masters of Soviet culture, loaded with awards in the 1930s, were brought to account. The greatest Russian film-maker of the era, Sergei Eisenstein, died in disgrace because of 'ignorance of historical facts' that he had demonstrated in the last part of his great film 'Ivan the Terrible'. World famous composers, such as Shostakovich and Prokofiev, were similarly criticised and penalised by the Soviet government.

More dangerous and disturbing was the fact that this climate of intellectual isolation also extended to industry and science. We have already seen some of the consequences of its operation in the field of biology and crop-science. Martin McCauley has summarised the intellectual atmosphere that existed in the Soviet Union at this time. 'It was suddenly found that Russians had discovered everything worth discovering. Anything their geniuses had not hit upon was not worth knowing or was simply false. Relativity theory, quantum mechanics, genetics were nothing more than pseudo-sciences.'

5.11 To what extent were Stalin's policies a logical continuation of the work of Lenin?
A CASE STUDY IN HISTORICAL INTERPRETATION

Totalitarian: A political system in which there is only one political party, and this party controls everything and does not allow any opposition parties.

Objective historical assessment of Stalin's work is relatively new. As recently as 1983, Martin McCauley, in *Stalin and Stalinism*, could still write that 'Stalin has left an indelible mark on Soviet development, and his shadow extends to the present day. The system of rule he evolved is essentially intact in the USSR.' So fundamental was Stalin's contribution to the construction of the Soviet Union, and to the superpower confrontation of the Cold War, that historical judgements were frequently influenced by the author's political standpoint.

This was never truer than in the Soviet Union itself during Stalin's period in power. Exercising complete control over a **totalitarian** regime, Stalin and his successors could ensure that his work was represented in whatever light was most desirable. It was essential to maintain Stalin's claims that he had been among the closest revolutionary colleagues of Lenin, and that he was now the right person to continue the ideology of Marx and Lenin. Such a claim conferred an enormous degree of political credibility and moral authority upon his policies and decisions. As early as

1924 Stalin published a short work entitled *The Foundations of Leninism*, in which he ascribed many of his own ideas, including the principle of 'socialism in one country', to Lenin. The re-writing of the history of the revolution was seriously underway by 1934, and culminated in 1939 with the publication of the *Short Course of the History of the Russian Communist Party (Bolsheviks)*, which remained the official version of the Party's and the revolution's history for the next two decades.

'Lenin's Banner'. Poster by Gustav Kluzis, 1933.

Со знаменем Ленина победили мы в боях за Октябрьскую революцию. Со знаменем Ленина добились мы решающих успехов в борьбе за победу социалистического строительства. С этим же знаменем победим в пролетарской революции во всём мире.   И. Сталин,

Upon Stalin's death in 1953, an important shift took place in the official Soviet view of the former leader. His successors in power were ready to condemn Stalin's methods, but not to reject the end-product of his work, nor to dissociate it from the work and aims of Lenin. Stalin, it was now declared, had pursued the same fundamental aims as the original Bolsheviks, although he had erred in the 1930s by allowing the **'cult of personality'** to develop and by taking savage and unwarranted actions against other Communists in the purges. This compromise was summarised by Nikita Khrushchev in a speech in 1957.

'Cult of personality': A term used to describe a form of political leadership in which the virtues and achievements (real or invented) of the leader are allowed to obscure the political principles on which the regime is based.

> 'It is, of course, a bad thing that Stalin launched into deviations and mistakes, which harmed our cause. But even when he committed mistakes and allowed the laws to be broken, he did that with the full conviction that he was defending the gains of the Revolution, the cause of socialism.'

In the last years of Soviet power, however, the rejection of 'Stalinism' became more explicit. In 1988 and 1989 the government of Mikhail Gorbachev went so far as to overturn the legal verdicts against many of those condemned as traitors and criminals during Stalin's purges.

Historians writing in western Europe, or in the USA, were not under direct political pressure of this kind, but many were impressed by the impetus, and sometimes by the achievements, of the Soviet revolution as a whole. It seemed undeniable, in the 1960s and 1970s, that Soviet leaders between the world wars had engineered one of the most monumental achievements of the 20th century. Besides, where these western writers adopted a '**determinist**' view of history, it was impossible to believe that the forces that created the revolution in Russia could have been deflected or re-routed to any significant extent by the will of one man. E.H. Carr, the most prolific English writer on Soviet history, certainly wrote with such assumptions in mind. In *A History of Soviet Russia and The Russian Revolution from Lenin to Stalin* (1979), he concentrated less upon the personal rule of Stalin, and more upon the dynamic impetus of the original revolution in Russia. Far from diverting those revolutionary forces, Carr concluded, Stalin was borne along by them, and to an extent they dictated the policies that he pursued and the outcome of those policies, just as they had done in Lenin's case. The biographer of Stalin, Isaac Deutscher, placed his subject in the context of even wider historical forces. Rather than concentrating directly upon the revolution, Deutscher emphasised the continuities in Russian social, economic and political development, seeing factors in these that explain the particular course taken by Soviet socialism. Lenin and Stalin both worked in a context in which there was no tradition of democratic decision making, and in which the rigid enforcement of the orders of central government constituted the norm.

David Lane, in *Leninism: a Sociological Interpretation* (1981), and Alec Nove, in *An Economic History of the USSR* (1969), are two more leading authorities who have examined Stalin's work in the context of wider trends in Russian history. Both placed their emphasis upon the agricultural and industrial backwardness of post-revolutionary Russia, which confronted the Bolsheviks with the alternatives of drastic action or ultimate political failure. In the long term, they conclude, the responses of Lenin and Stalin to these challenges differed only in practical detail, and not in their ideological priorities.

An alternative 'school' of thought, however, insisted that the future of Russian communism could have been secured by other means, without the enormous human cost that Stalin's policies entailed. Stalin's fiercest political rival, Leon Trotsky, can be regarded as the founder of this 'school'. In exile from the Soviet Union, and in such works as *The Revolution Betrayed* (1937), Trotsky portrayed Stalin as a political and intellectual mediocrity, whose whole career in power constituted a betrayal of the principles of Marx and Lenin. The essential features of the 'Stalinist' system – the building of the party bureaucracy, the development of personal leadership, the whole concept of 'Socialism in one country' – ran contrary to the ideological lines laid down by the founders of Communism. The man responsible for this perversion of the revolution was, in Trotsky's phrase, the 'gravedigger of the revolution'.

In the last years of the Soviet regime it became safer to express such views within the USSR, and a similar interpretation was put forward there by Roy Medvedev, in *On Stalin and Stalinism* (1979). An orthodox Leninist, Medvedev condemned Stalin as a perverter of Leninist principles, and as the man responsible for diverting the revolution from its correct course. In the west, criticism of this kind has been expressed in the work of historian Robert Conquest (*The Great Terror: a Re-assessment*, 1990). While

'**Determinist**': Used in the study of history to indicate the belief that historical events are broadly determined by forces that cannot be significantly changed by the actions of individuals. In particular, it is used to describe the Marxist view that historical events are predominantly determined by economic forces.

Conquest is no Marxist, and has no cause to commend the work of Lenin, he clearly recognises the need for industrialisation and modernisation in Russia after Lenin's death. He is convinced, however, that these goals could have been achieved without the brutality and repression of the 1930s. Above all, Conquest argues that what Stalin achieved was an increase in Soviet power, rather than an improvement in the living standards and the quality of life of Soviet citizens, which were presumably the prime objectives of Lenin's original revolution. These, he emphasises, were little better in 1953 than they had been on the eve of the First World War.

With the collapse of the Soviet system, it is no longer easy to view Stalin's excesses as justifiable steps along the road to 'inevitable' socialism. At the same time, the cooling of political emotions makes it easier to carry out a more objective comparison of the aims and methods of Lenin and Stalin. For many commentators, 'Leninism' and 'Stalinism' have much in common. The difference between the two men lay not in their aims or even in their methods, but simply in the circumstances that prevailed during their times in power. Indeed, in many respects, Lenin had already started out on the path that Stalin trod. It was Lenin, after all, who founded the political police, and who carried out the first purges of Party members. During the brief period of War Communism, Lenin's hostility towards the peasants, as a counter-revolutionary force, could be said to anticipate that of Stalin during collectivisation. It is also possible to blame Lenin for many of the problems that Stalin inherited. His opportunism in seizing power in 1917 forced the Bolsheviks to build communism in a society that had nothing like the industrial basis that Marx had considered a pre-requisite of any successful socialist revolution. In addition, Lenin was fundamentally wrong in assuming that the First World War would precipitate 'sister' revolutions across Europe. Lenin's early death then left his successors to find solutions to these problems. It might be convincingly argued that Stalin's policies and methods derived directly, not from Lenin's vision and insight, but from his mistakes.

Nevertheless, the fact remains that the nature of the Soviet Communist Party changed enormously between the death of Lenin and the outbreak of the Second World War. Although Lenin defined the Party in a relatively narrow way, and gave it an authoritarian role, it was the Party that directed policy in the early days of the revolution. The machinery of the Party was so important that Stalin had to gain control of it before he could secure his own authority. Over the next 15 years, however, Stalin changed the nature and role of the Party significantly. The purges did not only eliminate individual communists, they eradicated a type of communist politician. Lenin's colleagues were essentially 'western' thinkers, following the ideology of a western European thinker, and assuming that their revolution would be shared with the workers of western Europe. Stalin replaced them with men who knew nothing of western Europe, who were inward looking, exclusively concerned with the growth of Russia, and actively distrustful of socialist movements elsewhere in Europe. At the very least, this was a strategy so distinct from any that Lenin considered that it could hardly be regarded as 'Leninism'. Staffed by such men, the Party played little more than a bureaucratic role, and was clearly subordinated to Stalin's personal will. In Martin McCauley's words, 'the leader took over from the Party and collective wisdom was concentrated in him. He, and not the Party, became the guide and inspirer of the masses.'

1. What different views have been put forward by historians about the degree of continuity that existed between the work of Lenin and that of Stalin?

2. Why have historians in the Soviet Union and in the West reached so many different conclusions about the work of Stalin?

5.12 In what respects did Stalin's successors moderate his policies in the years immediately after his death?

Georgi Malenkov (1902–1988)
Communist Party official from early 1920s, and member of the Central Committee from 1941. Prime Minister of the USSR (1953–55), siding eventually with Khrushchev against Beria, and advocating economic reform. Ousted from power in 1957, he was assigned to manage a hydroelectric station in Kazakhstan.

Nikita Khrushchev (1894–1971)
Made General Secretary of the Communist Party of Soviet Union on Stalin's death in 1953. In the following power struggle Khrushchev first ousted Malenkov and then Bulganin to become Soviet leader. He created the Warsaw Pact (1955). Denounced Stalin at 20th Party Congress in 1956. Responsible for creating crises over Berlin (1958–61) and Cuba (1962), both foreign policy failures. Khrushchev was ousted from power in 1964 over failure of domestic agricultural reforms and foreign policy failures.

On 1 March 1953, Stalin suffered a massive stroke and died four days later. His death, like that of Lenin 30 years earlier, gave rise to genuine public grief, and to genuine popular concern that the state could barely expect to survive without the influence of its great leader. Unlike the death of Lenin, however, it did not lead to the creation of a 'cult of Stalin', to attempts to enshrine the leader's policies as a lasting ideology. On the contrary, certain elements of the Stalinist system were under attack within days of his death. Not only was it immediately announced that there was no substance to the 'Doctors' Plot', but an amnesty was quickly declared for many non-political prisoners serving shorter sentences in the prison camps. Over one million were released, including many close relatives of leading Soviet politicians. Between 1953 and 1955, over 10,000 prisoners were also released from prison camps as the result of appeals against illegal convictions.

The most striking change to the Stalinist system lay in the fact that, after his death, political power was no longer concentrated solely in the hands of one man. Stalin had named no specific successor, and on the face of it the Soviet Union was heading for a period of collective leadership. Among the prominent figures who seemed likely to exercise this leadership were Georgi Malenkov, Vyacheslav Molotov and Nikita Khrushchev, all close associates of Stalin over the years, but Lavrenti Beria appeared to occupy the most powerful position. As Minister of Internal Affairs he enjoyed control over the secret police, and had been a key figure in the enforcement of Stalin's will during the last 15 years of the dictator's life. Paradoxically, Beria's powerful position proved to be his undoing. So clear was the possibility that he might resurrect the methods and the authority of Stalin that other prominent figures were quick to ally against him. He was arrested at a meeting of the Party Presidium (26 June 1953), falsely accused of spying and shot shortly afterwards. The execution of a further 30 NKVD men between 1953 and 1956 effectively ensured the control of the Party over the secret police. This control was emphasised by placing the secret police under the control of a newly-formed Committee of State Security (KGB). The executions also marked the end of this form of blood-letting within the USSR.

The power struggle that resulted in the eclipse of Malenkov and the triumph of Khrushchev was more complex. In this Malenkov was handicapped by his initial alignment with Beria, while Khrushchev, like Stalin in the 1920s, benefited from his position within the Politburo and his office as Secretary of the Party's Central Committee. From this power base he was able, like Stalin before him, to place supporters – men like Leonid Brezhnev – in positions of influence. Malenkov's misjudgement in backing the 'Anti-Party Group', members of the government who wanted to limit the authority of the Party, played directly into the hands of Khrushchev. By 1957 the latter had emerged as the dominant figure in Soviet politics, and the political career of Malenkov was effectively at an end.

A further parallel with the 1920s lay in the fact that the power struggle centred around different visions of the economic future of the USSR. Both candidates envisaged measures that would ease the burdens of the working population, and improve Soviet standards of living. Malenkov's proposed 'New Course' placed an unparalleled emphasis upon the production of consumer goods. Well-intentioned, it nevertheless cost him the support of those in charge of, or dependent upon heavy industry, angry at the prospect of state funds being channelled away from traditional areas of industrial and military production. Khrushchev had a different strategy for

Nikita Khrushchev

the creation of higher living standards. His 'Virgin Lands' programme, launched in February 1954, envisaged a substantial increase in food supplies, not by placing further pressure upon the peasantry, but by exploiting vast areas of land that had never previously been used for agriculture. Between 1954 and 1956, young Party members and members of *Komsomol* helped to bring 36 million hectares of such land, equivalent to the total farmland of Canada, under cultivation. During this period, 300,000 people emigrated to areas of western Siberia, Kazakhstan and the Caucasus. At last agricultural production showed significant improvement: the grain harvest in 1956 stood at 125 million tons, compared with 82.5 million tons three years earlier. The policy also constituted a very important change in the balance of the Soviet economy, and a major departure from the practices of the Stalinist economy. As David Christian has written, 'the Soviet countryside ceased to be an exploited colony of the Soviet town. Instead, it became a massive recipient of investment resources and subsidies.'

A range of other reforms also indicated that the emphases of the Soviet economic and social systems were shifting. Tuition fees for higher education were abandoned, pensions were increased and housing was given higher priority in economic planning. The control of the Soviet economy was significantly decentralised, with much initiative removed from the ministries in Moscow and delegated to local officials.

What was the significance of Khrushchev's 'secret speech'?

The impression that the Soviet government was moving away from the precepts of Stalin was sensationally confirmed in February 1956. In a closed session of the 20th Party Congress Nikita Khrushchev delivered what has become known as his 'secret speech'. In it, he accused Stalin of excessive ruthlessness in his political purges, testified to the innocence of many of the victims, played down Stalin's role in the victory over Germany, and denounced the development by Stalin of a 'cult of the personality'. Particularly fierce criticism was reserved for Stalin's decision to purge the military leadership on the eve of war, and for his ignorance of agricultural realities within the Soviet Union.

To what extent did this 'secret speech' mark the abandonment of Stalinism? Critics have produced several lines of argument to claim that the speech was in part a calculated and self-serving attempt by Khrushchev to aid and consolidate his own rise to power. They emphasise that his criticism was restricted to the period between 1934 and 1953, and thus made no reference to forced collectivisation and industrialisation. These elements, the bases of the current Soviet society, continued to be praised as great achievements. The criticisms were also carefully phrased to discredit the absurdities of Stalinism, without discrediting the current politicians who had been instrumental in them. Equally, in the context of foreign policy, events in Hungary and Czechoslovakia over the next 15 years were to prove that the Soviet government had not departed from the priorities laid down by Stalin in 1945.

It is equally possible, however, to take a much more positive view of Khrushchev's actions. The evidence that has emerged since the collapse of the Soviet Union makes it clear that in delivering the 'secret speech' Khrushchev took a courageous and highly controversial step, the risks far outweighing the potential, personal advantages. His colleagues were extremely wary of the possible consequences of this rejection of Stalin's authority, of the danger of public disorder and of the questions that might be raised about their own roles in the crimes of the 1930s and 1940s. Fearful of the possible reaction to the speech, they insisted that it should not be delivered in the normal course of the Party Congress. Nor is it clear that Khrushchev cemented his own political position by taking this gamble. Many remained uneasy about the step that he had taken. Not only did it generate a short-term crisis in his leadership in 1957, it also gave rise to resentments and suspicions that followed him right up to his fall from power in 1964.

Source-based questions: Stalin's purges

Study the Sources and then answer questions (a) to (c) which follow.

SOURCE A

A statement by Yuri Pyatakov on the political trials held in 1935. A leading Bolshevik, Pyatakov was later executed during the purges

One cannot find the words fully to express one's indignation and disgust. These people have lost the last semblance of humanity. They must be destroyed like carrion that is polluting the pure, bracing air of the land of the Soviets; dangerous carrion which may cause the death of our leaders, and has already caused the death of one of the best people in the land, that wonderful comrade and leader, S.M. Kirov. Many of us, including myself, by our complacency and lack of vigilance, unconsciously helped these bandits to commit their black deeds.

SOURCE B

A report on the purges, made by Stalin to the Central Committee of the Communist Party in 1937

The espionage-diversionist work of the Trotskyite agents of the Japanese-German secret police was a complete surprise to some of our comrades. Our Party comrades have not noticed that Trotskyism has ceased to be the political tendency in the working class that it was seven or eight years ago. Trotskyism has become a frenzied and unprincipled band of wreckers, spies and murderers, acting upon instructions from intelligence service organs of foreign states.

(a) Study Sources 1 and 2.

What explanations do the authors of these Sources give for the political purges of the 1930s? [5 marks]

(b) In what ways did the scope of these political purges expand in the course of the 1930s? [7 marks]

(c) What were the major effects of the political purges of the 1930s upon the domestic politics and foreign policy of the Soviet Union? [18 marks]

Source-based questions: The peasantry in Russia and the Soviet Union

Study the Sources and then answer the questions that follow.

SOURCE A

A Soviet official reports on peasant attitudes in the countryside

The peasant uprisings develop because of widespread dissatisfaction on the part of small property-owners in the countryside with the dictatorship of the proletariat, which directs at them the cutting edge of implacable compulsion. The Soviet regime is identified with flying visits by commissars. In the countryside the Soviet regime is still predominantly military-administrative rather than economic in character. In the eyes of the peasants it is tyrannical and is not a system that, before all else, organises and ministers to the countryside itself.

Report sent to Lenin by the head of the CHEKA in Tambov province (20 July 1921)

SOURCE B

Stalin comments upon the lack of participation by peasants in the Soviet regime.

Our Party's growth in the countryside is terribly slow. I do not mean to say that it ought to grow by leaps and bounds, but the percentage of the peasantry that we have in the Party is, after all, very insignificant. Our Party is a workers' party. But it is also clear that without an alliance with the peasantry the dictatorship of the proletariat is impossible, that the Party must have a certain percentage of the best people among the peasantry in its ranks.

From a speech by Stalin delivered in 1927

SOURCE C

Stalin outlines his plans to transform the mentality of the peasantry through their employment on collective farms.

A great deal of work has still to be done to remould the peasant collective farmer, to set right his individualistic mentality and to transform him into a real working member of a socialist society. And the more rapidly the collective farms are provided with machines, the more rapidly this will be achieved. The greatest importance of the collective farms lies precisely in that they represent the principal base for the employment of machinery and tractors in agriculture, that they constitute the principal base for remoulding the peasant, for changing his mentality in the spirit of socialism.

From Stalin's speech 'Concerning Questions of Agrarian Policy in the USSR', December 1929

SOURCE D

Two comments by industrial workers upon the way in which food shortages affect the fulfilment of the industrial Five-Year Plan

i) The building of socialism is not done by Bolsheviks alone. It should not be forgotten that many millions of workers are participating in the building of socialism. A horse can drag seventy-five poods [a Russian measurement of weight], but its owner has loaded it with a hundred poods, and in addition he's fed it poorly. No matter how much he uses the whip, it still won't be able to move the cart. This is also true of the working class. They've loaded it with socialist competition, shock work, overfulfilling the industrial and financial plan. And what does the worker live on? One hundred and fifty grams of salted mutton, and soup without any of the usual additives, neither carrots, beets, flour nor salt pork. Mere dishwater.

ii) The press trumpets 'Give us coal, steel, iron, and so on and so forth. Shame on those who fail to fulfil the industrial and financial plan.' I say the following: 'Dear newspaper trumpeters, come and visit us in the Donbas. We'll treat you to a bottle of hot water, instead of tea, a hunk not of bread but of something incomprehensible, boiled water without sugar, and then, dear friend, kindly go and mine the coal quota.'

Letters written to *Pravda* by a worker in Tula, and by a coal-miner in the Donbas region, September 1930

(a) Study Source A.

From this Source and your own knowledge, explain the reference to 'the dictatorship of the proletariat'.
[20 marks]

(b) Study Sources A, B and C.

Compare the attitudes towards the Russian peasantry expressed in these sources. [40 marks]

(c) Study all of the Sources.

Using all of these Sources and your own knowledge, examine the judgement that 'the problems posed by the peasantry for the Soviet government between 1918 and 1932 were political rather than economic'.
[60 marks]

Source-based questions: Stalin and the Revolution

Study the following source material and then answer the questions which follow.

SOURCE A

Adapted from Nikita Khrushchev's 'secret speech', February 1956

Comrades: we must abolish the cult of the individual decisively, once and for all. It is necessary to condemn and to eradicate in a Bolshevik manner the cult of the individual as alien to Marxism-Leninism, and to fight inexorably against all attempts to bring back this practice in one form or another. In this connection we will be forced to do much work in order to correct the widely spread erroneous views connected with the cult of the individual in the sphere of history, philosophy, economy and other sciences, as well as in literature and the fine arts. We must restore completely the Leninist principles of Soviet socialist democracy, expressed in the Constitution of the Soviet Union, to fight wilfulness of individuals abusing their power. The evil caused by acts violating revolutionary socialist legality which have accumulated over a long period as a result of the negative influence of the cult of the individual must be completely corrected.

SOURCE B

From a speech by Stalin on the Five-Year Plan, 1931

It is sometimes asked whether it is not possible to slow down the tempo of industrialisation somewhat. No comrades, it is not possible. The tempo must not be reduced. On the contrary, we must increase it as much as is within our powers and possibilities. This is dictated to us by our obligations to the workers and peasants of the USSR. To slacken the tempo would mean falling behind. And those who fall behind get beaten. Old Russia suffered continual beatings because of her backwardness. We are fifty or a hundred years behind the advanced countries. We must make good this distance in ten years. Either we do it, or we shall be crushed.

SOURCE C

Adapted from Stalin: Triumph and Tragedy, by Dmitri Volkogonov, published in 1991

Stalinism took the primacy of the state over society to absurd limits. It was a system that depended upon a vast and powerful bureaucracy at all levels, and within this environment of political absolutism, the leader's decisions were increasingly divorced from economic reality. Much of what happened in the Soviet Union did so because freedom had been disregarded and scorned. One of the main aims of the October Revolution had been freedom, and yet its victory did not free the people. The deepest corruption of the Stalinist system lay in removing man as such from the centre of society's goals, and in replacing him with the state as a machine which magnified one man only.

SOURCE D

From Stalin, A Political Biography, by Isaac Deutscher, published in 1966

In 1945 Stalin stood in the full blaze of popular recognition and gratitude. These feelings were spontaneous, genuine, not engineered by official propagandists. Overworked slogans about the 'achievements of the Stalinist era' now conveyed fresh meaning not only to young people, but to sceptics and malcontents of the older generation. The nation was willing to forgive Stalin even his misdeeds and to retain in its memory only his better efforts. This new appreciation of Stalin's role did not spring only from afterthoughts born in the flush of victory. The truth was that the war could not have been won without the intensive industrialisation of Russia, and of her eastern provinces in particular. Nor could it have been won without the collectivisation of large numbers of farms.

(a) Use Source A and your own knowledge.

Explain what the author of Source A means by 'the cult of the individual'. [5 marks]

(b) Compare Sources C and D and use your own knowledge.

How do Sources C and D differ in the conclusions that they draw about the historical importance of Stalin's policies? [10 marks]

(c) Use Sources A, B, C and D and your own knowledge.

How convincing is the argument that Stalin's period in power served mainly to strengthen the Soviet state and to increase its chances of survival? [15 marks]

5.13 How successful was Khrushchev as Soviet leader?

Consolidation of power

Following his speech to the 20th Party Congress of the Communist Party of the Soviet Union (CPSU) Khrushchev was clearly seen as the more important member of the joint leadership of the USSR. From 1956 onwards Bulganin seemed to be joint leader in name only.

However, to win the leadership outright Khrushchev had to survive an attempt to dismiss him. In the wake of the 'secret speech' at the 20th Party Congress, Soviet power in eastern Europe faced its sternest challenge since the end of the Second World War. In Poland, there were demonstrations for political reform, but the most serious challenge came in Hungary, in October 1956. A full-scale uprising against Soviet influence was only put down by the brutal intervention of the Red Army.

Bureaucracy: administration by a complex network of state officials.

In addition, Khrushchev was profoundly suspicious of the large **bureaucracy** that existed in Soviet government. In the years 1955 to 1957 he introduced reforms to bring new blood into the Communist Party and the government apparatus. These moves threatened Bulganin's power base, and in June 1957 he asked Khrushchev to convene a meeting of the **Presidium**, the ruling body of the USSR. Bulganin believed he had sufficient support within the Presidium to dismiss Khrushchev, but Khrushchev demanded instead a meeting of the much larger Central Committee of the CPSU, where he knew he could get majority support. The Central Committee then met, and Khrushchev's opponents were soundly defeated – including Malenkov, Kanganovich and Molotov – who were dismissed from the Central Committee to be replaced by Khrushchev supporters, Brezhnev and Kosygin. Khrushchev's opponents were referred to as the 'Anti-Party Group'.

Presidium: The ruling committee of the USSR (similar to the Cabinet in the UK).

An important ally of Khrushchev in his victory over the Anti-Party Group was the wartime leader of the Red Army, Marshall Zhukov. However, within months of his Central Committee victory, Khrushchev and Zhukov clashed over Khrushchev's decision to reduce the size of the Soviet Army from 5.8 million in 1950 to 3.6 million by 1960. Khrushchev then ensured that Zhukov was denounced by the CPSU.

Finally, in 1958, Khrushchev replaced Bulganin as Prime Minister to make himself undisputed leader of the USSR.

Democratisation and decentralisation

Following the denunciation of Stalin in 1956, Khrushchev planned two major changes to the Soviet system of government. One was the democratisation of the Communist Party. From 1954 to 1964 the Party membership increased from 6.9 million to 11 million. Most of the new members were listed as workers and peasants. As part of the way to increase 'democracy' within the CPSU, Khrushchev revived 'comrades courts', led by ordinary party members, which dealt with minor offences.

Khrushchev also began the decentralisation of control. Part of the process was to transfer power from the Soviet central government to the governments of the fifteen republics which comprised the USSR. In 1957 the process reached its height, with the creation of the 'sovnarkhozy' – 105 regional councils given authority over economic development. Under Stalin all economic planning had been centrally controlled through Gosplan, which monitored the implementation of the 'Five-Year Economic Plans'. It was this change more than any other that led to the showdown between Khrushchev and his opponents in the 1957 Anti-Party Group affair.

Both these policies aimed at undermining the remnants of Stalinism and improving the standard of living of the Soviet people. The privileged position of Communist Party members under Stalin was widely resented and, to address this, Khrushchev introduced major changes to labour policy within the USSR. He narrowed the differences in pay between rich and poor, and he decriminalised absenteeism from work. Linked with these changes came reform of housing and education policy. From 1955 to 1964 a rapid housing construction programme doubled the amount of homes within the USSR. Most of the new homes, however, were in poorly made high-rise blocks of flats which appeared in the suburbs of Soviet cities. In education, Khrushchev abolished university tuition fees in 1958, allowing the children of ordinary workers to receive higher education.

Agricultural reform

The policy which had helped Khrushchev win the initiative in the race to be sole leader of the USSR was the 'Virgin Lands' policy, begun in 1954. Khrushchev believed the best food for livestock was corn. He hoped to transform the Ukrainian steppe into a corn-growing region. New 'Virgin Lands' in Kazakhstan and southern Siberia would be used for cereal growing. This plan opened up a further 41 million hectares of land for agricultural production. In the first years, the harvest was good and it seemed that Khrushchev's plans were going to pay off. Between 1950 and 1960, annual agricultural production increased by 43 million tones (29 million coming from the Virgin Lands). Khrushchev bragged that he could make the USSR self-sufficient in food production and even become an export nation. By the early 1960s, however, poor rainfall and soil erosion had destroyed the early gains of his programme. In addition, much of the mechanised equipment produced within the USSR was sent to the Virgin Lands, thereby delaying further improvements in agricultural output in European Russia.

Another setback for Khrushchev was his decision to abolish the Motor Tractor Stations (MTSs) in the countryside. During Stalin's time the MTSs had been important institutions in developing the collective farm method of agriculture through the provision of tractors and other mechanised machinery. They were also important centres for political control over collective farms. However, MTSs provided yet another layer of bureaucracy obstructing efficient farming. Collective farms had to negotiate with the MTSs for their services and farmers were never quite sure when the MTS would perform their work.

Removing this layer of bureaucracy made sense, but the speed at which the change was introduced – in just one year – badly affected agriculture.

Many collective farms did not possess the expertise to maintain machinery. As a result, agricultural-machine making actually declined during Khrushchev's period as leader.

Unfortunately for Khrushchev, 1963 was a drought year, which led to a shortage of bread right across the USSR. Khrushchev's failures in agriculture were an important contributory factor in his removal from power in 1964.

The space race

The optimism that characterised the early years of Khrushchev's leadership was epitomised by Soviet achievements in space. In October 1957 the USSR successfully launched the first satellite, Sputnik. This was followed by further Soviet successes, such as the launch of the first live animal in space (Laika the dog) and, finally, in April 1961 the successful launch of the first man in space, Yuri Gagarin. These successes greatly enhanced Soviet international prestige. They also supported the belief, held by Khrushchev, that the Soviet economic system was superior to the west. He took pride in boasting that it was inevitable that the USSR would overtake the USA and other western countries in economic wealth in the late twentieth century.

The USSR as a global power

In international affairs the USSR was seen as a truly global power. In 1949 the USSR had successfully tested its first atomic bomb. By the early 1960s the USSR had also developed the H-bomb, and had developed jet bomber fleets and missile forces which could deliver nuclear weapons across continents. All these developments greatly increased international tension with the USA.

Tension began to develop in 1958 when Khrushchev demanded an international treaty on the status of Berlin (where the four wartime allies – the USSR, USA, Britain and France – maintained military zones of occupation). The height of this crisis came in August 1961 when East Germany, with the support of the USSR, constructed the Berlin Wall, which permanently divided Soviet-controlled Berlin from the western sectors.

The Berlin Wall crisis greatly increased East–West tension, but it paled into insignificance compared with the 1962 confrontation between the USA and the USSR over Cuba. Cuba had become a communist country following the victory of Fidel Castro in the Cuban Revolution of 1958–59. In October 1962 the USA discovered the existence of Soviet nuclear missile sites in Cuba – only 90 miles from the coast of Florida. If fired, these missiles could hit most of the cities in the continental USA. The reaction of the USA was to impose a naval blockade of Cuba and demand the removal of all Soviet missiles. After a tense few days, the USSR acceded to the USA demand. At the time it seemed to be a great diplomatic victory for US President John F. Kennedy. However, the USA had been forced to agree to remove US missiles from northern Turkey, on the southern border of the USSR, and undertake never to invade Cuba. As a result, Khrushchev was able to remove an important US military threat to the USSR. He also ensured the survival of a Soviet ally, Cuba, in Central America.

One of the immediate consequences of the Cuban missile crisis was the installation of the MOLINK, a direct telephone link between the White House and the Kremlin. The aim was to prevent the escalation of any future crisis between the two superpowers. Also, in 1963 the USA and USSR signed the Partial Test Ban Treaty which limited the testing of nuclear weapons.

This 'thaw' in the Cold War in many ways reflected Khrushchev's own

Khrushchev and Mao Zedong in Beijing in 1959.

personal view. In 1959 he had put forward to the 22nd Party Congress of the CPSU the idea of 'peaceful coexistence' between the USSR and the USA. In his final year in power Khrushchev was moving the USSR in the direction of détente with the west, which was further developed by his successor, Leonid Brezhnev, in 1969.

In international affairs the denunciation of Stalin by Khrushchev also had effects on the world communist movement. The Communist Chinese leader, Mao Zedong, did not accept Khrushchev's analysis of Stalin's rule in the USSR. By 1959 Soviet relations with the People's Republic of China had changed from communist allies to rivals. It could be argued that a Sino-Soviet split was inevitable. Mao Zedong was unlikely to accept subordination to the USSR within the world communist movement forever. By the late 1950s Mao was developing his own road to socialism which was different from Khrushchev's USSR. In that year Mao began the 'Great Leap Forward' – his attempt at rapid economic modernisation. It ended in disaster within three years, causing the biggest man-made famine in world history.

1. What do you regard as Khrushchev's greatest success as Soviet leader? Explain your answer.

2. Do you think that Khrushchev was more successful in international affairs than in his domestic policies? Explain your answer.

5.14 Why did Khrushchev fall from power in 1964?

On 14 October 1964 the Central Committee of the CPSU 'freed' Khrushchev from his position as Prime Minister of the USSR and General Secretary of the CPSU. The reason given for Khrushchev's departure was 'deteriorating health'. In the entire history of the USSR this was the only time a coup was successful.

But why was Khrushchev dismissed? At the meeting of the Central Committee several accusations were levelled against Khrushchev, including mismanagement of the economy and 'errors' in foreign policy.

Clearly foreign policy was an issue which had gained enemies for Khrushchev. The Sino-Soviet split was regarded as a result of Khrushchev's 'revisionism' – his denunciation of Stalin, and Khrushchev had been forced

MODERN CLASSICS

Aleksandr Solzhenitsyn
One Day in the Life of Ivan Denisovich

The cover of *One Day in the Life of Ivan Denisovich* by Aleksander Solzhenitsyn. © 2000 Penguin Books.

to back down during the Cuban missile crisis. In addition, the USSR suffered another humiliation, in 1962, when India was defeated by China in the Sino-Indian War. India had received considerable Soviet military aid, and the outcome was seen as another triumph for Mao. Finally, Khrushchev was seen to have embarrassed the USSR by his antics when abroad. When visiting the UN in New York he interrupted a speech by British Prime Minister, Harold Macmillan, by taking off his shoe and banging it on the top of his desk. Macmillan used the occasion to publicly ridicule Khrushchev.

Khrushchev's cultural policy also seemed to have backfired on him. Following the denunciation of Stalin several literary works critical of the Stalinist system were allowed to be published within the USSR. These included *One Day in the Life of Ivan Denisovich* by Alexander Solzhenitsyn – a harrowing account of the Gulag concentration camp system of Stalin's USSR. Within one month of its publication in 1962, Khrushchev attempted to curb literary freedom. He also launched into attacks against the Russian Orthodox Church. By the time of his fall, Khrushchev had helped to undermine the Stalinist era and, at the same time, alienate the literary classes of the USSR by his subsequent clampdown on literary freedom.

However, none of these problems was as serious for Khrushchev as the claim of economic mismanagement. Economic problems began to appear by the early 1960s, with waste and inefficiency becoming increasingly evident. Although the government always claimed that the economy had full employment, productivity was obviously low compared to the west. In addition, the military budget was taking up a disproportionate amount of the Gross Domestic Product – and the military sector needed the best materials, workers and technology available. This led to the production of poor quality goods in other sectors, such as consumer goods.

The worst economic problems were in the agricultural sectors. In spite of Khrushchev's constant boasts, Soviet agriculture was inefficient and backward. It could also be argued that Khrushchev was plagued by bad luck. The 1963 drought, for example, created food shortages at the time when other problems were coming to a head.

Perhaps the main reason for Khrushchev's fall was his decentralisation policy and his attack on the party apparatus. His decentralisation policy loosened the control of the central government, and with it Khrushchev's power over the republics that comprised the USSR. Also, his reform of the party bureaucracy upset a large number of senior party members who saw their power bases reduced.

Finally, part of the blame must be laid at Khrushchev's personal style. His impulsive behaviour and his increasingly dictatorial manner alienated other senior members of the Communist Party. Added to this was his nepotism, giving jobs to members of his own family. An example was the promotion of his son-in-law, Alexei Adzhubei to the editorship of one of the USSR's leading newspapers, *Izvestia*.

By February 1964, senior officials – led by Nicholas Podgorny and Leonid Brezhnev – began plotting to dismiss Khrushchev. Khrushchev, however, decided to ignore the warnings he received about their activities,

1. Draw up a list of reasons why Khrushchev fell from power in 1964.

2. How far do you think Khrushchev was personally responsible for his own downfall?

1. Place the points in the mind map in order of importance, with the most successful first and the least successful last.

2. Do you think Khrushchev was, on balance, a success or a failure as Soviet leader?

and this arrogance would prove to be his undoing. In October 1964 Khrushchev was on holiday in the Crimea. In his absence his opponents convened a special meeting of the Central Committee which openly criticised his leadership. The degree to which Khrushchev had become an isolated and unpopular figure was the reaction of the Soviet public to the announcement of his 'retirement'. His fall from power was quick and bloodless, and within a matter of weeks he had disappeared from the public stage. He died in obscurity in 1971.

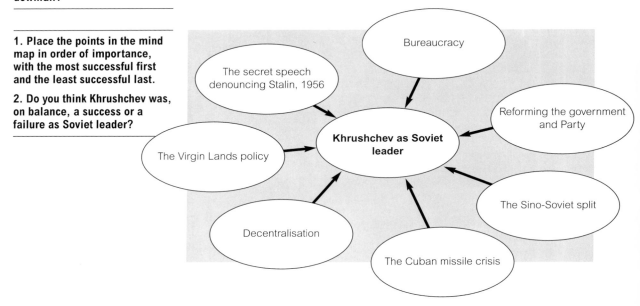

Further Reading

Texts designed for AS and A2 Level students

Stalin and Stalinism by Martin McCauley (Longman, Seminar Studies series, 1995)

Stalin and Khrushchev: The USSR 1924–64 by Michael Lynch (Hodder & Stoughton, Access to History series, 1990)

Stalin and Stalinism by Alan Wood (Routledge, Lancaster Pamphlets, 1990)

Stalin by John Philip (Collins Historymakers, 2005)

Communist Russia under Lenin and Stalin by Terry Fiehn and Chris Corin (John Murray, 2002)

More advanced reading

Stalin: a Political Biography by Isaac Deutscher (Penguin, 1966)

Hitler and Stalin: Parallel Lives by Alan Bullock (HarperCollins, 1991)

The Soviet Union 1917–1991 by Martin McCauley (Longman, History of Russia series, 1993)

The Great Terror: a Reassessment by Robert Conquest (Pimlico, 1992)

An Economic History of the USSR by Alec Nove (Penguin, 1969)

Stalin's Peasants by Sheila Fitzpatrick (Oxford University Press, 1994)

Imperial and Soviet Russia: Power, Privilege and the Challenge of Modernity by David Christian (Macmillan, 1997) provides a concise summary of recent writing on this period.

Index